"This Festschrift highlights the significant impact of Thomas R. Cole's pioneering research in humanistic gerontology, aging studies, and medical humanities. In its chapters, established scholars not only discuss the transformative power of Cole's contributions to their research but also reflect on his unwavering commitment to clarity, honesty, compassion, and care in his roles as an academic leader, colleague, teacher, mentor, and friend. The result is an outstanding kaleidoscope of chapters that bear witness to the large body of excellent work accomplished by Cole."
  —ULLA KRIEBERNEGG, professor of cultural aging and care research, University of Graz

"The outcome of a Festschrift conference held in April 2023, this book provides a rich sampling of the themes and thoughts that Thomas R. Cole has developed during his academic career as a scholar of aging and of medical humanities, woven around the biographical narrative of his own journey through life. The various chapters contribute both a kind of legacy of Cole's work and directions toward the future. Rich fare for all those interested in the link between age studies, the arts, and humanities."
  —CHRIS GILLEARD, honorary associate professor, University College London Division of Psychiatry

"When deep questions of value or meaning arise, we benefit from having companions in reflection, discernment, and action. This elegant volume offers readers a wise, generous, and discerning group of companions. Collectively, they honor the life and work of one who reminds us that the act of engaging timeless and timely questions of value and meaning, especially with trusted others, enriches our life journeys and our humanity."
  —ALLAN COLE, dean, Steve Hicks School of Social Work, University of Texas at Austin

Journeys of Life

Journeys of Life
Engaging the Work of Thomas R. Cole

EDITED BY
Nathan Carlin *and* Kate de Medeiros

INTRODUCTION BY
Craig Klugman, Nathan Carlin, *and* Kate de Medeiros

WIPF & STOCK · Eugene, Oregon

JOURNEYS OF LIFE
Engaging the Work of Thomas R. Cole

Copyright © 2024 Nathan Carlin and Kate de Medeiros. All rights reserved. Except for brief quotations in critical publications or reviews, no part of this book may be reproduced in any manner without prior written permission from the publisher. Write: Permissions, Wipf and Stock Publishers, 199 W. 8th Ave., Suite 3, Eugene, OR 97401.

Wipf & Stock
An Imprint of Wipf and Stock Publishers
199 W. 8th Ave., Suite 3
Eugene, OR 97401

www.wipfandstock.com

PAPERBACK ISBN: 979-8-3852-0362-8
HARDCOVER ISBN: 979-8-3852-0363-5
EBOOK ISBN: 979-8-3852-0364-2

Unless otherwise noted, all Bible quotations are taken from the New Revised Standard Version Bible, copyright © 1989 National Council of the Churches of Christ in the United States of America. Used by permission. All rights reserved.

Lines from the poem "A Clearing" by Denise Levertov appear in the epilogue. "A Clearing" by Denise Levertov is from *This Great Unknowing*, copyright ©1999 by The Denise Levertov Literary Trust. Reprinted by permission of New Directions Publishing Corp.

*For Thomas R. Cole—
mentor, collaborator, friend*

*And in memory of Andrew Achenbaum,
who succeeded in passing the torch*

Life is grace. Sleep is forgiveness. The night absolves. Darkness wipes the slate clean, not spotless to be sure, but clean enough for another day's chalking.

—Frederick Buechner, *The Alphabet of Grace*

Contents

Acknowledgments ix

Introduction 1
Craig Klugman, Nathan Carlin, and Kate de Medeiros

PART ONE: The Journey of Life—Two Perspectives

1. On Being Undisciplined and Subversive 15
W. Andrew Achenbaum

2. Re-Interpreting the Journey of Life 35
Roberta Maierhofer

PART TWO: Life Stories

3. Narrating Stories from the Perspective of Dementia 55
Kate de Medeiros

4. A Mutual Opportunity of Listening and Telling 73
Benjamin Saxton

5. Worthy to be Recorded 91
Craig Klugman

PART THREE: Cultural Studies—Literature and Film

6. Carrying the Fire 115
Woods Nash

7. Older Women's Sexuality—in Life and in Film 135
Renee Flores

PART FOUR: Religion, Spirituality, and the Anthropocene

8. The Fourth Age as a "Feared" Old Age   153
Paul Higgs

9. Aging in the Anthropocene   168
Larry Churchill

Epilogue   183
Craig Irvine

Appendix Essay   187
Annelise Berler and Isaac S. Chua

Bibliography   217
Index   241

Acknowledgements

WE WOULD LIKE TO thank the editorial staff at Wipf and Stock, especially Matt Wimer, managing editor, for believing in this project.

This book is the result of a Festschrift conference for Thomas R. Cole held at McGovern Medical School in Houston, Texas, on April 12-14, 2023. Friends and colleagues from around the world traveled to honor Cole. The tradition of the Festschrift is European, and its purpose is to pay tribute to significant academic figures as they approach retirement, to celebrate their contributions and accomplishments. At such events, it is custom for students and colleagues to give papers and write chapters that engage the work of the honoree.

The conference was supported by the Grant Taylor endowment, held in the McGovern Center for Humanities and Ethics at McGovern Medical School, generously provided by Dr. John P. McGovern in honor of his friend, Dr. H. Grant Taylor. We are grateful to the McGovern Foundation for their continued support. We also would like to thank Alma Rosas for organizing the logistics for this conference. Some of the participants said that it was the most well-organized conference that they had ever attended because of Rosas's efforts.

During the conference, the group came to feel that the best word to describe Cole's intellectual contributions was "undisciplined." We will sketch out what we mean by that term in the introduction, though we do want to note that others have used the term as well. It is not original with us. Indeed, Craig Irvine pointed out to us after the conference that one widely-cited text that employs the term "undisciplined" is Christina Sharpe's *In the Wake*.[1] While we use the term in our own way, we hope that this Festschrift can contribute creatively to other discussions about what it might mean to be or to become undisciplined.

1. Sharpe, *In the Wake*.

Of course, this volume is dedicated to our mentor, collaborator, and friend: Thomas R. Cole. We are indebted to Cole for accompanying us on our own journeys of life.

Nathan Carlin and Kate de Medeiros

Introduction

CRAIG KLUGMAN, NATHAN CARLIN,
AND KATE DE MEDEIROS

THIS BOOK IS A Festschrift for Thomas R. Cole. Cole was trained as a cultural historian of aging, but migrated to the field of medical humanities. He is perhaps best known for his *The Journey of Life*,[1] a book that was nominated for a Pulitzer Prize. Cole's work transcends formal disciplines and neat boundaries. He has taught and collaborated with students and colleagues in various academic settings—college students, medical students, graduate students, residents, scholars in various fields in multiple countries. Thus, the contributors to this volume (and the topics contained herein) are also drawn from a variety of fields and disciplines, though the majority focus on or are inspired by Cole's work on aging.

As is often the case with Festschrifts, the unifying thread of this book is the honoree. To be sure, these essays are representative of *his* journey of life, both academic and personal, for Cole often did not separate the academic and the personal. In what follows, we will: (1) provide a brief biographical sketch of Cole's life: (2) orient readers to the two major foci of Cole's academic work—aging and medical humanities; (3) offer some reflections on Cole's work as "undisciplined"; and (4) outline the contents of this volume.

A BRIEF BIOGRAPHICAL SKETCH

Thomas R. Michel was born on March 15, 1949, and he grew up in New Haven, Connecticut. His father, Burton David Michel, died by suicide via

1. Cole, *The Journey of Life*.

car accident in 1953, a fact that Cole only learned later in life. His mother Jacqueline Breslav remarried and the family name became "Cole." While culturally Jewish, Cole was not raised in a religious household. In his middle age, Cole reconnected to his Jewish roots. Later in life, Cole was ordained to work as a spiritual director at Congregation Beth Israel in Houston, Texas.

After college, Cole married Letha Birkholtz, who would go on to become a psychiatrist, and they had two children together: Jacob and Emma. The couple eventually divorced and Cole married Thelma Jean Goodrich, a psychotherapist, in 2007. Goodrich is a Christian—thus, their marriage is interfaith, with each regularly attending the religious services of the other.

Cole studied philosophy as an undergraduate at Yale University, after which he earned a master's in history at Wesleyan University and his doctorate at the University of Rochester. At Rochester, Cole studied with Christopher Lasch, a public intellectual who wrote *The Culture of Narcissism*.[2] The title of Cole's dissertation was "Past Meridian: Aging and the Northern Middle Class, 1830-1930." As is common for many graduate students, Cole struggled to secure an academic post as he was completing his dissertation. He applied to many jobs, often hearing nothing in return. But he received a lifeline when Ronald Carson, Director of the then Institute for the Medical Humanities at the University of Texas Medical Branch (UTMB) in Galveston, Texas, called him for an interview. Carson was impressed by the letter that Lasch wrote for Cole, and Cole was hired by Carson in 1982. The relationship proved to be transformative—for both the men and various academic fields, especially medical humanities.

Cole was a product of the 1960s, and he was a protestor of the Vietnam War and also stood up for causes such as civil rights, women's rights, and the rights of older persons. In his younger days, he considered himself a Marxist, in part due to the influence of his stepfather, but Cole no longer identifies as such. When Carson introduced Cole to medical humanities, he became a more pragmatic thinker, educator, writer, and scholar, because he had to be attentive to the needs of health professionals and patients. As Cole describes this transition, "As a graduate student and young scholar, I was constantly negating, but, when I moved into a health professional context, what was needed was not critique, but support. I was committed to the people right in front of me. This was very

---

2. Lasch, *The Culture of Narcissism*.

different from my experience in traditional universities. I became more practical in a vocational setting."[3]

In 2004, Cole left the Institute for the Medical Humanities to become the founding Director of the McGovern Center for Humanities and Ethics at McGovern Medical School. While many medical schools have bioethics centers, Cole was intentional about keeping the mission and vision of the McGovern Center oriented toward medical humanities. During his tenure, Cole raised a $25 million endowment—mainly from the McGovern Foundation—to sustain the ongoing work of the McGovern Center. He retired from his director position in 2021, and as *emeritus* continues to teach and write.

HUMANISTIC GERONTOLOGY AND AGING STUDIES

In *The Journey of Life*, Cole notes that his work at the Institute for the Medical Humanities required him "to become intimately involved in medical education and practice," enabling him "to develop strong working relationships with a broad network of colleagues in geriatrics and gerontological research, education, policy, and practice."[4] These relationships enabled Cole to make formative contributions to the emerging interdisciplinary fields of humanistic gerontology and aging studies. Cole's interest in philosophy of religion as an undergraduate, and later intellectual and cultural history, provided an ideal background through which to explore existential questions related to living into later life as well as how historical contexts shape current perceptions on the meaning of a good old age.

Recognizing that mainstream gerontology at that time lacked "an appropriate language for addressing basic moral and spiritual issues in our aging society,"[5] Cole pushed for perspectives on aging that recognized myriad ways that human experience and meaning were embedded in cultural practices. Humanistic gerontology, as he called it, drew from approaches primarily within the humanities that were focused on what it means to be human rather than on the bio-psycho-social approaches common in mainstream gerontology, which sought to explain and predict individual and societal behaviors and outcomes. While at the Institute for

3. Cole interview with Carlin, January 30, 2024.
4. Cole, *Journey of Life*, xi.
5. Cole, Kastenbaum, and Ray, eds., *Handbook of the Humanities and Aging*, xi.

the Medical Humanities, Cole facilitated cross-disciplinary, international research and scholarship on aging, and he authored and/or edited multiple publications that argued that the tension between an infinite self and an aging body was a core part of the human condition and an important site of knowledge and understanding, even in its obscurity.

In addition, Cole, along with Harry Moody and Andrew Achenbaum, became a strong voice for the importance of humanistic and interpretive approaches within mainstream gerontology through their advocacy within the Gerontological Society of America (GSA). In fact, Cole functioned as the face of humanistic gerontology, serving on panels and also as GSA's keynote speaker in 2018. He also presented to the President's Council of Bioethics of George W. Bush on June 24, 2004. His work is broadly cited in gerontology textbooks, and his seminal work on aging, *The Journey of Life*, is still widely read and taught.

Cole also remains an influential figure in aging studies, a field that emerged after humanistic gerontology, with a slightly different set of underlying assumptions about approaches to understanding old age than gerontology. Founded in the late 1940s, gerontology typically describes a multidisciplinary social science field that seeks to understand aging through social actors, institutions, and structures. Aging studies (or age studies) emerged in the early 2000s as a critical response to what many scholars in the field viewed as an overly biomedicalized view of aging. Drawing from approaches used in gender studies, race studies, media studies, and others, aging studies has sought to focus more on the cultural representations of age (e.g., in film and other media) to better understand aging as a cultural construction that is shaped by material and social circumstances. Like humanistic gerontology, aging studies scholars typically come from humanities-based or interpretive social science backgrounds. However, aging studies scholars often do not draw on earlier gerontological work to frame their inquiries, with few exceptions to include work by Cole and Achenbaum. As reflected by the scholarship in this current volume, Cole's influence can be seen in the diverse approaches used to understand later life.

MEDICAL HUMANITIES

In addition to his influence in gerontology and aging studies, Cole's impact was also felt in another burgeoning field: medical humanities. The term "medical humanities" first appears in an obituary the historian George Sarton wrote in 1948 in *Isis*, the journal of the History of Science Society.[6] The very first medical school in the United States, University of Pennsylvania, included medical history in its required curriculum and was taught by the physician-educators who owned large libraries of historical works. All American medical education changed after the 1910 release of *Medical Education in the United States and Canada: A Report to the Carnegie Foundation for the Advancement of Teaching*, or what is more commonly called "The Flexner Report."[7] Led by Abraham Flexner, the report cited the lack of rigorous, scientific, and evidence-based practices in U.S. medical education. Its release led to the closing of many medical schools and a reform of the curriculum toward the science-based one we know today. However, just a few years later, Abraham Flexner wrote "Medicine . . . is today sadly deficient in cultural and philosophic background."[8] Flexner had assumed that students would arrive at medical school with a four-year liberal arts baccalaureate background, but the liberal arts had been replaced by the undergraduate study of science and math. The new medical students were more versed in the sciences, but less in the human condition. In the following decades, this growing divide between the "two cultures" saw medicine gain in knowledge, technology, and power, while the humanities became more insular, isolated from real-world concerns.[9]

To connect medicine with the liberal arts, various medical schools attempted to bring more humanities into their curriculum: Johns Hopkins and Western Reserve (now Case Western Reserve) introduced medical history for brief periods, though this teaching was conducted by physicians. In 1972, four years after founding its Department of Humanities, Penn State College of Medicine hired the first humanist faculty member in a medical school: literary scholar Joanne Trautmann Banks.[10] A new generation of philosophers and literary scholars with interest in the humanities in medicine realized that "the humanities offered orientation to the power and challenges of medicine."[11] Through the humanities, medicine was re-grounded toward the larger human questions of life

6. Sarton, "Seventy-First Critical Bibliography of the History and Philosophy of Science."
7. Flexner, *Medical Education in the United States and Canada*.
8. Flexner, *Medical Education: A Comparative Study*, 18.
9. Engelhardt, "Birth of the Medical Humanities." Snow, *The Two Cultures*.
10. Oransky, "Obituary."
11. Engelhardt, "Birth of the Medical Humanities," 238.

and death, meaning and purpose. Medical humanities, thus, sought to bridge the divide between medicine and the liberal arts wrought by the Flexner Report by humanizing medicine and bringing new relevance to the humanities. The second half of the twentieth century saw the founding of national associations, journals, and institutional centers leading to an established field of medical humanities.[12] For example, the University of Texas Medical Branch founded the Institute for the Medical Humanities in 1973 and, fifteen years later, offered the world's first PhD in the field, a graduate program that Cole founded. Decades later, Cole later coauthored, with Carson and Nathan Carlin, *Medical Humanities*, the first textbook of the field,[13] and he also coauthored a choose-your-own-adventure book, titled *The Brewsters*,[14] for health professions students. *The Brewsters* is an example of a humanities-oriented approach to clinical ethics, professionalism, and research ethics.

BECOMING UNDISCIPLINED

While, as noted, the unifying thread of this book is Cole himself, we also have a particular interpretation of Cole that unites these essays—namely, that Cole is "undisciplined."[15] That is, Cole's work does not neatly fit into any single field or discipline, and he often pushes the boundaries of conventional thinking. He has meandered from place to place, intellectually speaking, moving far beyond his training as a professional historian.

But what does "undisciplined" mean? Before one can become undisciplined, one first must examine what that process rejects, in this case, being disciplined. The Australian sociologist Bryan Turner proposed five definitions of discipline: (1) a branch of knowledge; (2) a method or training and instruction; (3) a system of rules to maintain order in a religious organization; (4) obedience through punishment; and (5) medical regimen to ensure a patient follows a physician's orders.[16] In academic terms—Turner's branch of knowledge and method of training

12. Klugman and Jones, "To Be or Not."
13. Cole, Carlin, and Carson, *Medical Humanities*.
14. Spike, Cole, Buday, *The Brewsters*.
15. This is a term that was invoked during the wrap-up session of a conference for Cole, organized by Nathan Carlin on April 12–14, 2023, at McGovern Medical School in Houston, Texas. Craig Klugman suggested that this term applied to Cole and could be a useful organizing idea for this book.
16. Turner, "Discipline."

and instruction—disciplines share five characteristics: (a) a defined area of research; (b) a body of accumulated unique knowledge; (c) theoretical and conceptual paradigms; (d) jargon—its own technical language; (e) developed research methods; and (f) are manifested in academic departments and professional associations.[17] Disciplines are thus about power and control—to define an area of study, to draw the boundaries, to enforce a system, to grant entrance to the faculty, and sometimes to punish those who violate them.

Disciplines must be learned. Like the soldier learning how to dress, salute, march, fight, address an officer, and perform their assigned tasks, the graduate student must be trained into their discipline. Turner suggests that we must recognize that academic disciplines are "artificial constructs."[18] He adds that they do not occur in nature but rather are "intellectual divisions of the mind" and "are socially constructed perspectives" about what to think, what to consider, how to think, how to analyze, and how to present information.[19] Graduate students must learn the history, canon, research methods, scholarly jargon, reputations of departments and journals, how to address the faculty, grant sources, and writing formats of their discipline. Both being a soldier and an academic requires a refinement of the mind and the body toward a goal—one to fight and one to generate knowledge. We do not do these pursuits naturally; we must be trained into a discipline. There is nothing wrong with the disciplines, except when they are not aware of their biases and rootedness in a perspective. Disciplines can become trapped in securing their own continued existence rather than trying something new that might benefit other people or other areas of knowledge outside of the discipline.

So, to return to the question, what does it mean to be "undisciplined"? According to the Oxford English Dictionary, to be "undisciplined" is to be untrained or not subject to [military] discipline.[20] This connotation is negative—a person who is lazy, unproductive, a victim of their appetites, and morally suspect. This, of course, is not what we mean to invoke by using the term. Rather, to be undisciplined is to reject the structures that have become ingrained over time and to set out on a new path. In academia, this can mean moving from the formal, fixed, siloed structure of disciplines to find something new. The undisciplined scholar,

17. Krishnan, *What Are Academic Disciplines?*
18. Turner, "Discipline," 184.
19. Turner, "Discipline," 184.
20. *Oxford English Dictionary*, s.v., "Undisciplined."

then, is one who begins in a disciplinary setting with traditional training, but then chooses to leave and to explore new disciplines, new languages, and new ways of seeing the world. To become undisciplined is an act of rebellion, and of courage, since it means leaving a well-established and respected discipline for undiscovered territories.

Starting in the 1960s, scholars began rejecting the silos of the disciplines. Scholars from a variety of disciplines came together in programs, institutions, and centers that held in common an area of study, rather than a history, canon, or shared research methodology. These were working spaces where one would not be disciplined for coloring outside the lines. Literary critic Kenneth Burke talks about the "perspective of incongruity"[21] or, as noted by Tod Chambers, using the lens and language of "one discipline to study the subject matter of another."[22] Clifford Geertz calls this "genre mixing."[23] Examples include when one uses: literature to examine medical records (narrative medicine); comics to communicate scientific and medical ideas (graphic medicine); or narrative to explain moral issues in the life sciences (narrative ethics). What these innovations have in common, as Geertz would say, is they reject a divide between theory and data—they pay attention to the applied, they embrace subjectivity, and they reject claims to moral neutrality. In moving away from departments and disciplines, medical humanities became multidisciplinary. As Chambers observes, "Distinct disciplines, each contributing individually to the medical humanities, but neither so intertwined that the loss of one would radically reshape the other."[24]

Undisciplining scholarship shifts focus away from what is normal and privileged. This decentering makes evident power dynamics, implicit biases, and the construction of normativity. For example, in medicine, the patient's story is often ignored, whereas in medical humanities it becomes a central focus that shows the lack of control sick people have in their care. Kumagi and Wear refer to this process as "making strange":

> An integral part of this orientation is the critical questioning of taken-for-granted assumptions, unconscious biases, and unquestioned attitudes that may distort and dehumanize relationships and interactions in medical care. To stimulate this type of critical questioning . . . literature, movies, art, and interactive

21. Burke, *Permanence and Change*.
22. Chambers, "Virtue of Incongruity in the Medical Humanities," 152.
23. Geertz, "Blurred Genres."
24. Chambers, "Virtue of Incongruity in the Medical Humanities," 152.

theater [can be used] to engage students and faculty in reflective exploration and discussions and have made use of a key pedagogical tool, that of provoking a state of cognitive disequilibrium—that is, the sense of discomfort one may feel when encountering a person, an experience, or a perspective which is unfamiliar. Through this state of disquiet and discomfort, one is prompted to reflect on personal values, beliefs, perspectives, and life experiences in an attempt to incorporate this new entity into one's understanding, and in doing so, reflection.[25]

Becoming undisciplined requires not only throwing off the limitations of disciplinary thinking, adopting a critical and reflective approach, and making strange, but also being willing to use these insights to create change in the world. Medical humanities evolved to not only know about something—often an injustice or bias—but requires that we act upon it, similar to Cole's own personal evolution when he moved from the traditional university setting to the context of medicine. Thus, it is not a surprise that medical humanities is aligned with feminist studies, disabilities studies, and queer studies (think Foucault's *Birth of the Clinic*[26]), all of which share similar aims of education and action.

Becoming undisciplined does not just happen. It is a conscious choice, a recognition that the limited view of a discipline does not provide a full picture to answer a question. To be undisciplined is an act of rebellion against the usual way of doing things and risks sanction from those vested in preserving the status quo. In summary, becoming undisciplined means that one:

a. Recognizes and identifies the limitations of solely disciplinary approaches;

b. Embraces subjectivity and rejects moral neutrality;

c. Recognizes and rejects the power structures that have limited knowledge generation and its application;

d. Decenters the narrative to adopt a strange perspective;

e. Seeks collaboration with others from different disciplines;

f. Develops new and constantly evolving ways of working;

g. Embraces application of the theoretical;

---

25. Kumagi and Wear, "Making Strange," 976.
26. Foucault's *Birth of the Clinic*.

h. Becomes generalists in the new field; and

i. Seeks to educate students in interdisciplinarity.

Of note, this succinctly describes how Cole has operated over the decades. Because being undisciplined often entails reacting against disciplines, there is inherently a subversive element in being undisciplined, which fit neatly with Cole's 1960s radicalism that, as noted, became transformed when he entered the context of medical education. This will be explored in much greater detail in chapter 1, where Andrew Achenbaum delves into Cole's work on aging, showcasing how Cole was undisciplined and subversive.

But perhaps the most undisciplined of Cole's projects began in 1984, in a psychiatry case conference focused on Eldrewey Stearns, a psychotic Black man whom nobody believed when he claimed to be the original Texas integration leader. After more than a decade of interviews with all those involved, Cole published the book *No Color Is My Kind: The Life of Eldrewey Stearns and the Integration of Houston*.[27] Part history, part psychobiography, and also introspective, the book wove together Stearns's life, the untold story of desegregation in Texas, and Cole's relationship with Stearns. To cap it off, he produced an accompanying documentary film, *The Strange Demise of Jim Crow*,[28] which aired on over sixty PBS stations. Collecting life stories became a key form of his research in later films and in his later work, most notably *Old Man Country*.[29] These projects and topics will be explored in various chapters in this volume.

LOOKING AHEAD

The chapters for this book were originally written for a Festschrift conference for Cole organized by Nathan Carlin on April 12–14, 2023, at McGovern Medical School in Houston, Texas. The chapters were circulated prior to the meeting so that each chapter could be workshopped.

---

27. Cole, *No Color Is My Kind*.
28. Cole, *The Strange Demise of Jim Crow*.
29. Cole, *Old Man Country*.

FIGURE 1

Conference for Thomas Cole
April 12, 2003
Photograph by Dwight Andrews

The conversations were stimulating, fun, and productive, and, as a group, we shaped the structure of the book. Also, the chapters here were revised based on the feedback from the conference. We are deeply grateful to Wipf and Stock for publishing this Festschrift, something that few publishers are willing to do anymore.

This book is divided into four parts. Part one focuses on the journey of life. In chapter 1, Andrew Achenbaum views Cole as a *puer-senex*, both a young boy and an old man searching for meaning, exploring this theme throughout Cole's career by focusing on a wide-range of his body of work as an historian, culture-driven gerontologist, medical-humanities trailblazer, film maker, and mentor. In chapter 2, Roberta Maierhofer provides a feminist and anocritical perspective on the journey of life. Part two of the book focuses on life stories. In chapter 3, Kate de Medeiros focuses on Cole's work related to narrative gerontology and dementia. In particular, she considers in detail Cole's interview with Walter Wink, while Wink was experiencing dementia. In chapter 4, Benjamin Saxton writes about Cole's "dialogical sensibility" by reflecting on their ongoing work together. In chapter 5, Craig Klugman analyzes the four documentary films that Cole created, especially in light of Cole's affirmation of Martin Buber's I-Thou relationship. Part three of the book focuses on cultural studies. In chapter 6, Woods Nash writes about generativity in light of two of Cormac McCarthy's novels: *No Country for Old Men* and *The Road*. In chapter 7 Renee Flores, a geriatrician and sexual health specialist, writes about research on older women's sexuality and analyzes two films that depict older women's naked bodies in light of this research. Part four of the book focuses on religion, spirituality, and the Anthropocene. In chapter 8, Paul Higgs writes about issues relating to religion and spirituality in the Fourth Age, and in chapter 9, Larry Churchill writes about intergenerational justice in light of climate change. The book concludes with an epilogue by Craig Irvine. As an appendix, there is an impact review of *Medical Humanities*, written by Annelise Berler and Isaac Chua.

In *Old Man Country*, an undisciplined book that is part oral history, part journalism, and part memoir, Cole writes about a future time when he will step down as Director of the McGovern Center:

> This will not be easy for me: What will I do? Who will I be? I want to feel less pressured by the demands of full-time work. I want to spend more time with Thelma Jean, to visit my children and to play with my grandson, to strengthen old friendships. And, like each of the men to whom I talked, I will still need to feel needed, to serve others, to feel that I am making a difference in the world.[30]

That future time has arrived, as Cole did step down as director, with Carlin succeeding him as director. And, as this book attests, Cole still is making a difference in the world, both with his ideas and his actions. These essays are a small token of appreciation for the difference he has made in our lives and countless others.

---

30. Cole, *Old Man Country*, 167.

PART ONE

The Journey of Life—Two Perspectives

1

On Being Undisciplined and Subversive
Thomas Cole's Search for Meaning

W. Andrew Achenbaum

As THOMAS COLE's FRIEND and colleague for forty-six years, I am both privileged and challenged to interpret transformative components and contrarieties that punctuate his lifelong search for credible, meaning-laden insights.[1] Traumatic memories framed Cole's creatively balancing unique qualities of a *puer* (undisciplined and idealistic) and a *senex* (subversive yet authoritative). "These diverging, conflicting tendencies are ultimately interdependent, forming two faces of the one configuration, each face never far from the other."[2] Cole still acts like an archetypal *puer-senex*, blessed and burdened.

Cole's first and last single-authored books attest to his dual-faced journey:

1. I am indebted both to Thomas Cole for illuminating his life story over lunches and in emails, and to Kate de Medeiros for sharing her 2003 interview with Cole. They, along with Nathan Carlin, Larry Churchill, and Roberta Maierhofer, offered sage comments on earlier drafts of this essay. I am enormously grateful to Stephen Katz for his continuing efforts to convert me, a tribal elder, into a Cole-like nomadic gerontologist.

2. Hillman and Elder, eds., *Senex and Puer*. Hillman's notions of *puer-senex* are elaborated in Slater, ed., *James Hillman Uniform Edition*. "The senex consolidates, grounds, and disciplines; the puer flashes with insight and thrives on fantasy and creativity," notes Slater. Slater, ed., *James Hillman Uniform Edition*, 8–9. "These diverging, conflicting tendencies are ultimately interdependent, forming two faces of the one configuration, each face never far from the other."

When my father died at the age of twenty-seven, I was immediately transformed into an aged four-year old, a *senex puer* (sic). For many years, I carried a burden of guilt and depression, punctuated by primal flashes of wisdom. The sequence of generations in my life had been broken . . . . Perhaps, if I am blessed, I may someday become a *puer senex*, an innocent and playful old man.³

My thinking about aging has always been shaped by the image of life as a journey. . . . *Old Man Country* seeks to reclaim and enhance the humanity of men in the Fourth Age. . . . *Old Man Country* is also a personal book. Each chapter tells a story of my conversation with an elder, including my observations, insights, reactions, and feelings. In a sense, the book is an autobiographical field report, a memoir of my own journey toward an uncertain wisdom, and the final payment on my childhood's psychic debt.⁴

Amidst piercing disclosures Cole envisions himself as a childlike, sagacious sojourner. His *puer-senex* life story narrates suffering psychic pains in a search for uncertain meaning.

As a trailblazer in both age studies and medical humanities, Cole undercut bio-medical-psycho-social paradigms through critical thinking and political activism. Later, he was called to be certified as a spiritual director, relentlessly coupling interior reflections, practical notions, and intimate experiences in order to surmount obstacles with ethical breakthroughs.⁵ Now an elder of the tribe and a "child of God,"⁶ Cole faces finitude through personal, spiritual, and cultural identities that transform

---

3. Cole, *Journey of Life*, xv, xvii. Here, Cole inverts *puer senex* and *senex puer*. For consistency's sake, I shall refer to Cole being a *puer-senex* throughout this essay.

4. Cole, *Old Man Country*, 7, 11, 20–21.

5. Other contributors to this volume ably fill gaps here in this essay about Cole's contributions to medical humanities, pedagogy, film-making, radical social advocacy, and activism. I cannot and do not attempt to compose what would seem to be a straight-forward biographical sketch in order to impose a neat reconstruction of Cole's eclectic professional foci and personal wanderings. They arose through primal awakenings, internal doubts and questioning, and formidable obstacles. Nor, I suspect, would Cole expect me to try to do so. Cole's interplay of being a *puer-senex* reminds me of what Ralph Waldo Emerson wrote about subjectivity in "Experience": "We do not see directly, but mediately [sic] . . . . We must hold hard to this poverty, however, scandalous, and by more self-recoveries, after the sallies of action, possess our axis more firmly." Emerson, *Essays*, 307.

6. Howard Thurman best defines my characterization of Cole as a "child of God," despite never feeling personally loved. Thurman, *Growing Edge*, 17–18.

interpersonal relations, themselves suffused with his senses of the meaning of love, sacred, and earthy.[7]

THE FORMATIVE YEARS

"I first became interested in aging when I was in middle school.... There was an article in *Scientific American* on aging that somehow really got my attention.... And I think I was frightened by that," Cole recalled in an interview 20 years ago with Kate de Medeiros, then one of his graduate students.[8] "I spent a lot of time with my grandparents and I was very attracted to the image of older people as wise, able to provide guidance about how to live in the world," added Cole. "So it was a combination of fear and desire, really."[9] Cole, at age fifty-four both a precocious *puer* and playful *senex*, recalled his fear and desire of being intrigued by older people's capacity to be mentors, despite the ravages of age. Herein lie the symbiotic foundations for his enduring *puer-senex* quest to amalgamate and energize elements of his thoughts and deeds into a holistic authenticity.

Cole frequently relates the painful, poignant backstory of his father's 1953 accident, but recalls that, at age four, he could not make sense of details. Not until the late 1990s did an aunt acknowledge a truth Cole had long feared—that his father had died by suicide. During years of grief, Cole's grandmothers lovingly doted on him as the firstborn Jewish male; next, his grandfathers died; and then the adolescent fought with his mother and stepfather. Cole's undergraduate years at Yale (1967–71) were partly spent trying to reconcile traumatic guilt while struggling to make sense of their consequences.

An anti-war, civil-rights protestor and champion fencer, Cole majored in philosophy. Cole "learned how to think" conceptually and to engage in political activism, he told me, under the tutelage of two Yale professors. Merold Westphal, a "preacher's kid," widened Cole's intellectual horizons with a steady diet of Hegel, Kierkegaard, and Buber. Nine years his senior, Westphal "went on to write important books on

---

7. Twigg and Martin, "Challenge of Cultural Gerontology," 1–7.

8. de Medeiros, interview with Thomas Cole," November 12, 2003.

9. de Medeiros, interview with Thomas Cole," November 12, 2003. Here, I believe, is an instance in which Cole refracts and qualifies remarks in an intentional effort to pull threads of thought and meaning together.

the phenomenology of religion (versus studying systematic theology)."[10] Cole wrote his senior thesis under William McBride, a Marxist political philosopher eleven years his elder. He gratefully loved these two men for awakening intellectual, spiritual, and political impulses.

Westphal the phenomenologist and political scientist McBride urged Cole to go to Wesleyan University to study with historian Donald Meyer, "an expert in offering a vigorous challenge to prevailing views, especially about sectors of our society that figured much too little in our history."[11] Meyer (1924–2018) encouraged "a 60s know-it-all radical . . . always taking up causes, things that needed to be set right" to progress as an outspokenly relentless subversive.[12] Deciding to investigate "older people as marginalized and social policy . . . [a] kind of border crossing [that] was comfortable," Cole wrote his master's essay on the history of state pension plans. Social Security "from the left-wing perspective that it didn't go far enough, it didn't cover enough people, and that the levels were too low."[13] Recognizing that Cole remained more interested in radical politics than primarily to be an intellectual historian, Meyer then "passed me off to Christopher Lasch who had been one of his mentees."[14]

"Kit" Lasch (1932–94) served as both a father figure and kindred rebellious spirit. An "incredibly literate person, he loved fiction, poetry, creative writing. And I enjoyed all that," Cole told de Medeiros. Above all they shared a "love of learning."[15] The pair stayed up drinking the night before Cole received his doctoral hood. As a graduation present, Lasch autographed a score of Schumann's lieder, songs they had sung together.[16]

---

10. Cole conversation, and follow-up email, with Andy Achenbaum, March 25, 2022. Cole's preference for Westphal's phenomenology and McBride's Marxism helped to crystalize his undisciplined, subversive persona as both an experiential thinker and radical activist.

11. Curiel, "Meyer Remembers for Shaping Curriculum in History Department."

12. de Medeiros interview, November 12, 2003; Cole email to Achenbaum, March 24, 2022.

13. de Medeiros interview with Cole, November 12, 2003. While I present an interpretation different from Cole's in Achenbaum, *Social Security*, as well as in Achenbaum, *Safeguarding Social Security for Future Generations*, I salute Cole's pathway to justice and compassion. Relying on his discerning moral imagination, Cole pictured in his mind what believed was missing in the present moment.

14. Cole email to Achenbaum, March 24, 2022. Here again, Cole passively accedes to mentors' lead.

15. de Medeiros interview with Cole, November 12, 2003.

16. Cole conversation with Achenbaum, February 8, 2023.

Quickening the friendship and mentorship was Lasch's willingness to share gifts as an historian and social critic. The author of *The New Radicalism in America* and *Haven in a Heartless World* saw "the past as a political and psychological treasury from which we draw the reserves . . . that we need to cope with the future."[17] How fortuitous for Cole to be guided by a fellow traveler who appreciated and fed his political and philosophical cravings manifestly present at Yale and Wesleyan.

Cole was moved by Lasch's *The Culture of Narcissism: American Life in an Age of Diminishing Expectations*, a perfectly timed best seller for readers unsettled by stagflation, besieged by an energy crisis, and (in the aftermath of Vietnam and Watergate) grappling with a growing distrust of institutional leaders. President Carter, himself mired in a cultural malaise, invited Lasch to Washington to explain why "every society reproduces its culture, its norms, its underlying assumptions, its modes of organizing experience—in the individual, in the form of personality."[18]

One passage in *The Culture of Narcissism* undoubtedly spoke to thirty-two-year old Cole, a *puer-senex* who remained haunted in fear about death. Like Lasch who declaimed old age's relation to dying, Cole discerned distinctive meanings that few young men grasped:

> In a society that dreads old age and death, aging holds a special terror for those who fear dependence and whose self-esteem requires the admiration usually reserved for youth, beauty, celebrity, or charm. The usual defenses against the ravages of age—identification with ethical or artistic values beyond one's immediate interests, intellectual curiosity, the consoling emotional warmth derived from happy relationships in the past—can do nothing for the narcissist.[19]

Other historians in addition to Lasch influenced the emerging professional's growth. Cole participated in David Van Tassel's cross-disciplinary conference on "Human Values and Aging: New Challenges to Research on Aging"; devoured my two-volume doctoral history of aging; and read two monographs, one by Peter Stearns, *Old Age in European Society*, and one by David Hackett Fischer, *Growing Old in America*.

---

17. Mattson, "Historian as a Social Critic," 381.
18. Lasch, *Culture of Narcissism*, 34.
19. Lasch, *Culture of Narcissism*, 209.

There was more to be written about the cultural history of senescence, reckoned Cole, as he began work on a dissertation.[20] He spent a year at Father Flanagan's Boys Home in Omaha, where he delved into thousands of sermons preached between the colonial period and antebellum America. Before finishing his thesis in 1980, Cole was emotionally drawn and spiritually touched by Henri Nouwen's *Aging: The Fulfillment of Life*. The priest-philosopher stirred Cole's deepening ruminations on the human condition: "We have only one cycle to live, and that living it is the source of our greatest joy."[21] Individuals, declared Nouwen, are distinctive parts, spokes on the wheel of life.

All these sparks were unconnected, however. Clusters of images, feelings, and experiences between his New Haven childhood and first academic job were coalescing slowly without fusing. Pain and guilt colored his search for meaningful truths in inkhorn sermons and premodern texts. Cole imaginatively muddled through what today is called intersectionality within the context of a tectonic shift in academic landscapes: "The conditions of postmodern knowledge have disrupted the modern projects of disciplinary progress and universal representation."[22] Figuring out how to integrate radical truths within cross-disciplinary elements became for Cole an undisciplined, subversive although frustrating venture. Buoyed with assistance from several father figures, Cole nonetheless was ready to translate his gerontological knowledge and to leap into concepts and constructs set forth by bioethicists in medical humanities.[23]

Academic borders, like fluid cultures and liminal individuals, are porous enough to be bred by knowledge exchanges across an ever-widening spectrum. "To compare, to exchange ideas, to learn and to build from differences to mix, not to keep things separate."[24] Cole in 1982 desired a congenial multidisciplinary home wherein he, the perennial *puer-senex*,

---

20. Cole to Achenbaum, email, June 15, 2022.

21. Nouwen and Gaffney, *Aging*. Cole was reminded of the book as he composed *Old Man Country*, 165.

22 52 I see parallels in Katz, *Disciplining Old Age*, 139–40. See also Katz and Whitehouse, "Legacies, Generations, and Ageing Futures," 245–47.

23. Cole's work as a critical gero-historian (unlike mine) was manifestly subsumed into medical humanities. His inquiries into the meaning of old age had cogent parallels to work in medical humanities. Cole's career proceeded for decades in the Galveston medical center to bridge two paths of research, writing, and advocacy—gerontology and medical humanities.

24. Rovelli, *There are Places in the World Where Rules are Less Important than Kindness*, 18.

could comprehend and compensate for losses in childhood and fears in adolescent angst. That search for Absolute Truth was vain, Cole gradually perceived, insofar as uncertainties could be diminished, but never totally eradicated.

Instead of seizing on definitive conclusions, Cole wanted to pursue ideas with a high degree of credibility. He was ready to engage the cluster of subjective and probabilistic, subversive and undisciplined polarities that would arise at Galveston's medical-humanities center within the University of Texas Medical Branch (UTMB). Cole was keen in 1982 to deal with the perplexities of a philosophical-political approach to scientific models and methodologies.

THE FIRST FRUITS OF COLE'S SEARCH FOR OLD-AGE MEANING

Ronald Carson, Cole's UTMB mentor, was only nine years older, so theirs was a partnership more fraternal than paternal. Having studied at Colgate Rochester Divinity School under Death-of-God theologian William Hamilton, Carson built the Institute for the Medical Humanities into one of the premier multidisciplinary centers for research and teaching. Shortly after hiring Cole, Carson asked him to spearhead the first U.S. doctoral program in medical humanities. In this capacity, Cole probed cultural-aging knots of "meaning," personally and academically, which bore first fruits in practice.[25]

With generous foundation support, Cole and his colleague, Sally Gadow,[26] invited inter-disciplinary, inter-professional scholars to UTMB in 1983 to discuss and critique the uneasy relationship between aging and meaning. "For Sally Gadow, the meaning of aging is to be found in individual subjectivity," noted Carson. "Throughout the course of this project, the editors' perspectives on aging and meaning have remained in creative tension. In Thomas Cole's view, aging must be understood within

---

25. Cole, Carlin, and Carson, *Medical Humanities*. Cole email to Achenbaum, February 8, 2023. Carson served as Director of the Institute for the Medical Humanities at UTMB until 2005.

26. The organizers' differences in training, Carson observed, were significant: Cole was a cultural historian; Gadow was doing research on theories of nursing. Two dozen graduate students as well as scholars in the social sciences, humanities, law, and medicine participated in the 1983 conference.

an intersubjective web of cultural meanings that are embedded in social relations and practices."[27]

Cole formulated a profound exegesis of the keyword "meaning" in the volume of conference essays, which was published as *What Does It Mean to Grow Old?* He writes:

> What is meaning? Why does it matter? ... The concept of meaning contains a crucial ambiguity. It is ... a point of intersection from which one may move either into living or into theories about our living.... We human beings must enter into our own webs of meaning to understand ourselves.... This seminal ambiguity allows one to connect the world of public understandings with the inner struggle for wholeness.[28]

Although it is tempting to connect the existential dots wherein "meaning refers to lived perceptions of coherence, sense or significance of experience,"[29] Cole amplified his own definition of meaning's "seminal ambiguity" in editor's "Introduction" to his part of the book.[30]

To preface ethicist William F. May's provocative and contrarian "The Virtues and Vices of the Elderly," Cole wrote that "taking old people seriously as members of the moral community means understanding their obligations as well as their rights .... May helps initiate the long overdue reconstruction of guidelines for moral and spiritual life in old age."[31] About Harry R. Moody's "The Meaning of Life and the Meaning of Old Age," Cole opined that "all thought is historically conditioned—that is related to changing structures of power and patterns of culture."[32] Other conference scholars in the humanities, social sciences, law and medicine who assessed the "tattered web of cultural meanings," bolstered Cole's attack on "ageism, which currently passes for an enlightened view of aging [that] is both conceptually and existentially inadequate, as well

---

27. Ronald Carson, "Foreword," xiii-xiv. The contents of the book *What Does It Mean to Grow Old* were divided into two halves. Cole labelled his part "The Tattered Web of Cultural Meanings"; Gadow titled her part "Subjectivity: Literature, Imagination, and Frailty."

28. Cole and Gadow, *What Does It Mean to Grow Old?* "Introduction to Part One," 4.

29. Cole and Gadow, *What Does It Mean to Grow Old?* "Introduction to Part One," 4-5.

30. Cole and Gadow underscored their differences in editorial perspective in their editorial prefaces.

31. Cole and Gadow, *What Does It Mean to Grow Old?* "William F. May," 41.

32. Cole and Gadow, *What Does It Mean to Grow Old?* "Harry R. Moody," 9.

as politically dangerous."³³ Working within a medical complex, Cole quickly realized that peer-reviewed publications in prestigious scientific journals counted more than writing history monographs to obtain tenure in history departments. Writing pieces that enlivened his mental acumen and emotional impulses, Cole demolished constructs in the anti-aging movement in "The Fall of Daedalus," part of a special issue of *Generations* that he co-edited with Barbara Thompson,³⁴ and in other peer-reviewed essays before Cambridge University Press issued *The Journey of Life*.

"In one sense," declared the author, "the book results from my own engagement with these motifs [the ages (or stages) of life and the journey of life], my personal and intellectual grappling with their significance."³⁵ Cole rejected dualistic thinking and rebuked scientific paradigms about processes of aging in postmodern, graying culture:

> In rebuilding a moral economy of an extended life course, we must not only attend to questions of justice within and between different stages of life, we must also forge a new sense of the meanings and purposes of the last half of life.³⁶

Cole in his early forties decided to spearhead political, philosophical, and ethical projects that underscored "why humanistic perspectives critically mattered in the field of gerontology."³⁷ Editing handbooks on the humanities and aging presented a complement to bio-medical-psycho-social constructs deployed by mainstream members advancing gerontology. That said, the project, which over the course of four volumes became more patently undisciplined and subversive. It facilitated the *puer-senex*'s influence on experts in geriatric medical humanities.³⁸

---

33. Cole and Gadow, *What Does It Mean to Grow Old?* "Introduction to Part One," 4.

34. Cole, "Fall of Daedalus," 66–68.

35. Cole, *Journey of Life*, xix. Part One of the book traces "The Ages of Life and the Journey of Life: Transcendent Ideals" in western culture. Part Two explicates "The Dualism of Aging in Victorian America." Part Three assesses twentieth-century visions of "Science and the Ideal of Normal Aging."

36. Cole, *Journey of Life*, 237. Larry Churchill elaborates Cole's sense of aging transcending dualities; he italicized a reference to Cole: "Aging is a moral and spiritual frontier because its unknowns, terrors, and mysteries cannot be successfully crossed without *acceptance of physical decline and mortality*, and a sense of the sacred." Stating that "this should alert us that meaning in aging and meaning in death are a package, best explored together," Churchill punctuates his essay's critique of the ethics of global warming. Cole, *Journey of Life*, 243.

37. Cole, *Journey of Life*, 243.

38. See, for instance, O'Neill, "Geriatric Medical Humanities," 337–38. In between

COLE AUGMENTS HIS SEARCH FOR MEANING

To leaven and advance the aging enterprise's blossoming research, teaching, and outreach, Cole, over the next thirty years, published four handbooks focusing on the humanities and aging. The project had been suggested by Robert Kastenbaum (who had staged a play at the 1983 UTMB conference), and was seconded by David Van Tassel (with whom Cole had remained very close). These father-figures played important roles in making editorial decisions, but it was Cole who managed the serial project's overall scope and articulated its original tone.

The first *Handbook of the Humanities and Aging* (published in 1992, the same year that Cambridge released *The Journey of Life*) was originally designed as a counterpoint to "handbooks on aging" and encyclopedias on biology, psychology, and the social sciences compiled by several cohorts of gerontological leaders who critiqued the latest work in aging studies.[39] The "overview" in Cole's presentation attests to this *Handbook's* undisciplined subversive intent:

> This *Handbook of the Humanities and Aging*, in contrast, approaches aging with a different epistemological stance—one that strives for contextual understanding and interpretation along with explanation and that considers scientific method to be one way of knowing among others. Again, the humanities have become important in late twentieth century gerontology precisely because conventional scientific and professional gerontology has retreated into a formal, technical rationality that lacks a shared discourse for addressing moral, aesthetic, and

---

Cole, Carlin, and Carson published *Medical Humanities*, the first and only textbook in the field. Since it was published during the period in which Cole was editing the four aging-and-humanities handbooks, I count it as the fifth such compendium, though this textbook is not an edited volume (it is a coauthored book). Cole told me on August 5, 2023 that "it was a kind of familial collaboration: Carson mentored Cole, and Cole mentored Carlin."

39. The first volume of the *Handbook of the Humanities and Aging* was designed to expand an important publishing outlet that became essential in updating gerontology's research. Cowdry's *The Problems of Ageing* set the standard precedent for the biomedical scientists who founded the Gerontological Society of America (GSA) in 1945, then amplified by Nathan Shock and Edward Stieglitz in the 1950s. The next wave of GSA luminaries—including but not exclusively Vern Bengston, James Birren, Dale Dannefer, Linda George, Malcolm Johnson, and Chris Phillipson—followed suit. For more, see Achenbaum, *Crossing Frontiers* and Park, *Old Age, New Science*.

spiritual issues or for appreciating their historical and cultural contexts.[40]

The twenty articles were placed in four parts—historical; world religions and spiritual; artistic expression, creativity, and representations of aging; and commentaries on the state of the art by historians, a literary critic, a philosopher, and a coordinator of a gerontology program. In an "Afterword" I concluded that "the scope of the humanities, as the articles in this *Handbook* attest, is wide-ranging, but some topics attract greater attention than others . . . the record is uneven."[41]

Cole dedicated the second edition of the *Handbook* to David D. Van Tassel, the generous senior historian who mentored most of our generation of scholars in the humanities.[42] The updated volume's format resembled the first edition, but Cole made noteworthy editorial changes. A third of the twenty-one chapters (with fourteen new contributors) were written by scholars trained in one of the social sciences. Cole underscored the value critical thinking, especially if tied to a political agenda, in an Introduction coauthored with Ruth Ray:

> This volume demonstrates the many ways that humanistic gerontology both necessitates and promotes interdisciplinary thinking. We have divided the chapters into four sections: 1) Disciplinary approaches; 2) Interdisciplinary perspectives; 3) Humanistic themes in the study of aging; 4) Reflections . . . . Besides crossing *academic* borders, interdisciplinarity in gerontology functions critically and politically. Critically, interdisciplinary scholars respond to the intellectual limits of disciplinary

---

40. Cole, "Humanities and Aging," xii-xiii.

41. Achenbaum, "Afterword," 465. Full disclosure: I have never emulated, but have long admired, Cole's subversive, undisciplined approach to scholarship.

42. At David Van Tassel's memorial service, Cole expressed concerns about the generational succession overseen by his beloved father-figure. After praising Van Tassel's devotion to doctoral students Carole Haber, Brian Grattan, Judith Cetina, me, and himself, Cole said that he didn't see "a natural cohort of people coming after me, people my age in their 40s and 50s . . . . And that troubles me. . . . I don't think we're attracting enough good people to carry this on. I don't know why this is, but we're not going to be as productive as we've been." de Medeiros interview with Cole, November 12, 2003. I agree that there are not enough younger stars like de Medeiros advancing interdisciplinary humanistic perspectives, which is one reason why many in GSA marginalize the humanities and arts (see my essay, "The Humanities and Arts in The Gerontological Society of America"). Cole remained very productive in age studies, but he also followed disparate (and seemingly unrelated) projects in writing about race as well as producing works of art and collaborating in film making.

thought; politically, they insist on social and intellectual change in order to move beyond these limits.[43]

My "Afterword" reinforced Cole's carefully parsed emphasis on the intellectual divergence:

> The second edition of the *Handbook of the Humanities and Aging* manifests excellence in research that both resembles and differs in important ways from what is found in successive editions of . . . gerontologic handbooks [that] are becoming narrower and narrower. We know more and more about less and less . . . . Paradoxically, [this second edition] is richer in detail. Its contributors seem more assured in making their assessments with an eye to disciplinary-specific conventions—even though they realize that that the canons that used to govern humanistic inquiry are in flux.[44]

At the turn of the century, I, too, knew that the fields of gerontology, which aspired to be a Big Science, and the humanities, grappling with interpretive flips, were undergoing critical turns.[45]

Cole, along with co-editors Ruth Ray and Robert Kastenbaum, designated the third edition not as a *handbook*, but as *A Guide to Humanistic Studies in Aging: What Does It Mean to Grow Old?* Keeping the four-part format and adding a dozen new contributors, Cole and Ray traversed dimensions of the *humanistic* realm to permeate a broader didactic intent:

> Humanistic study comprises not only humanistic studies but also the recently developed human sciences or interpretive social sciences. . . . Humanistic gerontology was born during a period of sweeping social and intellectual upheaval—just as the wave of postmodernism reached American shores. . . . Rediscovery of narrative as an essential form of seeking and representing knowledge has profoundly shaped gerontology's understanding of the search for meaning and identity.[46]

Interdisciplinary humanities, the quest for meaning and identity were central themes in the third edition's conceptual landscape. Age studies was penetrating disciplinary upheavals, contended Cole and Ray, as it

---

43. Cole and Ray, "Introduction," *Handbook*, xii.
44. Achenbaum, "Afterword," 421.
45. Like Cole, I did not anticipate at the time how much wider that gap would become.
46. Cole and Ray, "Introduction," *Guide*, 8, 10.

underscored the importance of narrative gerontology and other cultural fields "whose boundaries escape the confines of any specific community of interest."[47] The coeditors' overall intent is encapsulated in their fearless judging Robert Kastenbaum's distinctive role to be:

> We present the final chapter, written by our coeditor Robert Kastenbaum [. . . as] a kind of spiritual ethnography, filled with characters who are struggling to hold onto life while also learning to let go. Kastenbaum's fellow travelers have no energy to spare and no reason to fool themselves or anyone else...Describing these travelers and their existential grit, Kastenbaum helps us imagine our own future travels to an "authentic destination."[48]

This paean pivots to a turn to "spiritual ethnography" in thanking the polymath-mentor for preparing the pair to imagine future passages in their continuing search for authenticity.[49] What, I ponder, was behind Cole's self-reflections on meaning's "existential grit?" Why does he now identify coeditor Robert Kastenbaum as a "fellow traveler" instead of another father-figure resembling mentors at Yale, Lasch, and David Van Tassel? To my mind, Cole was spurred by age-irrelevant commitments to a shift that positioned his distinctively *puer-senex* persona: he was to begin advocating critical gerontology and then affirming the spiritual dimensions of maturity as he reconfigured fragments of Self all the time grappling with cultural changes.[50]

47. Gilleard and Higgs, *Contexts of Aging*, 8.

48. Cole and Ray, "Introduction," 23. I call it "fearless" because it was a subversive, undisciplined editorial invitation urging readers to not be afraid of future uncertainties.

49. Here is Cole's commentary about the 4th edition of *Critical Humanities and Ageing*: "After the publication of the third addition [of the handbook] in 2010, the gap between the gerontologists and humanists remained as wide as ever; worse, misunderstandings and distrust of each discipline's research and methodological approaches deepened . . . . Realizing that remedying this division would require a change in the editorial approach, Cole invited two new scholars to the team," Goldman, de Medeiros, and Cole, *Critical Humanities and Aging*, 3. Cole's role as third editor, I speculated over lunch on May 5, 2023, may have indicated his undisciplined disengagement masked as subversive passivity. As argued further on in this essay, however, I later sensed the *puer senex* was coming to terms with his spiritual bond to God.

50. This tack, which builds on the approach presented in the previous footnote, was consistent (I surmise) with Cole's acting out his undisciplined, subversively intellectual advocacy of *meaning* in critical gerontology, which preceded his spiritual awakening. For more, see the roundtable that Stephen Katz moderated between Cole, Brian de Vries, and me on "aging masculinities" in the *Journal of Aging Studies*. In *Disciplining Old Age*, Katz, framing the shift in sociological terms, posits that the study of "old age is caught in gerontology between the efforts to discipline, calculate, and manage it, and

FRESH MEANINGS OF CRITICAL GERONTOLOGY

Cole with three other editors issued a sequel, *Voices and Visions of Aging: Toward a Critical Gerontology*, to the first aging-and-humanities handbook. It signaled a nascent *critical* humanistic perspective on age studies. In the collection's Preface, Cole wrote:

> Stock-in-trade of the humanities—self-knowledge, historical understanding, imaginative communication, and critical appraisal of assumptions and values—can promote a more intellectually rigorous gerontology in several ways: *heuristically*, by offering new hypotheses for empirical inquiry; *critically*, by revealing values and power relations often concealed in existing methods and findings of empirical research; and *practically*, by offering reflection on the intentions and values realized by human actors in particular cultural settings. . . . Such engagement remains a central task for a socially responsible and intellectually vibrant "critical" gerontology.[51]

Critical gerontology became Cole's lens through which ideas about applying the humanities proved more than a heuristic, philosophical complement challenging GSA and anti-aging scientists. The new thrust, he hoped, would undercut an increasingly obsolescent, morally oblivious research agenda. This meaning-laden tack shepherded Cole's undisciplined, subversive approach to listening to older person's voices, intentions, and values as rigorous, sentient, and socially-conscious individuals articulating personal views on aging's strengths and decrements.

Contributors to *Voices and Visions of Aging* shared Cole's contention that critical gerontology had to be a dispassionate, activist paradigm counterbalancing putatively ageist narratives, traditional models of intergeneration justice, and existing modes of scientific measurement.[52] "Do we need a gerontology that is more informed by critical theory? Yes, of course. But is it sufficient to cultivate critical theory as provided by sideline academics?" asked coeditor and psychologist Robert Kastenbaum. "Perhaps not. To avoid 'the separation of warm emotion and cool intelligence . . . we might address the critical theory implicit in the thoughts,

---

the forces that undiscipline, diversify, and fragment it," 139.

51. Cole, in Cole, Achenbaum, Jakobi, Kastenbaum, eds., *Voices and Visions of Aging*, i.

52. Cohler, "Aging, Morale, and Meaning"; Jecker, "Justice and Mother Love"; and Bookstein and Achenbaum, "Aging as Explanation."

actions, and dreams of the aged men and women among us."[53] Medical ethicist Laurence B. McCullough argued that "the disciplines of gerontology fail to identify and take account of one possibility for human aging: the possibility that time, the past in particular, has the power to arrest some lives, to bring them to a stop, without death occurring."[54] Jaber Gubrium, editor of the *Journal of Aging*, asserted that "this new gerontology is against theoretical integration . . . in the 'real world,' a new gerontology might best tolerate the tension rather than attempting to integrate voice and context into an analytically unified vision of aging, totalizing experience."[55]

Cole asked Harry R. Moody to define the importance of critical gerontology as it permeated the current culture war over concepts and practices. The postmodern life course, pronounced Moody, demanded fresh, bold images of age, truth, power, and policy:

> Critical gerontology is concerned with identifying possibilities for emancipatory social change . . . in opposition to the conventional positivism and empiricism so prevalent in social gerontology. . . . Recapturing the moral dimension of old age means that *unsuccessful* aging is also a possibility, a very real moral hazard . . . . So for scientific gerontology, just as for individual life narratives, the task is to maintain coherence if science and the life course are to make sense. . . . But for critical gerontology, the problem here is that the political economy perspective and the literary evidence still remain apart.[56]

Cole noted that "Moody's theoretical vision of critical gerontology is not shared by all authors and editors."[57] In this understated observation, I feel, Cole was bracing to anticipate the theory's ephemeral malleability and possible demise as it assaulted specialists' gerontological models

53. Kastenbaum, "Encrusted Elders," 182.
54. Laurence B. McCullough, "Arrested Aging," 185.
55. Gubrium, "Voice and Context in a New Gerontology," 82.
56. Moody, "Overview," xv-xvi, xxix, xxxvi, xxxix. Moody was building on his essay, "Toward a Critical Gerontology." There, Moody (building on Jurgen Habermas and the Frankfurt School) analyzed the multiplicity of fragmented theories of aging, and "the ideal of a *critical gerontology*, that is, theories of aging that contain self-reflexive rules for their construction, interpretation, and application to the life-world. We can understand best what critical gerontology is in terms of its opposite: *instrumental gerontology* [which] serves to legitimate professional interventions that reinforce a pattern of domination in both the theory and practice of the bureaucratic state," 231.
57. Cole, in Cole, Achenbaum, Jakobi, Kastenbaum, eds., *Voices and Visions of Aging*, x.

amid the academic community's fraying yet intensely socio-politically competitive turf wars.[58]

Prominent GSA idea brokers noted and then marginalized interpretations by others who set forth bold insights about critical gerontology.[59] Jan Baars claimed that "the problem of social constitution . . . is seen as the principal theoretical challenge that is implicit in the different approaches to 'critical gerontology.'"[60] Ruth Ray envisioned kindred authors taking "a reflexive, as well as a reflective approach, making themselves an object of study."[61] Insisting on micro-macro sociological and cultural levels of narrative gerontology, Stephen Katz invoked Michel Foucault and Jacques Derrida to adumbrate its limitations in fluid, hybrid panoply of ideas:

> [There is] an internal debate regarding the sub-field's constitution, accomplishments, and future directions. However this debate has generally delimited criticality to research directly associated with radical theoretical traditions (e.g., Marxism, phenomenology, social constructivism) or radical social movements (e.g. feminist, anti-poverty, pension reform), thus overlooking the intellectual and discursive contexts in which critical ideas attain their criticality within gerontology [and] within the contextual dynamics of its own development. . . . The predominance of bio-medically-driven funding policies, the privatization of health care resources, the priorities of corporate and pharmaceutical research, the popularity of an alarmist demography that blames growing aging populations for the fiscal collapse of social programs, all contribute to the marginalization of critical thought.[62]

I cannot ascertain the extent to which Katz's exegesis jibed with (much less reinforced) Cole's self-reflexive perspective on critical gerontology's promises and shortcomings. Cole did not refer to critical gerontology's

---

58. For later affirmations, see Bass, "Gerontological Theory"; Liang and Luo, "Toward a Discourse Shift in Social Gerontology."

59. For useful summaries of the state of the art in critical gerontology, see Baars, Dannefer, Phillipson, and Walker, *Aging, Globalization and Inequality*; Andrews, "Critical and Reflective Gerontology"; and Twigg and Martin, "The Challenge of Cultural Gerontology."

60. Baars, "The Challenge of Critical Gerontology," 239. Also see Baars, *Aging and the Art of Living*.

61. Ray, "Foreword," 99.

62. Katz, "Critical Gerontology for a New Era," 396–397.

underpinnings in his 2003 interview with de Medeiros. Instead, Cole simply stated that "I'm moving more into spirituality."[63]

Also left unmentioned in the interview with de Medeiros was his quest for meaning in the arts. In his coedited *Oxford Book of Aging: Reflections on the Journey of Life*, Cole claimed that "our era offers new opportunities for reclaiming the moral and spiritual dimensions of later life, for bridging the gap between existential mystery and scientific mastery, for reconciling the modern value of individual development with the ancient virtues of accepting natural limits and social responsibilities."[64] Cole, however, identified later on with the conflicted portrait of aging masculinity presented in Sheriff Bell, the protagonist in Cormac McCarthy's *No Country for Old Men*: "The oscillating movement, which swings between the events of the story and Bell's interpretation of them, illuminates his gradual process of transformation as a man."[65] Like the sheriff, Cole attempted to shred midlife's masculinity script to redefine his late-life identification with meaning. Concurrently, following up his *puer* religiosity, he rediscovered his connection to God and took his place as an elder—a *senex*—in the powerful and haunted tradition of his Jewish ancestors.[66]

COLE'S REVITALIZED SPIRITUAL JOURNEY

Cole sought a psychotherapist after moving to Houston, because he harbored distressingly complicated questions regarding his current existence and its evolving purpose during the second half of life. Cole had hoped to work through his spiritual struggles with an experienced, trustworthy clinician, but he left not long after: "Therapists work with

---

63. Cole, in his November 12, 2003, interview with de Medeiros. The lapses in Cole's presentation of his moral and intellectual development can be revealing. For instance, in this interview he did not mention his book, *No Color Is My Kind*, nor a movie, *The Strange Demise of Jim Crow*, which he produced with David Berman in 1998. Cole and I had many phone calls in the 1990s, however, about how his meetings with Stearns disrupted his family life and UTMB relations.

64. Cole, in Cole and Winkler, *The Oxford Book of Aging*, 4.

65. Quoted in Saxton and Cole, "No Country for Old Men," 108.

66. Saxton and Cole, "*No Country for Old Men*," and Cole and Saxton, "No Country for Old Men." I thank Saxton for sending me these articles. In writing the last sentence of this paragraph, I reworked Cole's phrasing in a July 2023 critique of an earlier version of this essay. On thoughts about being manly, Cole contributed four essays in Stephen Katz's round table discussion published in the *Journal of Aging Studies*.

interior conflicts and troubles, while spirituality requires that we open ourselves to the mysteries of the divine which must enter us from the outside."[67] Cole had been pondering whether he wanted to become a hospital chaplain; subsequently he Zoomed with Yale's Rabbi James Ponet between 2008 and the present to pursue the Torah and become a Jewish Spiritual Director.

Cole had thrived in New Haven's religious culture beyond family observances as a child. There, he learned the meaning of "at-one-ment." As a young adult he honored both tradition (sitting in the back row of an Omaha synagogue) and the prophetic teaching of Jeremiah and Amos, but he could not hear God's voice. Cole sensed that he needed a mentor to lead him to God's presence everywhere and in everything.[68] He found such a guide in Rabbi Samuel Karff. One of Houston's "three amigos"— the other two were a Roman Catholic archbishop and a Baptist minister and civil-rights comrade of Rev. Dr. Martin Luther King, Jr.—advocating for vulnerable minorities, including the aged. Rabbi Karff, like Cole, benefited from an Ivy-League education after a childhood of mediating family members' disputes and anger. For decades the prolific writer and congregational cleric shepherded Houston's two thousand-member Reform Temple Beth Israel.

Karff throughout most of his life rose at 5:15, to pray in Hebrew and English to a faithful Sovereign who gave him *Permission to Believe* with the compassionate *Soul of a RAV*. "During the 25 years we've known each other, Karff has been my rabbi, my colleague, and friend. Now he is somehow all three at once," Cole wrote in *No Country for Old Men*. "Whatever the motivation, Karff's indirect gaze reduces your ability to engage him directly and limits emotional intimacy. It also allow him to formulate his thoughts unimpeded so that his brilliance and wisdom wash over you."[69] Karff discerned that the key to faith lies not in doctrine, but in telling

---

67. Cole to Achenbaum email, February 8, 2023. Jon Allen states that the humane relationship to a patient requires ethical practices that balance experience, common sense, science, and trust. Allen, *Trusting in Psychotherapy*. See also Pargament and Exline, *Working with Spiritual Struggles in Psychotherapy*.

68. Cole to Achenbaum, lunch conversation, February 8, 2023.

69. Cole, *Old Man Country*, 106. Through Cole, I also met Rabbi Karff (1931–2020), a sagacious, gracious, and generous soul friend to all he met. Karff was someone Cole interviewed in this book as part of an effort to enjoy the blessings and endure the sufferings anticipated in retirement and physical woes during the Fourth Quarter of Life. To my mind, Karff was a father-figure as Cole, setting out to pursue a spiritual quest, sought meaningful answers lost to his own dead father.

stories that tied individual lives to Biblical passages, which according to Cole, made the rabbi a spellbinding counselor and wise raconteur.

The personal bond turned professional, when Karff tapped Cole in 2004 to be founding director of the McGovern Center for Humanities and Ethics at the University of Texas Health Science Center. Karff served as an ever-present father-figure, a steadfast mentor and soul friend who integrated faith and meaning, and thus nurtured a spiritual reawakening in Cole, now himself an elder of the tribe. Here is what Karff said about being old in Cole's conversation with him for the book, *Old Man Country: My Search for Meaning Among the Elders*:

> I *am* an old man, and I bear the name honorably. . . . And I am very grateful to be an old man who is still functioning as well as I am. . . . We can feel enormous pleasure and intense pain. Suffering is the price we pay for the blessings of creation. . . . My faith is robust enough that my ultimate source of meaning—apart from love and being needed and useful—is the sense of Covenant with the ultimate One and a personal God.[70]

Cole in 2021 founded the Center for Healing, Hope and the Human Spirit at Beth Israel; he teaches part-time at the McGovern Center, now directed by longtime colleague Nathan Carlin.[71]

THE JOURNEY CONTINUES

Cole cannot possibly know how long his transformational roles as a *puer-senex* will continue to ripen and thrive. Neither his inward search for meaning nor outwardly fruitful career paths have unfolded in consecutive order. Instead the facets of his quest weave in and out time over time toward a boundless authenticity within God's embrace. Being both religious and spiritual, Cole knows that "ideas are disclosed in a long and unnerving traffic with the margins of knowledge."[72] Having outlived most father-figures and mentors, he relies mainly on support and consolation from his beloved wife, psychotherapist Dr. Thelma Jean Goodrich. Seeking clarity amid uncertainty in embracing the luminosity of life,

---

70. Cole, *Old Man Country*, "Sam Karff and the Power of Stories," 110.

71. Other participants in this conference will talk about his work in medical humanities, but here it is worth citing, again, Cole, Carlin, and Carson, *Medical Humanities*.

72. Rovelli, *There are Places*, 74.

Cole remains ever curious and enchanted about embarking on paths to meaningful, ones he knows that he will never totally understand.

I cannot predict how the last acts of this *puer-senex* will play out. Cole may alter his undisciplined, subversive ways of promoting radical change to fit them into a humane mode of experiential transcendence through soulful aging.[73] He may determine that what he has been searching is already here; he will continue to be a critic and activist—his time lived in clockwork *chronos* passes into to time actually lived in mystical, mysterious *Kairos*. Cole still has time to reconsider serving as a hospital chaplain, or to relive being a champion fencer.[74] As he faces finitude, he may choose bold intersectional ways to express his diversely revolutionary persona.[75]

May God bless Cole with extra years, to rejoice with a sense of nearly completing his life's journey to meaning. May he continue to get to know himself better in the Presence of Divine Love, creatively designing ways spiritually to care, mentor, and provoke. May he adapt Judaic sensibilities with a therapeutic model of humanity. May Cole remind us to talk humbly and walk honestly, for "this story is but a vehicle for sharing with you . . . the living faith in what is possible."[76]

---

73. Cole's unstinting love for Thelma Jean Goodrich is a transformative spiritual intimacy, which extends to others. Cole read a first draft of "My Journey into Conscious, Spiritual, and Soulful Aging," and, in an email to me on April 11, 2023, Cole (who referred to himself as "Your Brother") said that the piece "is just as inspiring as the first time I read it. 'The Unfolding of Divine Love' . . . the effort of a lifetime."

74. Cole had a hospital chaplaincy in mind as an option before he pursued Torah studies with Rabbi James Ponet.

75. Cole told me over lunch on August 2, 2023 that he meets with Jeff Kripal, a Rice professor who wrote about the *Superhumanities*. Cole is now at work on a spiritual-laden book about paranormal experiences.

76. Cole, *Old Man Country*, 150.

2

Re-Interpreting the Journey of Life
Gendered Meaning over the Life Course—
An Anocritical Perspective

ROBERTA MAIERHOFER

VOICES AND VISIONS OF MEANING

IN A 1986 ANTHOLOGY of essays, Thomas Cole references Harry R. Moody's essay "The Meanings of Life and the Meaning of Old Age," and Cole demands a recognition of the importance of cultural images of aging, for numerous practical decisions in professional ethics and public policy rely on the cultural and theoretical meanings we give to aging, such as the bureaucratization of the life cycle, the displacement of the search for meaning onto old age, the trivialization of leisure, and the covert ideology that underpins the study of life span development.[1] All of these need philosophical study and public engagement in the search for more human meanings of age and aging. Likewise, Ronald Carson speaks of a necessity for both young and old to recognize and articulate the implicit meaning of aging.[2]

---

1. Cole and Gadow, *What Does It Mean to Grow Old?*, 5–6.
2. Carson, "Foreword," *What Does It Mean to Grow Old?*, xii.

Cole has always centered his scholarship around meaning: in his choice of topics, his interweaving of personal details into explaining his scholarship and his writing, as well as his often abstract and philosophical contextualization in his work. Cole defines this meaning as a "notoriously vague concept,"[3] as "tattered,"[4] and adds a strong sense of skepticism into the mix, where meaning-making is understood as both a process *and* an experience—an embodied journey in time determined by paradox, ambiguities, and ambivalences.

When reading and writing, articles and publications become companions on one's own (academic) journey through life. In my case, the collaborative essay "In Whose Voice? Composing an Ethics Case as a Song of Life"[5] was one of the early inspirations for my own journey into the field of age/ing studies in the 1990s. In more specific terms, the essay points to the dilemma of giving a voice to a person without a voice, who can neither sing her own song of life—in Cole's metaphor—nor can evaluate and consent to other's intoning the song.

In this essay, Cole describes the case of a patient with Alzheimer's disease in which two colleagues, Barbara Thompson (a family physician) and Linda Rounds (a geriatric nurse practitioner) asked him for his opinion about the moral factors involved. The ninety-year-old patient, Mrs. Green, was strapped to the bed to prevent her from pulling out a feeding tube that sustained her life. Not only did Cole offer an opinion, but was also the one who constituted meaning for an incident in time by providing a narrative frame and allowing these voices to be remembered. As the title of the short essay suggests, Cole, who defines being "fully human" as having the "capacity for relationships . . . intact,"[6] is the story-teller, the narrator and not the singer of the song. For us as an audience, the multi-voiced song of life needs an interpreter, a translator, to understand this choir of existence. Cole as the story-teller that he is, is not a distant, "objective" recorder of events, but is actively involved and connecting different voices, not necessarily in harmony, but in an awareness of their distinct individualities, which then make up a "meaningful" song.

Cole approaches the case not from an academic and formal philosophical position, but from his own personal involvement with his 87-year-old grandmother, for whom he was then legally responsible, who

3. Cole, *Journey of Life*, xviii.
4. Cole, "Tattered Web of Cultural Meaning," 3–7.
5. Cole, Thompson, and Rounds, "In Whose Voice?," 23–31.
6. Cole and Gadow, *What Does It Mean to Grow Old?*, 30.

was also suffering from advanced Alzheimer's disease. Cole's interest in narrative and phenomenological dimensions of both aging and ethics leads him to an approach to the "case" of Mrs. Green as a "multi-voiced narrative"[7]:

> Mrs. Green could not tell us what she wanted, but perhaps if we thought of her voice as the silent melody in a larger musical composition, we could hear the voices of others who provide the harmonies and descant lines. Perhaps we could even hear the silent melody by listening closely to the other voices singing together, each contributing something important to the song of Mrs. Green's life, no one voice drowning out any of the others.[8]

As intact as Mrs. Green's capacity for relationship is, so intact is Cole's capacity to interpret and narrate the interactions and connections of others and position these in relation to his own past and present. It is not only in terms of cognitive deficiencies where we are invited to challenge our own feelings of worth and identity and define them in the connection to others. Based on her very practical and concrete experience of working with patients, the nurse's aide, Mrs. Brooks, thus, finds her own voice to express her identity as grounded in an interaction with others:

> I'd like somebody, even if I'm demented, to treat me like a person and talk to me. This might be the happiest time of my life. . . . I just might be happy. I have this feeling about being old.[9]

Similar to Donna Haraway's feminist understanding of "objectivity," Cole's approach is not abstract and distant, but a position of simultaneity. Therefore, Cole speaks of the fact that knowledge in humanistic gerontology is useful because it deepens understanding and enhances opportunities for human flourishing, and insists that publications should be less scientific and instrumental and encourages focusing on questions of representation, meaning, and value by centering the historical as well as the limits and conditions of knowledge.[10] Concerning the relationship between material realities and their cultural representations, Cole's understanding of this dialectic echoes Haraway's feminist positioning:

---

7. Cole and Gadow, *What Does It Mean to Grow Old?*, 23.
8. Cole and Gadow, *What Does It Mean to Grow Old?*, 24.
9. Cole and Gadow, *What Does It Mean to Grow Old?*, 29.
10. Cole, *Journey of Life*, xii.

> So, I think my problem, and "our" problem, is how to have *simultaneously* an account of radical historical contingency for all knowledge claims and knowing subjects, a critical practice for recognizing our own "semiotic technologies" for making meanings, *and* a no-nonsense commitment to faithful accounts of a "real" world, one that can be partially shared and that is friendly to earthwide projects of finite freedom, adequate material abundance, modest meaning in suffering, and limited happiness.[11]

When Cole speaks of the fact that the problem is not so much the phenomenon of ageism, as this in all times performs important social functions, but in the splitting apart of negative and positive aspects of growing old, his position resonates with demands of feminists of the 1980s of deconstructing the dichotomy of female and male. Rather than acknowledging ambiguity and contingency, so Cole claims, the ideological and psychological splitting into negative and positive aspects of growing old has long-lasting effects in establishing a dualism of old age—a positive and a negative pole.[12] He writes: "Unable to infuse decay, dependency, and death with moral and spiritual significance, our culture dreams of abolishing biological aging."[13] In a similar vein as Cole's multi-voiced song, Haraway defines science as a "search for translation, convertibility, mobility of meanings, and universality,"[14] which only becomes reductionism when only one "language" is enforced. As Cole has repeatedly stated, both the most pessimistic and optimistic views of old age are part of the same agist ideology.[15] When the reader resists a simple understanding of the texts based on the binary of "good" and "bad" images of aging, the confining binary scale of young and old can be transcended and lead to an acceptance of what Cole has called the "paradox."[16] He writes:

> Aging, like illness and death, reveals the most fundamental conflict of the human condition: the tension between infinite ambitions, dreams, and desires on the one hand, and vulnerable, limited, decaying physical existence on the other–between the self and the body. This paradox cannot be eradicated by the

11. Haraway, "Situated Knowledges," 579.
12. Cole and Gadow, *What Does It Mean to Grow Old?*, 121.
13. Cole and Gadow, *What Does It Mean to Grow Old?*, 129.
14. Haraway, "Situated Knowledges," 580.
15. Cole, *Journey of Life*.
16. Cole and Gadow, *What Does It Mean to Grow Old?*, 5.

wonders of modern medicine or by positive attitudes toward growing old.[17]

When Haraway—analyzing the category of gender—speaks of reductionism, Cole in his own search for meaning in age/ing has implied that "the search for new meaning in old age will have to grapple more directly with the limits of bourgeois value."[18] When considering that Cole's texts were published in 1986, today the demand for understanding ageism and its critics "in relationship to each other"[19] sounds like an intersectional approach. Referencing Sandra Harding in terms of a "postmodern insistence on irreducible difference and radical multiplicity of knowledges," Haraway reaches the conclusion that "all components of desire are paradoxical and dangerous, and their combination is both contradictory and necessary."[20] As Haraway writes:

> But we do need an earthwide network of connections, including the ability partially to translate knowledges among very different—power-differentiated—communities. We need the power of modern critical theories of how meanings and bodies get made, not in order to deny meanings and bodies, but in order to build meanings and bodies that have a chance for life.[21]

JOURNEYS OF (GENDERED) LIVES: FINDING MEANING IN A RE-ASSESSMENT OF MASCULINITY

Few publications can be found where Cole does not situate his scholarship in his own personal life story. In the "Introduction" to *The Journey of Life*, for example, Cole uses metaphors of seafaring to explain that his personal encounter with family members growing old encouraged his search for personal meaning in aging: "I have been exploring the cultural shoreline of later life, chartering its historical forms and sounding their philosophical depths."[22] In his early work Cole describes this as "not so much a history of *attitudes toward old age* as it is a study of the historical

---

17. Cole and Gadow, *What Does It Mean to Grow Old?*, 5.
18. Cole and Gadow, *What Does It Mean to Grow Old?*, 116.
19. Cole and Gadow, *What Does It Mean to Grow Old?*, 120.
20. Haraway, "Situated Knowledges," 579.
21. Haraway, "Situated Knowledges," 580.
22. Cole, *Journey of Life*, xvii.

meanings of aging."²³ As his questions are "existential and moral," the answers should lead to a "renewed awareness of the spiritual dimensions of later life."²⁴ When reading the progression of Cole's work from the early 1980s to 2020, it becomes evident that his focus moved from a gender-neutral position of man-kind to a gendered position and to an understanding of the life-course as determined by intersectionality. By 1997 Cole speaks of the fluidity of identity; he positions the definition of self within the political frame of race, class, and gender:

> Identity, loosely defined as a sense of who one is, is not a unitary thing that one simply finds and wears—like overalls, a dashiki, or a pin-striped suit. Identity is rather an unstable, relational process, a story always in flux, negotiated in difference and relationship. Identities . . . are historically conferred, subject to redefinition, resistance and change. They are ambiguous, produced through multiple identifications, some of which are salient in certain contexts and hidden in others. These insights are crucial to the future of a democratic culture and to the creation of new cognitive maps of identity which will allow individuals to form selves that are not mutilated by cultural domination of the powerful or by exclusive claims of any group.²⁵

When talking about time, we fall back on spatial metaphors, in order to express our embodied lives determined by both time *and* space. But as Cole's own work has shown, it is not just the movement that we have to look at—the moving from one place to the next—but the starting points and the in-between-places, and—at least envisioned and imagined: the maps that determine the routes that we take. Whereas the term "journey" entails the time element, already depictable in the root of the word, *jour* (day), a movement in abstract terms, the term "travel" seems to imply more concretely the act of moving. Positioning *The Journey of Life* "in between my daughter and my grandmothers"²⁶ in an awareness of the passing of time as embodied through individual lives and already using the metaphor of song for his analysis ("basic musical phrases for those who sing about aging"²⁷). The spatial metaphor of a journey allows Cole to position his quest in defining not so much the direction or path, but

---

23. Cole, *Journey of Life*, xvii.
24. Cole, *Journey of Life*, xx.
25. Cole, *No Color Is My Kind*, 200.
26. Cole, *Journey of Life*, xxxv.
27. Cole, *Journey of Life*, xix.

a possibility to see "life as a whole"—not as "a separation of body and self."[28] By emphasizing "the fluid and unique qualities of individual experience, the spiritual drama of the traveler's search,"[29] Cole in performative language brings together the motif of ages of life with that of the journey in order to determine aging as a process *and* an experience.[30] He writes:

> Existentially adequate and culturally powerful meanings of aging emerge when artists, writers, theologians, philosophers, or scientists hold these two motifs together in creative tension and weave them into their culture's view of the relations between cosmos, society, and self.[31]

The Merriam-Webster Dictionary suggests that the term "travel" would allow for a more specific understanding of journey ("travel: a journey especially to a distant or unfamiliar place").[32] While in 1992, Cole's *The Journey of Life* (which began as a dissertation in the late 1970s) can be read as a departure to a distant and unfamiliar destination, his *Search for Meaning Among the Elders* in *Old Man Country*, published almost half a century later, signals an arrival. Calling for "criticism and evaluation in social, moral, and existential terms" of "unacknowledged middle-class, masculine ideals" in 1992,[33] Cole now—in all its ambivalences—self-confidently and specifically locates a meaningful gendered (male) life. Invoking *No Country for Old Men*[34] by Cormac McCarthy, Cole, in his search for meaning, has not only found a country for old men, but has defined the country using "old man" in grammar terms as an adjective, a qualifier, a specific place to be old and male. Having set out to "look for what . . . his fathers couldn't find,"[35] Cole reaches the conclusion that, "being an old man, I learned can mean many things. Or it can mean nothing at all."[36] However, he is now in a position to put a country *for* old men on the map by creating a male community of diversity, a country *of* old men:

28. Cole, *Journey of Life*, xxi.
29. Cole, *Journey of Life*, xxxiii.
30. In my own work, I have spoken in this context of the matrix of time and experience.
31. Cole, *Journey of Life*, xxxiii.
32. Merriam-Webster, https://www.merriam-webster.com/. Accessed on November 1, 2023.
33. Cole, *Journey of Life*, xxviii.
34. McCarthy, *No Country for Old Men*.
35. Cole, *Old Man Country*, 4.
36. Cole, *Old Man Country*, 166.

> I found things to emulate and things to avoid, inspiring examples and cautionary tales. . . . My encounters leave me with greater courage to live my own unfolding and uncertain story. I am less afraid of the future. I feel enlarged and more compassionate and often surprised by the joy and the sheer beauty of music, family, conversation, and nature.[37]

Whereas the gendered aspect becomes more prominently displayed in his later publications, the intersectional aspect is already apparent in his early writing, when Cole speaks of ideals as "always socially located and implicated in relationships of power and authority" and stating that "medicine and science since the Renaissance have generally been infused with unacknowledged middle-class, masculine ideas."[38] Already in his book *No Color Is My Kind*, Cole emphasizes his dialogical storytelling and acknowledges the difficult task of this collaboration over divides. As the book cover states, it is "an uncommon chronicle of identity, fate, and compassion of two men—one Jewish and one African American—set out to rediscover a life lost to manic depression and alcoholism."[39] Although the book tells both an individual and collective story, the struggle of Eldrewey Stearns, an unrecognized civil rights leader and lawyer who initiated Houston's desegregation movement between 1959 and 1963, it is also a positioning of Cole himself in this narrative in his own recognition of an intersectional identity by exploring the emotionally charged collaboration in terms of race, class, and gender.

However, the aspect of age and the passing of time is also a crucial element of this life-course narrative. Despite the focus on Stearns, this book reveals not only an approach to life, but provides important lessons for researchers and academics working in the field of age studies. It carries—albeit unaware—a feminist stance, as it reflects the vulnerabilities of the interviewer in connection to those of the interviewee, and establishes a painful and troubling relationship that at times reveal a co-dependency and inter-dependency that allows no sugar-coating or romanticizing. Cole as the academic that he is, is aware of this dilemma in the writing of this book:

> In *Writing Lives*, Leon Edel suggests that a biographer must identify and analyze the private mythology of his or her subject,

---

37. Cole, *Old Man Country*, 165.
38. Cole, *No Color Is My Kind*.
39. Cole, *No Color Is My Kind*, back cover.

the hidden self-concept motivating the public figure. To write Stearns's life as honestly as I could, I had to discern not only *his* mythological self-construction, but my own as well. Identifying, acknowledging, and analyzing these intertwined self mythologies has been a long arduous task.[40]

In 2020, Cole overcomes this divide between intertwined self-constructions by acknowledging his self in others: "Today, when I see an old man bent over or limping, I do not see an Other. I see my future self."[41] When in the 1980s, Cole defined being "fully human" as having the "capacity for relationships . . . intact" in terms of an old incapacitated woman, he can now in the 2020s, accept his own gendered life as a man as determined by paradox, ambiguities, and ambivalences: "I know that my body will suffer more insults in the future, and that I will struggle emotionally. Yet I accept my vulnerability as part of being human. I do not feel less of a man."[42]

In her essay "Rehearsing Age,"[43] Elinor Fuchs relates the experience of aging—not only as an acknowledgement of its potential for resistance—to Brecht's theory of estrangement (*Verfremdungseffekt*), when she views the human condition of old people as feeling estranged and excluded from the familiar. Fuchs sketches Brecht's life-course patterns: from birth to midlife as the making familiar; the middle years as a possible perfect fit; the later years as the "fitting-out," defamiliarizing.[44] In this sense, the theatre theorist Fuchs does not compare, but equates, life to a stage, and positions aging as a "progressive estrangement," or an "estr*ag*ement"[45]as it gives us something to *do* about aging. The theater's dialectical habit allows for an understanding of the embodied aspect of aging as "estranged by performance."[46] Positioning the Aristotelian plot scheme as the decline narrative, Brecht's "dialectic habit" allows an acceptance of the paradox, ambiguities, and ambivalences of the life-course. Similar to Cole in his study of the cultural history of aging in America, the actor can stand aside from the character, as the action is framed by commentary—in

40. Cole, *No Color Is My Kind*, 194.
41. Cole, *No Color Is My Kind*, 166.
42. Cole, *No Color Is My Kind*, 166.
43. Fuchs, "Rehearsing Age."
44. Fuchs, "Rehearsing Age," 144.
45. Fuchs, "Estragement."
46. Fuchs, "Rehearsing Age," 151.

Brecht's term "literarized"[47]—to avoid sentimental fusion of the spectator and spectacle through the manipulation of "empathy." She writes:

> To this end, [Brecht] wanted the spectator to stand back from the performance and think about it critically, adopting the laid-back "gest" of the cigar smoker at a sports event.[48]

Now, Cole, in his writing, is not the laid-back cigar smoker at a sports event, but he does offer a laconic, level-headed, almost wry perspective and a flexible account of the life trajectory where "process" and "experience" meet. In Fuchs's take, "a life on this side of the ledger moves in surprising ways, in 'curves and jumps,' not simply in foretold steps leading to the grave," where the human subject is seen as both "alterable" and "able to alter."[49]

In many ways, Cole's less recognized book, *No Color Is My Kind*, is possibly the most revealing in terms of his approach and understanding of the subject of aging as different forms of entanglement, of the individual and the collective, as both concrete and abstract, as a material reality and its cultural representation, and in terms of a conventional understanding of his gender identity. In an anocritical reading, however, Cole's work emphasizes resistance to the status-quo, the grand narrative of aging, and postulates process *as* experience: "Eldrewey and I are neither the same nor intractably alien. We are separate, unequal, and related. . . . No cure emerged for either of us, but real healing continues."[50] When in 1997, Cole declares his exploration of his own life in relation to Eldrewey Stearns's as "too deep to fathom" and the "service of healing" in contrast to limited knowledge as endless, he relies on deconstructing a dialectic positioning determined by both similarities and differences.[51]

Beginning his academic journey by referencing the Greek mythologies of the *Iliad* and the *Odyssey* and positioning his own personal story as an (ambivalent) progress novel of a masculine heroic quest and male adventure, almost fifty years later, *Old Man Country* ends with a contemplation on Noah's protective ark representing both Jewish and Christian traditions. Similar to the conclusion that Fuchs reaches in terms of

---

47. Fuchs, "Rehearsing Age," 146.
48. Fuchs, "Rehearsing Age," 146.
49. Fuchs, "Rehearsing Age," 148.
50. Cole, *No Color Is My Kind*, 199.
51. Cole, *No Color Is My Kind*, 199.

Brecht's Epic Theatre that "there is no finish"[52] and giving up the "certainty of drama for open path of epic,"[53] Cole in his academic journey moves from the stories of displacement in Greek mythology to a picture of his and his grandson's hands "holding onto each other for dear life,"[54] thus, accepting the loose ends of Epic Theater by taking on "the risk of improvisation and discipline of rehearsal."[55]

FINDING AN OLD MAN COUNTRY IN AUSTRIA: A CASE STUDY

As Cole's work demonstrates, personal encounters and experiences are part of academic investigations and influence others in the field in sometimes unexpected ways. I would like to offer here such an example by presenting my own collaborative work with my colleagues Barbara Ratzenböck and Nicole Haring analyzing focus groups with men sixty-five-plus and a reading of the Austrian writer David Schalko's novel *Bad Regina*,[56] as an exploration of social and cultural narratives of aging masculinities in the early 2020s.

Addressing intersections of masculinities and aging, Cole was invited to present his book *Old Man Country* at the Madrid meeting of the EU Gender-Net project *MascAge–Analyzing Social Constructions of Aging Masculinities and their Cultural Representations* in *Contemporary European Literatures and Cinemas* in November 2019.[57] Theoretically and methodologically, this project is situated in critical studies on men and masculinities (CSMM), in which masculinities and men's lives are understood as explicitly gendered and are explored considering feminist and gender scholarship.[58] As Jeff Hearn emphasizes, "Men and masculinities are recognized as intersectionally gendered, with unequal, sometimes contradictory, relations to gendered power . . . and as variable and changing across time (history) and space (culture), within societies, and

---

52. Fuchs, "Rehearsing Age," 153.
53. Fuchs, "Rehearsing Age," 153.
54. Cole, *Old Man Country*, 169.
55. Fuchs "Rehearsing Age," 153.
56. Schalko, *Bad Regina*.
57. See https://gender-net-plus.eu/mascage/.
58. Hearn, "Place and Potential of Crisis/Crises," 3.

throughout life courses and biographies."[59] As a transnational endeavor, the European *MascAge* project explored social constructions and cultural representations of aging masculinities in Austria, Estonia, Ireland, Israel, Spain, and Sweden, always in acknowledgement of and indebted to work done in previous decades on the topic of masculinity and aging.

Similar to Cole's previously mentioned reference that relationships of power and authority inform our knowledge of aging, the collaborative analyses suggest that *negotiations of (declining) power* are central to understanding contemporary constructions of aging masculinities in Austria. While in 2020, about a fifth (19.2 percent) of Austrians were aged sixty-five or above, older adults will likely represent more than a fourth of the population by 2050 (27.7 percent).[60] While aging has gained recognition as a local and global social phenomenon, intersectional aspects, such as gender and age, have so far received less attention. Especially, older *men* as a topic of analysis have been neglected, whereas there has been some research on women and age[61] and some on "ungendered" portraits of aging.[62] The exploratory focus group study investigated experiences and perspectives of Austrian men aged sixty-five and above. In addition to collecting personal accounts of what it means to be an older man in Austria in the early 2020s, the study explored how media representations of older men were perceived. Inclusion criteria were gender (male), age (65 and above, representing statutory retirement age in Austria), and place of residency (Austria). Beyond these criteria, sampling aimed at diversity in terms of location (urban vs. rural), educational and professional backgrounds, family status, sexual identity, and health status. Recruitment of participants relied on both contacting local institutions for seniors and personal contacts of the research team.

In total, eight men, aged sixty-five to eighty-two, participated in four online meetings. Discussions on aging masculinities and media representations of aging men charted in diaries were complemented by a questionnaire on socio-demographics. Analysis of the transcribed material was inspired by practices of grounded theory,[63] Udo Kuckartz's

59. Hearn, "Place and Potential of Crisis/Crises," 3.
60. *Statistik Austria*, 2020, https://www.statistik.at/fileadmin/publications/Demographisches-JB-2020.pdf, 56.
61. Segal, *Out of Time*; Maierhofer, "Feminism and Aging in Literature"; and Calasanti, Slevin, and King, "Ageism and Feminism."
62. Saxton and Cole, "*No Country for Old Men*."
63. Corbin and Strauss, *Basics of Qualitative Research*.

"qualitative content-structuring content analysis,"[64] as well as my own theoretical approach of "anocriticism," which encourages exploration of social and cultural entanglements of age and gender.[65] Specifically, anocriticism encourages readers of literary texts as well as interview transcripts to examine in detail: (1) age and aging's collective cultural construction and relation to gender; (2) aging's individual dimension; (3) people's interpretive power and narrative performance regarding age and aging; as well as (4) age and aging's inherent potential for resistance and change.[66]

Based on the results of the focus group study, we three researchers put forward the hypothesis that older Austrian men's understanding of aging and of aging masculinities, in particular, revolve around the idea of *power*.[67] Notably, Austrian men sixty-five-plus conceptualize the process of aging as a "power game," in which one frequently loses, ideally maintains and—only in exceptional cases—gains power. Notions of *losing power* were often framed in terms of social status and related to both abstract concepts of aging masculinities as well as concrete personal experiences. The men's accounts on their experiences of aging were nuanced and multi-facetted. However, comparatively, more negative than positive aspects of aging were mentioned. Accounts of loss and decline included, for example, the death of friends similar in age, loss of professional roles, declining health, and diminished physical strength. The experience of Kurt (eighty-two), a retired postal worker and widower with three adult children, is exemplary: "But when I have to drive the Akia [rescue sledge] with a colleague on the mountain—that is a device to transport those injured—one realizes that one physically no longer has the strength of a young person."

Even more prominent than stories aligning with what age critic Margaret Morganroth Gullette has called the "decline narrative" of aging,[68] were accounts on efforts to *maintain power* while growing old. To successfully maintain power as they age, the men developed different tactics. Firstly, they portray themselves as still middle-aged, and not old, since within the hierarchy of ages it represents the most powerful position.[69] At

64. Kuckartz, *Qualitative Inhaltsanalyse*.
65. Maierhofer, "Graying of American Feminism"; Maierhofer, *Salty Old Women*.
66. Ratzenböck, *Media Relations*.
67. Ratzenböck, Pirker, Haring, and Maierhofer, "Aging Masculinities in Austria."
68. Gullette, *Aged by Culture*.
69. Pickard, *Age Studies*, 66; Woodward, *Figuring Age*; Maierhofer, "Aging as

the same time, they are careful not to portray themselves as too "young," by, for example, disapproving of older adults' attempts of "dressing too youthfully." Efforts at maintaining power also involve avoiding serious vulnerabilities, particularly in terms of becoming ill and requiring care. Similarly, the men discuss "staying busy" as a tactics to uphold social status while growing older, adopting and reproducing the powerful contemporary discourse and cultural imperative of "active aging."[70] The men also self-empower through self-reinvention in retirement, a key concept related to old age in western cultures.[71] They find and shape new social roles for themselves.[72] Ludwig (seventy-eight), a former consultant in the non-profit sector and married with three adult children, poignantly summarized—resonating Elinor Fuchs's concept of rehearsing age—this tactic as creating "a good supporting role" for oneself. He states: "I now have other roles, grandfather, visits in hospitals and so on. So, one has to find a role for oneself and like one knows from films and theater, one can also play a good supporting role. So, playing the clever supporting role is also something very beautiful, right?"

Notably, throughout the discussions, participants show high levels of self-reflexivity, also when discussing efforts to maintain power. They are, for example, acutely aware of their privileged social and cultural position as old *men* in comparison to old women. Also, participants emphasize that "old men" are not a homogenous social group and acknowledge differences in resources, influence, and status among different groups of men. Similarly, participants critically address social expectations of older adults, mostly of older men, to represent figures of authority. Maintaining power is thus discussed by the participants in a nuanced and complex manner.

In contrast to losing and maintaining power, *gaining power* while growing older was almost exclusively discussed in the context of media contents. In the second meeting, "powerful old men" were the most important topic. Participants discussed an impressive range of influential old politicians. The normative idea of old men as figures of authority was thus foregrounded even more decisively than before. Hans (sixty-five), a former delivery driver in a rural area of Austria, married with one adult

---

Continuity and Change"; van Dyk, *Soziologie des Alters*; and van Dyk, "Zur Interdependenz und Analyse von Alter(n) und Geschlecht."

70. Katz and Calasanti, "Critical Perspectives on Successful Aging."
71. Cruikshank, *Learning to Be Old*.
72. Calasanti and Slevin, *Gender, Social Inequalities, and Aging*.

child, summarizes this by explaining: "Many ... [old people] do not represent anything anymore and that is also the case, I say, in old age, now he [Joe Biden] has had the opportunity to become president, that's the biggest office of America and that's then the biggest ambition. But fifty years or even longer, he's been in politics and now he's at the peak."

WHEN MEN GROW OLD, EMPIRES FALL: DAVID SCHALKO'S *BAD REGINA*

Contrasting and expanding the social science part of the project, David Schalko's recent novel *Bad Regina*, can be analyzed as a cultural representation of the material realities revealed by the focus group study in terms of "aging as a power game." Published in 2021, Schalko's *Bad Regina* received wide-spread public attention in the German-speaking countries for its surprisingly strong and inappropriate language, its mostly failed attempts at satire and irony, and—despite or possibly because of its politically incorrect stance—its accurate references to Austrian past and present and its current social and political positioning. Set among the decayed and decaying buildings of the belle époque in the fictional Alpine spa town of Bad Regina, easily recognizable as the former glamorous and fashionable town of Bad Gastein, which is still a popular tourist destination, the novel presents a bleak and stark decline narrative of a once fashionable and elegant resort now presented as a symbol of a fallen and failed civilization. All western fears are symbolized in the mysterious Chen, a Chinese real estate tycoon from Hallstatt buying up properties to further their decay. Despite the few remaining inhabitants' decision to fight the hostile takeover, their own moral deficiencies and past actions are revealed in the course of the novel as the motivational drive of this destruction. Led by gout-plagued Othmar, the former owner of the most famous party club of the Alps, the few remaining inhabitants under the leadership of the otherwise unpopular mayor Heimo Zesch abduct Chen. When Chen is found dead, the true cause of the willful destruction of the town is revealed, which like in the "tragic comedy" of Friedrich Dürrenmatt's *Der Besuch der alten Dame*[73] is determined by past actions. Gideon Blomberg, who had to flee Austria during the Nazi regime, because he was allegedly the son of the Jewish psychiatrist of the town's sanatorium, has come back a rich man to destroy Bad Regina, motivated "Not out of

73. Dürrenmatt, *Der Besuch der alten Dame*.

revenge. Or fear. Rather out of contempt. And respect towards himself."[74] Eventually, Gideon succeeds in buying up all the town's property leaving them to African immigrants willing to settle in Bad Regina. Thus, by acquiring the place as an act of regained power and control, he turns locals into foreigners, and foreigners into locals.

Despite the reception of the novel as a general contemporary account of our times, Schalko's novel is very much a gendered reflection on male aging, time passing, and (nostalgic) memories of past (male) powers. Its central topic is aging at a specific moment in time, in a specific place, where both the place and its inhabitants have individual (hi)stories. The decay of buildings, the decay of the town's reputation and attractiveness, as well as the erosion of stability are symbolically intertwined with the aging of the town's population. *Bad Regina* also represents a pointed account of the pretentious and male dominated history of Austria as a tourist destination. Despite the novel seemingly centering on the *grand narrative* of Austria's hypocrisy in not acknowledging the past and its agency in the atrocities of the Nationalsocialist regime, as well as the present in its rejection and exploitation of asylum seekers and migrants, it is men aging that can be read as the main topic. Symbolically, the novel illustrates that empires have to fall and eras have to end, in order to narrate a male life-course and to give cultural meaning to men growing old. The novel uncovers the entanglement of the individual and the collective in terms of aging masculinities. Gendered male aging can only be made sense of—and thus narrated—in a larger frame of reference. In this sense, Margaret Morganroth Gullette's term "decline narrative" takes on a very specific meaning and extends from the experience of an individual life-course to the fall of an empire and the end of an entire era.

Following this logic, loss and decline are central motives of the text. Cell phones no longer work to connect lovers, the dentist goes out of business because he treated only healthy teeth, and the only policeman in town cannot prevent that his lover, Petra, who used to be a man named Peter, dies by suicide. Therefore, it is the priest that takes on the executive role of the police to conduct the investigations into the alleged murder of the investor Chen. Even the town's priest, however, loses his faith when he recognizes that no sacred code of honor exists and, thus, symbolically murders the already dead Chen to reconstruct an order which paradoxically never existed in the first place. Schalko's novel creates a polemic,

---

74. Schalko, *Bad Regina*, 344.

vicious, and cynical world by presenting old men situated in a place of decay. Places and people alike are determined on the one hand by their materiality, on the other by their past. The former spa town determined by the façade of wealth and power is no different to the remaining inhabitants, whose past actions catch up with them. All is now quiet in the former "party heart"[75] of Europe:

> Was it arrogance which was their doom? Was it the arrogance, which one could already detect in the buildings? . . . The valley like a deep cutting wound. The rushing waterfalls a bloodletting, which drove out the last energies of life. Inactively, everybody watched their own disappearance.[76]

By focusing on the fundamental connectivity between material realities and their cultural representation, literary texts as multi-versed arrangements of understanding the here and now, can open up a discussion of what it means to live determined by paradox, ambiguities, and ambivalences in a certain place, at a certain time, as an affirmation of the individual and the collective. Telling such a story from an individual perspective and positioning it in a specific social political, historical, and cultural context, helps us transgress traditional and limiting modes of understanding. Despite this ending of doom, the novel can be read as a voice of resistance and expression of meaning, thus, supporting the ongoing healing of individuals and society. To reference Cole, no cure emerged for anyone, but real healing continues.

---

75. Schalko, *Bad Regina*, 10.
76. Schalko, *Bad Regina*, 10.

PART TWO

Life Stories

3

Narrating Stories from the Perspective of Dementia

Considerations for Narrative Gerontology

KATE DE MEDEIROS

IN THIS CHAPTER, I consider the narrative construction of Walter Wink,[1] the subject of chapter 13 in Thomas Cole's *Old Man Country*.[2] At the time of Cole's interview with Wink in 2011, around fifteen months before his death in May 2012, Wink had been living with a diagnosis of dementia with Lewy bodies (DLB) for five years. By comparing content from Cole's interview transcript with a close reading of the chapter, I consider the tension between Wink's personal narrative and the dominant cultural narratives of dementia present in the chapter. My purpose here is not to criticize Cole's handling of the interview itself, or the chapter, but rather to use the two formats as a way to point out the disconnects that many people have regarding conversations with people living with dementia. Overall, I consider and challenge many of the limits and possibilities of narratives in the context of storying dementia.

---

1. In his obituary, Walter Wink, was described as "an influential liberal theologian whose views on homosexuality, nonviolence and the nature of Jesus challenged orthodox interpretations." Martin, "Walter Wink, theologian and author, dies." Wink died in 2012 at age seventy-six.

2. Cole, *Old Man Country*.

I begin with a broad overview of scholarship in narrative, self, and identity to clarify and situate my position and use of terms. I then consider cultural and personal narratives in the context of dementia to include memory and narrativity, dementia narratives and narrators, and the imposition of story. Finally, I turn to Wink as a participant in an interview and the focus of a chapter. I suggest that current views of narratives by people with dementia position them as broken or flawed, leading to the ventrilooquilization of their experiences. Yet, small stories by people living with dementia offer an important opportunity to examine how selfhood and identity are maintained despite narrative challenges.

NARRATIVE, SELF, AND IDENTITY

Definitions and features of narrative, self, and identity differ by discipline. At its most basic, personal narratives describe a "telling of some aspect of self through ordered symbols."[3] Here, self refers to the "culturally constituted individual"[4] who is sensitive to their own being, is aware of their uniqueness from others, is shaped by the cultural rules that surround them, and whose sense of uniqueness is experienced and confirmed through the reactions of others.[5] Although the ordered symbols of narrative are not limited to language and can include gestures, images, movements and so on, the focus in this chapter will be on narratives expressed through language since language and dementia are integral to the interview with and chapter about Wink.

Linear personal narratives describe a type of discursive act involving setting, characters, emplotment, coherence, complicating actions, and retellability.[6] For Labov and Waletzky, temporal organization is necessary to distinguish narrative from discourse. Narrative analysis, from their perspective, typically involves understanding the narrative as a set of relationships between linguistic structures between teller and listener, with an eye toward details such as what characters are involved, what event puts the complicating action into play, and what resolution, if any, is achieved. Retellability is also important in Labov's and Waletzky's construct. The more retellable a story, the more often it is to be told. In a

---

3. de Medeiros, *Narrative Gerontology in Research and Practice*, 2.
4. Rubinstein and de Medeiros, "Ecology and the Aging Self," 61.
5. Goffman, *The Presentation of Self in Everyday Life*.
6. Labov and Waletzky, "Narrative Analysis."

slightly different way, Polkinghorne describes narrative as both a process and a product.[7] Rather than focus on the structural components of the narrative, he is more interested in the meaning behind narrative choices, that is, why these characters and not others, why this particular story, why this particular array of ordered symbols? Also interesting is how the story may change its retelling: What details are included or excluded? How do details change in retellings?[8]

Cultural narratives are the stories embedded within a culture that reinforce norms, values, expectations, roles, and interpretation of meaning through unspoken and deeply engrained rules. Cultural narratives shape not only what stories are told and which are silenced, but also provide the storylines and metaphors that communicate values and expectations.[9] As Laceulle and Baars argue, dominant cultural narratives "are carriers of values, they provide the horizon against which we situate our own life narratives. They provide us with a reservoir of both narrative form and content on which to model our own stories."[10] In this way, selves and narratives are shaped and interpreted in terms of cultural values.

Also important is the distinction between "big stories" and "small stories."[11] Big stories refer to the overarching, more fully developed grand narratives about our lives—the storyline of the biographical myths to which we might align ourselves or others.[12] Big stories are typically rehearsed through retellings and revisions, with plotlines that remain relatively stable over retellings, although smaller details may change. Because big stories are well formed, they are heavily influenced by the cultural narratives that shape the context of their telling. An example is the common plotline of life stories in the U.S. that align with the cultural narrative of success as a personal effort: With enough effort, anyone can lift themselves up by their bootstraps to fulfil the American dream of rags to riches.

In contrast, Bamberg and Georgakopoulou describe small stories as "an umbrella term that captures a gamut of underrepresented narrative

7. Polkinghorne, *Narrative Knowing*.

8. Maschler and Schiffrin, "Discourse Markers *Language, Meaning, and Context*."

9. Laceulle and Baars, "Self-Realization and Cultural Narratives about Later Life"; de Medeiros, "The Complementary Self."

10. Laceulle and Baars, "Self-Realization and Cultural Narratives about Later Life," 36.

11. Bamberg, "Stories"; Freeman, "Life on Holiday?"

12. McAdams, *The Stories We Live By*; Bamberg, "Stories."

activities, such as tellings of ongoing events, future or hypothetical events, and shared (known) events."[13] Small stories also capture refusals and deferrals to tell, as well as allusions to other tellings. Unlike big stories, small stories are more akin to asides or fleeting moments in talk. As such, small stories have been described as a site for emerging identities to be negotiated,[14] something that will be addressed in further detail later in the chapter. Because small stories are typically not well rehearsed, well-formed or complete, they may offer insights that counter dominant cultural narratives. Given that cultural narratives about dementia influence what big stories are told about the experience of living with dementia, small stories offer opportunities for relational insights that may counter or resist big stories.

Narrative and Identity

While "self" describes the awareness one has of being a unique, culturally constituted individual, as mentioned earlier, "identity" describes the part of the self that is constituted by the dominant cultural view of the individual based on a variety of characteristics such as actions, physical appearance, participation in groups, and others.[15] In other words, identity includes attributes which the individual may claim (e.g., I am a kind person) and those which are ascribed to them (e.g., You look like an irresponsible person.) How one identifies themselves and how they are identified by others may not align. As Laceulle and Baars have suggested, "identity is fundamentally social. Our opportunities to be who we want to be, and the way we perceive and experience ourselves, are inextricably bound up with our social positioning."[16]

Within the context of narrative, McAdams and Guo have described narrative identity as the autobiographical author.[17] However, Esteban-Guitart, recognizing the role of cultural narratives on narrative identity, have a more complex view of identity.[18] They write:

13. Bamberg and Georgakopoulou, "Small Stories as a New Perspective," 381.
14. Georgakopoulou, "Small Stories Research."
15. de Medeiros, "Complementary Self," 5.
16. Laceulle and Baars, "Self-Realization and Cultural Narratives about Later Life," 36.
17. McAdams and Guo, "Narrating the Generative Life."
18. Esteban-Guitart, "Towards a Multimethodological Approach to Identification of Funds of Identity."

> Identity is not something supposedly private, that one possesses, but something that is made by using a particular cultural resource. That is, identity requires the use of cultural resources —such as language, significant others, a certain flag or an ideology—which is expressed and transformed into life scenarios and exchanges with the world.[19]

Narrative forms, situations such as interviews and essays, and attitudes towards attributes such as cognitive decline are cultural resources through which identities are negotiated and understood. The narrative "I" does not exist outside of an exchange with another within a cultural context; identity exists in communicative spaces. As I will explore in the next section, the experience of living with dementia is an important site through which to consider self, narrative and identity. Building on some key ideas in the current section, I will consider how changes to cognition including memory and language are positioned within cultural narratives of dementia and how those narratives shape views of self and identity both for and by people living with dementia.

DEMENTIA AND NARRATIVE

Laying out an overview of dementia and narrative is a bit more complicated than for narratives in general since memory and language are integral parts to narratives and are important in determining whether a person living with dementia is the subject, author, or co-creator of a narrative. In this section, I'll first consider dementia, language, and self before looking at the intersection of personal and cultural narratives of dementia.

Dementia is a general term that describes a constellation of conditions resulting in memory loss greater than is typical for one's age and educational status, disorientation to time and place, changes in personality and/or social behavior, and changes in language.[20] However, it is important to underscore the fact that each the experience of each person living with dementia is unique.

Alzheimer's disease is the most common form of dementia, accounting for around 70 percent of dementia diagnoses. Some common

---

19. Esteban-Guitart, "Towards a Multimethodological Approach to Identification of Funds of Identity," 175.
20. "2019 Alzheimer's Disease Facts and Figures."

features of Alzheimer's-type dementia (AD) are forgetfulness and changes in language. Consider, for example, the following excerpt from a person with moderate AD: "And they were all doing it. And they'd have someone come over and grab me. And tell me what to say and do. They'd give me all of that and then I could do it. And then my mother would come in and she would help me out." Of note is the use of nonreferential pronouns, common in in later stages in AD, which makes understanding the meaning of the passage somewhat challenging.[21] Around 30 percent of people with early stages and 100 percent of people in late stages of AD and vascular dementia, which has a different etiology, experience some form of aphasia or the loss of ability to speak.[22] Incorrect word choice, and non-sensical language appear relatively early in the course of disease for many but not all people.[23]

DLB is the second most common type of dementia, comprising 3–7 percent of all dementia types.[24] It is characterized by cognitive symptoms, which typically emerge first and accelerate quickly, followed by behavioral and motor symptoms. In DLB, language use such as syntax, grammar, and overall cohesion typically remains unchanged, although word finding, naming ability, or other memory-related features of language may decline over time.[25]

Because of the progressive and profound loss of memory and changes to language found in all dementia types, dementia has been described as a "loss of self,"[26] "the long good-bye,"[27] and other similar metaphors which equate living with dementia to having a meaningless existence.[28] This reinforces the notion that memory and verbal communicative ability are necessary to have a meaningful life and that one must be able to communicate "self" in socially recognized ways, thereby linking "loss of language" to "loss of self." Since self and meaning are connected in the

21. Hamilton, "Language and Dementia."

22. Fraser, Meltzer, and Rudzicz, "Linguistic Features Identify Alzheimer's Disease."

23. Henry, Crawford, and Phillips, "Verbal Fluency Performance in Dementia"; Blair et al., "'A Longitudinal Study of Language Decline."

24. Macoir, "Cognitive and Language Profile of Dementia"; Bentley et al., "Exploring the Experiences of Living with Lewy Body Dementia."

25. Macoir, "Cognitive and Language Profile of Dementia"; Drummond et al. "Narrative Impairment"; and Pistono et al. "Discourse Macrolinguistic Impairment as a Marker."

26. Small et al., "Discourse of Self in Dementia."

27. Hamilton, "Language and Dementia."

28. Taylor, "On Recognition, Caring, and Dementia."

research literature on dementia, it is important to consider what self and identity mean in the context of dementia and how we might reconsider both within the larger question of meaning in life.

Self in Dementia

With regards to conceptualizing "self" in dementia, Sabat and colleagues suggest three types of selves to consider with regards to the person living with dementia, all three of which are made known through language.[29] They write:

> Self 1 refers to the self of personal identity and each person experiences this aspect of selfhood by being one and the same person from moment to moment, day to day, month to month. Self 1 is expressed through the use of first person grammar.[30]

Self 1 remains intact throughout the course of dementia through indexical use of first-person pronouns, which signals the existence of an "I," even if a person cannot recall autobiographical details associated with that "I." Sabat and colleagues use the example of a person who may not recall where they were born. However, by saying "I don't know where I was born," the person indicates that they know they were born somewhere (i.e., are the one and the same person from moment to moment) and that they are a unique individual who is different from others.

In contrast to the introspective, indexical aspects of Self 1, Self 2 describes characteristics that are outwardly evaluated by others, such as through autobiographical details (e.g., Am I able to relate key autobiographical details?) as opposed to Self 1 (e.g., Do I experience myself as me?). Sabat and colleagues argue that people with dementia are often viewed in terms of Self 2 attributes rather than Self 1, whereby people living with dementia are positioned as "demented other" and are viewed as having lives devoid of meaning, or as the embodiment of a much-feared Fourth Age.[31]

Self 3 describes the public personae that people maintain with the help of others. Examples include being a loyal friend, a loving parent, and an academic.[32] Each personae involves behaviors and actions that are not

29. Sabat et al. "'Demented Other' or Simply 'A Person'?"
30. Sabat et al. "'Demented Other' or Simply 'A Person'?," 287.
31. Higgs and Gilleard, *Rethinking Old Age*.
32. Sabat and Collins, "Intact Social, Cognitive Ability, and Selfhood."

identical to the other and speak to the presence of Self 3 in people living with dementia.[33]

Narrative in Dementia

If personal narratives are the way the self is made known through ordered symbols, and self in dementia can have multiple types of presentations, it's important to consider how selves are expressed in narratives by people living with dementia. As Phinney has observed, since "the ability to narrate is presumed to be contingent on memory, language, and awareness. Therefore, it is little surprise that illness narratives in dementia have been mostly overlooked or discounted, for such stories would indeed be difficult to tell and understand."[34] Because of the challenges with language, grammar, syntax and memory described earlier, dementia narratives can be classified as what Frank calls the chaos narrative or a narrative which reflects a loss of control, challenges with self-reflection, and difficulty putting suffering into words.[35] As Donnelly observes:

> The chaos narrative is rarely encountered by audiences because the chaos narrative is usually erased. This "anti-narrative" can only be lived and cannot be told. The individual living with chronic physical or mental illness or a disability, who cannot be stoic and turn their story into a quest narrative, is rendered mute. Since restitution narrative is also unavailable to these individuals, their stories are left unspoken or unwritten. Their stories have largely been controlled by external agents. Failure to meet normative expectations has meant rejection.[36]

Although Donnelly was not referring to narratives in the context of dementia in particular, people living with dementia are at risk of being silenced since changes to memory and language are assumed to limit narrative possibilities for people living with dementia. The inability to recall autobiographical details can be interpreted as an inability to put experience into words or a lack of self-reflection. Simply characterizing narratives by people living with dementia, however, overlooks Self 1 and

---

33. Caddell and Clare, "Impact of Dementia on Self and Identity."
34. Phinney, "Fluctuating Awareness," 331.
35. Frank, *The Wounded Storyteller*.
36. Donnelly, "Claiming Chaos Narrative," 1.

Self 3, something which will be further explored later in the interview with Wink.

Hydén uses the term "broken stories" to characterize narratives told by people living with dementia.[37] Broken stories "are perceived to be broken and fail because in contrast to other stories they are fragmented, partial, jumbled, and repetitive; they lack temporal and thematic coherence, and shift between characters, places, and times without any notice."[38] Consequently, many dementia narratives focus on dementia as experienced by another such as a parent or spouse.[39] In this way, the experience of living with dementia is "ventriloquized" since it is assumed that "since dementia patients can no longer speak for and of themselves—at least not in the ways ordained by our culture—others must take over the job."[40]

The overall message is that others must repair the broken narratives of people living with dementia due to challenges associated with language and cohesion. These challenges then become equated with loss of self. Common cultural narratives and images associated with dementia include the "loss of self," "the long good-bye," and "a living shell"[41] which characterize people living with dementia as non-people or living corpses.[42] Zeilig points out cultural narratives such as the "rising tide of dementia" or "silent tsunami"[43] to describe vast devastation that we cannot fully anticipate. She also adds that there are biblical aspects to dementia metaphors, such as dementia as a "millennium demon" and the need to crusade against it, suggesting metaphysical aspects of dementia that can be battled against and won. These and other framings of dementia (e.g., war-like metaphors), position dementia as something frightening and all-encompassing.

Overall, metaphors and cultural narratives reinforce the idea that people living with dementia are unreliable narrators of their own experiences.[44] Because they may have difficulties retelling their big stories, they are discounted. As Thomas has noted, the need to fit the experiences of

37. Hydén, *Entangled Narratives*.
38. Hydén, *Entangled Narratives*, 4.
39. Hartung et al., *Ageing Masculinities*.
40. Hartung et al., *Ageing Masculinities*, 7.
41. George, "Overcoming the Social Death of Dementia," 586.
42. Behuniak, "The Living Dead?"
43. Zeilig, "Dementia as a Cultural Metaphor," 260.
44. Young et al., "Expanding Current Understandings of Epistemic Injustice and Dementia."

people living with dementia into a linear narrative has ignored the many opportunities for expression (e.g., small stories) that are still possible in the context of dementia.[45]

THE CASE OF WALTER WINK

I now turn to take a closer look at the narrative construction of Wink from two sources: the transcript of an interview that Cole did with Wink in 2011 and the subsequent book chapter that emerged from that interview. I recognize a few limitations to my analysis. The transcript is limited to verbatim spoken text. It does not include any linguistic features such as voice inflections or timing of pauses. I am also not certain if the talk has been "cleaned up" to remove false starts or vocal disfluencies (e.g., um, uh). I have no visual information to look at gestures, posturing, emotional responses, or other clues that unfold during interviews but are likely absent from the transcript. My reading of the transcript is therefore not meant to be a critical research evaluation. Instead, I use the transcript as a point from which to consider the presentation of Wink as a person living with DLB in the chapter who is then reconstructed as the subject of a chapter. Finally, I realize that my presentation of Cole's interview and chapter represent *my* construction of Wink and Cole and my own narrative which includes limitations, biases, inclusions and omissions.

With regards to the chapter, I note that Cole's purpose was *not* to understand Wink's experience of living with dementia. Instead, in keeping with Cole's other interviews for his book, Cole writes, "*Old Man Country* seeks to reclaim and enhance the humanity of men in the Fourth Age . . . To learn about men in the Fourth Age, I decided to talk to those who were living it . . . To begin with, I made a list of men I admired and wanted to talk to."[46] My analysis is therefore not meant to be a critique of Cole, but rather an illustration of how many people make sense of conversations with and stories by people living with dementia and to suggest new ways of understanding and making sense of these stories.

Wink's chapter is titled, "The Story of Walter Wink: Nonviolent Resistance and Dementia." It is the only chapter in the book that ends with the subject's name rather than begin with it (e.g., "James Forbes: *Old Man by the Riverside*"; "Ram Das and Me"). Although arguably all the book

---

45. Thomas, "Whose Story Is It Anyway?"
46. Cole, *Old Man Country*, 11.

chapters are as much of a biographical rendering by Cole as the Wink chapter, the title immediately suggests that Cole is telling Wink's story, because Wink's dementia renders him unable to do so himself. Cole, not Wink, is the one telling the story.

The interview begins as follows:

> TC: Today is February 18, 2011, and we are having a conversation with theologian and preacher and scholar, Walter Wink, at his home in Sandersville. That's just a formal—so I know at the head of the tape.
>
> WW: Sandis—
>
> TC: Sandisfield, yeah. And it's a gorgeous day out. The sun is out, and the snow is piled up all around. The creek—what's the name of the creek that goes by your house?
>
> WW: Buck.
>
> TC: Buck Creek? It's a lovely creek.

Wink is having difficulty with word recall. Cole gently helps him.

Like the interview, the chapter begins with a description of the sunny day, a bit about the house Wink shares with his wife June, and a short biographical description of Wink:

> Walter is a prominent theological, radical critic of the church, and peace activist from Dallas, Texas. At age 76, he seems already to have spent more than one lifetime of pastoring, writing, teaching, speaking, protesting, and loving. In recent years, though, he has struggled with restless leg syndrome (RLS), prostate cancer, and pneumonia. Now dementia, exacerbated by medication for RLS, is taking his mind and his life in terrifying pieces.[47]

Cole goes on to describe the routines that Wink undergoes to slow the dementia progression, adding "but the dementia is a steady slide."[48] Here, "the dementia" suggests that dementia is a particular entity robbing Wink of "his mind and his life."

As a social scientist who studies dementia, I was taken aback by tragic tone whereby dementia (specifically DLB) seemed to eclipse all that Wink accomplished. Words like "exacerbated," "terrifying" and "steady slide" dominate the first two paragraphs. There is also the added

---

47. Cole, *Old Man Country*, 141.
48. Cole, *Old Man Country*, 141.

description of Wink's study: "We are surrounded by a lifetime of learning and by files for future books that will never be written and lectures that will never be given."[49] This description fits the metaphors of an empty shell and loss of self. Wink is presented to readers as a shadow of himself, someone whose life is being torn into "terrifying pieces." These and other similar depictions incorrectly reinforce the idea that the person living with dementia is somehow "less than," incapable of understanding or articulating their experiences.

Returning to the interview, after commenting on the place and explaining the purpose of the interview, to Cole's credit, he does what many people do not but should: asks Wink about his dementia. Cole says, "But let me just start with this question for you, and it's not an easy question because of the dementia that you're in the middle of. How would you—? How different are you from the self that you were ten years ago? How would you characterize yourself today compared to ten years ago?" Wink explains that he was told by friends and experts that he would be "dead at some point . . . There is one line probably—preliminary. I can't do it."

Part of this verbatim exchange is included in the chapter. Cole writes, "He [Wink] stops in frustration and says, finally, "I can't do it."[50] Cole goes on to write:

> We keep going, but our conversation is disjointed. Sometimes I can't get what he is trying to say. Sometimes there is nothing to get. Walter drifts between the present and the past, between presence and absence. He can't finish most of his thoughts or stories. I try to bring him back, gently.[51]

The interview is filled with many false starts, forgotten words, broken lines of thinking. Yet, Wink demonstrates Self 1 through the indexical positions of "I." However, Cole, as the outward evaluator, seems to see Wink as "lacking" through use of the image of Wink drifting away. From Cole's perspective, Wink is someone unable to construct a cohesive narrative. Consequently, Cole, as someone without dementia, tries to align Wink to the narratives and insights for which Wink was known.

Cole continues in the interview: "So you— The doctors, when they gave you a diagnosis of dementia, they said that you would be dead sooner than you otherwise would have been, or did they have a certain

---

49. Cole, *Old Man Country*, 141.
50. Cole, *Old Man Country*, 142.
51. Cole, *Old Man Country*, 142.

number of years?" A few minutes later, after a brief exchange, Cole says, "You look quite alive to me." Wink responds, "I'm actually more alive than I was 10 years ago." Wink continues by describing his routine for staying healthy. Cole, who clearly states in his book's introduction that he is not a trained qualitative interviewer nor was his purpose to gather research data, does miss the opportunity to delve a bit deeper into Wink's comment about being alive.

Being the thoughtful and caring person that he is, Cole is careful throughout the interview to respectfully restate his interpretation of Wink's comments for Wink's input and correction if necessary. This strategy seems to help Wink with word recall, the most common feature of dementia which is often mistaken for memory loss. Cole does fall prey to a common mistake that people make when talking with people living with dementia: presenting too many language processing tasks at once, which can lead to confusion. Language processing tasks include word and event recall. Multiple, back-to-back questions often do not leave the person living with dementia enough time to process one question fully before another is presented. In addition, following a train of thought from beginning to end, retrieving the information necessary to respond to a question, processing and expressing ideas, and transforming memory resources into language is difficult.[52] Multiple questions increase the difficulty of responding. Also, by being unable to recall names and details or by making other grammatical errors, the speaker becomes positioned as somewhat unreliable and potentially as "less than." For example, toward the beginning of the interview, Cole asks:

TC: And what really matters to you now?

WW: Well, one thing is that I have three books that I'm trying to finish before I give it up.

TC: Okay. What are they?

WW: One is a collection of—

TC: Essays?

WW: I don't think I can do this.

TC: You can't do it? It's hard to remember the books?

WW: Yeah.

52. Hydén, *Entangled Narratives.*

In this exchange, Cole, first asks Wink to name the three books, which is clearly a challenge for Wink. Cole gently helps Wink by filling in words like "essays" when Wink is unable to finish his description of the first book. Then Wink says, for the second time, that he doesn't think he can "do this." It's unclear if he is referring to remembering the book names, completing the interview, or both. The exchange does suggest that Wink is frustrated by the difficulties he is having, part of which are an unintentional result of the types of information he is being asked to produce.

Another exchange involving memory recall and processing multiple questions that is retold in the chapter involves the following:

> TC: One of the things that you love is your scholarship. You've written so much and influenced so many people over the years. Do you remember today what the most important contributions—what the most important insights—that you've given us—the biblical exegesis or nonviolence? Or will you let your books do the speaking for you now?
>
> WW: I may have no choice in that. (Laughs) But if I do have a choice, I would say it's the passage in the Sermon on the Mount—"walk the second mile."

In this exchange, Cole asks several questions of Wink at once. First, does Wink remember his most important contributions, which Cole quickly changes to "insights" midsentence? Cole adds, "biblical exegesis or nonviolence" but then follows with "or will you let your books do the speaking for you now?" As mentioned, processing multiple questions can be complicated, even more complicated while also being asked to recall names and other data can add further pressure.

After Cole finds the passage and asks Wink to read it aloud, Cole then asks Wink to explain its importance:

> TC: What does that mean? Why is it so important? Why is it so radical?"

In this example, Cole asks three separate questions in succession related to the interpretation of a text.

> WW: Well, because the passage has been used over these 2000 years in such a way that it would be oppressive, rather than liberation. There's a little word in there, "If anyone slaps you on your right cheek"—
>
> TC: Let him slap you on your left cheek.

WW: And that's the back of the hand that's being described there, and everybody knows that that's got any scholar. And what we're dealing with here is not a blow to injure; it is to—

TC: To humiliate?

WW: To humiliate, yeah. Good. And then, the soldier then— you see why that— There's no mystery there. One of the soldiers could— So thinking of those passages all together, they are the most radical statements about the future of humanity.

TC: The most radical statement about the future of—?

WW: Humanity.

As mentioned earlier, it's unclear from reading the chapter how much time elapses between question and response. Cole is almost certainly unaware of the complexity of his multiple questions. Yet, despite the challenge, Wink makes his thoughts known in an intelligible way. Referring to the previous exchange, however, Cole writes in the chapter: "Walter can't really explain his radical interpretation of this passage or why it is the grounding of his fundamental message of Christian nonviolent resistance to oppression. Later, I find the answer in chapter 5 of his book . . . ."[53] From Cole's narrative position in the chapter, Wink is not able to provide the details that Cole would like. Wink is living a chaos narrative. However, Wink's response suggests that he understands the meaning of the passage, even if he is unable to clearly express that to Cole. Going back to Sabat's work on the three selves of dementia from earlier in the chapter, Wink, with Cole's help, lives up to his personae of scholar, Self 3 although Cole seems to see Wink more in terms of Self 2.

Throughout the chapter, Wink cannot seem to give Cole the answers that he is looking for that align with what Cole perceives to be Wink's big story. Yet, the interview includes several small stories that seem germane to Wink. For example, in talking about an autobiography that Wink is working on, his big story, Cole asks, "Is there one story in particular that's funny that you'd like to tell, or should we all wait until the autobiography comes out?" Wink responds, "Well, I can just tell a short, quick one." He then tells the following story.

WW: We had a bunch of kids together to make a bus, and there was a bully on the bus. He has terrified the kids—just

53. Cole, *Old Man Country*, 143.

petrified. I'm actually reenacting this story, and it is a true story. Finally— And on the bus there's also a—I don't know. I can't remember how to do it. But the little kid— there was a little kid on the bus that had— I can't even tell.

TC: There's a little kid on the bus. There's a bully.

WW: And there was a kid who just had a runny nose all the time, just snot, and he jumped to his feet and goes— (blowing noise)—and blew his nose. And he says, "I want to shake the hand of a real bully."

TC: (Laughs.)

Understandably, the story doesn't appear in the chapter since the chapter was really focused on Cole's larger purpose of the book: Learning from accomplished men he admired. However, this small story has lessons to be learned and does relate to Wink's writings on non-violent resistance. For example, in his 2009 talk entitled "Nonviolence for the Violent,"[54] Wink explained that Jesus, in his Sermon on the Mount (Matt 5:38–42) offers a third way for people to resist their oppressors, not by meekly acquiescing, as is often assumed in the expression "turn the other cheek" or through violence but by turning the system of oppression on itself. "Turning the other cheek," argued Wink, was a way to force the oppressor to move beyond the intended act of humiliation caused by slapping someone on their right cheek with the back of one's right hand (the only dignified way that one could slap a "lesser" person in that historical period). Instead, turning one's left cheek would force the oppressor to lose *their* dignity. Wink said, "The left cheek now offers a perfect target for a blow of the fist. But only equals fought with fists as we know from Jewish sources. And the last thing the master wishes to do is to establish this underling's equality. This act of defiance renders the master incapable of asserting his dominance in this relationship. He can have this little slave beaten, but he can intimidate him no longer."[55]

The story of the bully that Wink tells to Cole during the interview is also an example of turning the table on the oppressor. Although Wink could not clearly articulate his past and complicated scholarship regarding the Sermon on the Mount passage, he could illustrate, though the

---

54. The talk, delivered on September 24, 2009, was co-sponsored by the Chicago Theological Seminary (CTS). A video recording and transcript of Wink's talk is located at https://www.lutheranpeace.org/articles/nonviolence-for-the-violent-walter-wink.

55. Fellowship, "Transcript of Walter Wink's Nonviolence for the Violent."

small story, what he meant by "going the second mile" through nonviolent resistance. The "little kid" in the story blows his nose into his own hand, then holds it out to shake "a real bully's hand." In this way the "little kid" humiliates the bully while also seemingly acknowledging his "power." The bully would be faced with no-win situation and would subsequently be undone through a very simple act. Through this small story, Wink re-positions himself in the conversation as someone who has thought deeply about nonviolent resistance even in small, everyday gestures. Wink's story is a reminder of the importance of really listening to narratives by people living with dementia.

CONCLUSION

The purpose of the chapter was to consider self and identity in dementia narratives by looking closely at an interview with and subsequent chapter about Wink. As noted, cultural narratives about dementia influence how we interpret the narratives by people living with dementia. Much of the focus on dementia narratives is on how much the person with dementia has lost. Slips in memory, problems with word recall, reinforce the idea that someone is "slipping away" or becoming less than. Overlooked are the narrative features that point to the person's reaffirmation of self in spite of their condition, not because of it. As Phinney has argued, shouldn't we be considering in what ways people who are experiencing the course of dementia are able to continue having a meaningful life rather than assuming that their lives are without meaning?[56]

Instead, we often employ confirmatory approaches that involve judging the person living with dementia in terms of evidence of symptoms or attributing all actions and statements to dementia.[57] This is not to say that dementia is without profound and real consequences and that the experience of dementia should be romanticized despite the real challenges that do exist. Instead, it is important to recognize how the imposition of story onto a person living with dementia silences narratives that can and do emerge.

As Falcus and Sako have observed, "We are living in what we call the 'time of dementia,' a cultural context dominated by a sense of crisis about dementia and the ageing population . . . . But time is also central

56. Phinney, "Fluctuating Awareness."
57. Reid, *Doing Relationship-Centered Dementia Care*.

to the experience of dementia itself. Illness can represent a disruption to the smooth progression of life and the way we imagine the life course, but dementia, in particular, fundamentally upsets our imagining and experience of time itself."[58] Although they are referring to literary texts that attempt to convey the experience of dementia, the same thought can be applied to personal narratives of dementia by people living with dementia. The disruptions to narrative that suggest chaos should not be abandoned because they lack conformity to cultural expectations of complete narratives. Instead, narratives, especially small stories, by people living with dementia offer a wealth of insight that challenges common stereotypes such as loss of self and give voice to people who are often spoken for.

58. Falcus and Sako, *Contemporary Narratives of Dementia*, 20.

4

A Mutual Opportunity of Listening and Telling

Thomas Cole's Life Writing

BENJAMIN SAXTON

"Those who know ghosts tell us that they long to be released from their ghost life and led to rest as ancestors. As ancestors they live forth in the present generation, while as ghosts they are compelled to haunt the present generation with their shadow life."[1] —HANS LOEWALD

FIRST CONVERSATIONS

The first thing you saw, when you walked into Thomas Cole's office at the McGovern Center for Humanities and Ethics, was a polished round brown table: a perfect place for conversation. It was the fall of 2009 and I was visiting from across the street, at Rice University, where I was studying modern American literature. Cole had brought me on as a research associate who could hopefully help him think through the tropes of the "wise old man" and the "dirty old man" in literature and pop culture; we had started with Phillip Roth's late fiction. After reading a half-dozen of

---

1. Many thanks to Thomas Cole for his continual support and suggestions (the Hans Loewold quote being one of them), as well as his willingness to share some of his unpublished writings with me.

his novels, I couldn't get past the ferocious dogmatism of Roth's narrators. "They're just so . . . . " I struggled to find the right word, and finally spit it out—"*monologic.*"

Cole raised an eyebrow and asked me to say more.

I launched into a summary of Mikhail Bakhtin's work, speaking with the false confidence of a lit nerd who had read much and understood little.[2] Bakhtin was an early twentieth-century Russian thinker who had transformed how I thought about stories and literary freedom. An individual is never a single, isolated person in full possession of their speech, in Bakhtin's view, but rather a person among persons whose voice gains meaning only with others: "Life by its very nature is dialogic. To live means to participate in dialogue: to ask questions, to heed, to respond, to agree."[3]

Even if life is irreducibly dialogic, this doesn't prevent us from defining each other and the world monologically—that is, as the condition in which "another person remains wholly and merely an object of consciousness, and not another consciousness."[4] Monologic discourse shuts out the voice of the other, turning him or her into a lifeless object rather than a living subject. The monologic author, standing outside the novel as an omnipotent judge, knows everything about his characters and can evaluate, contrast, and juxtapose them as he pleases. An internal connection—a connection *between* consciousnesses—is completely absent. "The characters," Bakhtin writes, "are self-enclosed and deaf; they do not hear and do not answer one another. There are not and cannot be any dialogic relationships among them. They neither argue nor agree."[5] With very few exceptions, Bakhtin argues, monologism has characterized the history of the western novel, with Tolstoy as the classic example of a monologic author.

In resistance to monologism and its corollaries—manipulation, domination, even totalitarianism[6]—Bakhtin looked for an alternative

---

2. I have written about Bakhtin elsewhere, and here apply some of my previous work. See Saxton, "Tolkien and Bakhtin on Authorship." Also see Saxton, "Grotesque Subjects."

3. Bakhtin, *Problems of Dostoevsky's Poetics*, 296.

4. Bakhtin, *Problems of Dostoevsky's Poetics*, 293.

5. Bakhtin, *Problems of Dostoevsky's Poetics*, 70.

6. Bakhtin's insistence on the transformative potential of dialogue is surely tied to living in a society in which millions of human voices were permanently silenced in the name of totalitarianism. Barely escaping execution during the Stalinist purges in 1929, Bakhtin was exiled to a remote area of Kazakhstan for six years, where he subsisted as a bookkeeper. See Clark and Holquist, *Mikhail Bakhtin*, 144.

relationship between authors and characters, which he found in the fiction of Dostoevsky. This special relationship, which he called "polyphony," can be considered an intense, very rare kind of dialogism. In the polyphonic novel, according to Bakhtin, the strict hierarchy between author and hero is somehow dismantled: "A plurality of consciousnesses, with equal rights and each with its own world," engage on equal terms with the author, who is one voice among many.[7] Characters can disagree with the author, surprise her, and develop in ways that the author herself could never predict. Bakhtin compares the polyphonic author to Goethe's Prometheus, who "creates not voiceless slaves (as does Zeus) but free people, capable of standing alongside their creator, capable of not agreeing with him and even of rebelling against him."[8]

I talked on and on, carried away by my enthusiasm as Cole listened quietly and attentively. At the time, I didn't know that he'd already thought long and hard about the delicate power dynamics between authors and subjects, between friends and foes, between fathers and sons. "It took me a long, long time to actually have a genuinely dialogical way of thinking about things," he told me later.[9]

On September 22, 1953, Cole's father Burton woke up early at their house in New Haven Connecticut and wished his wife a happy 28th birthday. He went into the next room, gave four-year-old Cole a kiss, and ate breakfast. Then he got into his brown four-door Packard, headed north on the Merritt Parkway, and drove his car into a bridge.[10] For years, in both his published work and private journals, Cole dwelled on the meaning of that fateful day. The sequence of generations in his life had been broken. Putting himself in his father's shoes, Cole wondered why Burton had chosen suicide. "The only way to exert control over his own life was to take it," Cole wrote in an unpublished essay.[11] "Finally he'd have some peace, some freedom from his father Irving, who could never let him alone. He slipped into the netherworld and silently became a ghost yearning to be understood by a family that remembered his sweet and gentle ways but could never fathom his suffering."

7. Bakhtin, *Problems*, 6.
8. Bakhtin, *Problems*, 6.
9. Cole, interviewed by Saxton, New Orleans, Louisiana, July 13, 2017.
10. Cole, *Old Man Country*, 1.
11. Cole, "The Flames of Oblivion." Although Cole's family refused to talk about Burton's death, treating it for many years as a tragic accident, in the late 1990s Cole learned from his aunt Carole that it was in fact a suicide. See Cole, *Old Man Country*, 1–3.

Burton wasn't a silent ghost. In 1998 Cole wrote to his father, and Burton answered. Then and now, through dozens of epistolary exchanges, they've enjoyed a long and fruitful correspondence. The tone of these letters is supportive and compassionate. In one of them, Cole wrote from a ski resort where he was staying with his daughter and family friends. Although he was having a great time skiing and admiring Utah's snow-capped peaks, he was also feeling guilty that he'd left his wife at home as she was recovering from foot surgery. Cole signed the letter "Tom Avie," a nod to his given Hebrew name Avram Michel.[12]

> "Dear Avie," Burton replied,
> I can sense that you are a little wound up, your body armor in place, feeling guilty about leaving Letha in Houston, feeling guilty that you're not at Temple today on the Sabbath, guilty about spending money, guilty about having fun, worried about your children and your trip to Duluth and Central Michigan next week.... I could go on. Relax. There's plenty of guilt and anxiety to go around; don't try and hoard it all for yourself. You know how your ski instructors tease you about being "Frankenstein," all tensed up, trying too hard? And did you notice how great it felt when you figured out how to stand up straight and allow your weight to lean downhill? Less strain and effort, more enjoyment. Good metaphor for you. Up there at 8,000 feet. Enjoy the air, the wonderful people you're with, my granddaughter I never met, the breathtaking scenery, just breathing, in-spire-ing! And allow yourself to rest. You need to strengthen your vessel in order to bear the glimpses of divine light that are coming your way. Your ancestry on Jackie's side is fascinating, and I look forward to what you learn about us. You are painting a larger picture of my life than I ever imagined. Keep it up. Love, Dad[13]

Even as he processed Burton's haunting absence, Cole also grappled with the domineering presence of his stepfather Bert, a brawny World War II veteran who'd fought in the Battle of the Bulge. As bellicose as he was big, Bert always had to be right. Eventually, after Bert died in 2006 at 88 years old, Cole would write him letters too. Unlike the loving back-and-forth with Burton, these exchanges are explicitly combative. "I went into academics partly to beat you at your own game," Cole told Bert. He added:

---

12. Cole, letter to Burton Michel, March 17, 2000.
13. Burton Michel, letter to Cole, March 18, 2000.

> I wanted to get the credentials and do the scholarly work that you were unable to do. You once acknowledged that you were trying to write but couldn't finish things. I was in no position to help you. I remember one night in Toronto, when I had read Isaac Deutscher's biography of Stalin and we walked up and down a long cold street by the lake arguing about Stalin's policies and life. Neither of us backed down. What a pity we couldn't talk to each other and listen to each other's arguments. I never learned how to have a real conversation from you.[14]

Bert's response was similarly combative. What did Cole want from him? To say that he was sorry? That he was a failure? That he wished he had made more money and been a better father? Maybe Cole had forgotten that Bert had lived a hard life. Bert grew up poor and started working at an early age, helping his father deliver oil to customers who burned the stuff to heat their homes. When he was six years old, his parents' grocery store and their apartment burned to the ground on a freezing cold night. That night left him forever fearful of becoming poor and homeless. From that day on, he woke up every morning with a knife between his teeth.

"You were given things on a silver platter and I fought through life to get where I was," Bert told Cole. "I changed my name from Cohen to Cole to get a job when they weren't hiring Jews. It didn't work."[15] Despite his bitterness and defensiveness, Bert ends the letter with a quasi-apology and a confession:

> This is a partial Apologia, in both senses. It is an apology for the things I've done that hurt you and a defense of the way I looked and still look at the world of the living. Take it or leave it.... No, I don't really mean that. I still haven't learned the art of give and take, of listening to the arguments of others and taking them seriously in my responses. Anyway, there's not much I can do now about my life anyway. It is what it was. Maybe this exchange of views in letters can help our relationship. But you know that I don't really believe in relationships or correspondence between the living and the dead. On this point, though, I am willing to listen to your next letter, since I do hope we can get on better terms. We're talking about eternity here, and unless we make peace or come to some sort of terms before you die, it will not happen. Progress in Olam Haba depends on the work of the living. The dead are dead. We can see things from the perspective

---

14. Cole, letter to Burton Cole, January 24, 2016.
15. Burton Cole, letter to Cole, January 24, 2016.

of eternity but cannot change things that were done in life. So the burden is on you.[16]

I think that one of these "burdens," for Cole, was the desire to achieve through writing what he couldn't achieve with Bert: a partnership of equals. That was easier said than done—especially when Cole met Eldrewey Stearns.

One day in 1984, Cole attended a weekly psychiatry case conference that introduced medical students to the characteristics of major mental disorders.[17] The patient, Eldrewey, was a short fifty-two-year-old man with fierce gleaming eyes that betrayed great pain and loneliness. His mustachioed mouth churned out rapid-fire sentences, punctuated by awkward silences. Eldrewey complained that he felt very important—indeed he *was* important, having been a central member of Houston's desegregation movement—but no one understood him. "It sounds like you have an important story to tell," Cole said. "I'd like to help you get it down on paper."[18]

"An interesting proposition," Eldrewey skeptically replied. "I doubt you're up to it.... But then, I'm not exactly in a position to refuse."

In 1985, the unlikely collaborators began meeting two or three times a week at Cole's UTMB office to tape Eldrewey's life story, which they envisioned as an autobiography. The process was an endless struggle. Eldrewey often wandered randomly from topic to topic, leading to mutual stress, disappointment, and recrimination. He was often disorganized, and sometimes he roamed drunk through the hallways, hitting on female colleagues and office staff.[19] He goaded Cole into arguments about race. Once, as they were driving to lunch, Cole asked Eldrewey what it meant for a white man to write about the life of a Black man.

"You're not white," Eldrewey told him. "You're a Jew."[20]

Overcommitted and resentful at Eldrewey's lack of gratitude, Cole felt like he was trapped in a continual tug of war. He half-wished they'd never met.[21] But he refused to give up.

---

16. Burton Cole, letter to Cole, January 24, 2016.
17. Cole, *No Color Is My Kind*, 1.
18. Cole, *No Color Is My Kind*, 3.
19. Cole, *No Color Is My Kind*, 5.
20. Cole, *No Color Is My Kind*, xii.
21. Cole, *No Color Is My Kind*, 151.

What we find here, I think, isn't a productive marriage of speaking and hearing but rather a shouting match in which the tellers argue, interrupt, and undercut each other; revise or re-imagine details of the story; jostle for control over the conditions of the telling; or, sometimes, refuse to talk at all in favor of silence and isolation. Conversation exists in a precarious state of flux between dialogue and monologue, polyphony and cacophony.[22] As one of William Faulkner's characters puts it,

> You are born at the same time with a lot of other people, all mixed up with them, like trying to, having to, move your arms and legs with strings only the same strings are hitched to all the other arms and legs and the others all trying and they don't know why either except that the strings are all in one another's way like five or six people all trying to make a rug on the same loom only each one wants to weave his own pattern into the rug.[23]

To confront the dangers of authorial domination, Cole tried to express Eldrewey's views as accurately as he could. After long stints of working with him during manic swings and psychotic breaks—and after receiving his permission—Cole decided to tell the story as he saw it, using his own judgment and integrity as a historian, medical humanist, and writer. This included his decision to write about Eldrewey's mental illness—something Eldrewey opposed. "Other writers—white or Black—would have made different decisions," Cole wrote in the preface to the revised edition of the book. "I leave readers to judge the strengths and weaknesses of my approach."[24]

TOWARDS A DIALOGIC MASCULINITY

By 2009, when we began regularly meeting and working together, Cole had established himself as a versatile storyteller. In addition to his academic work, he'd made four documentary films and launched, with Kate de Medeiros, a life story writing workshops for elders.[25] Now, at sixty,

---

22. While Bakhtin was very good at accounting for the way in which Dostoevsky orchestrates the voices in his novels, he rarely considered the negative, destructive potential of dialogic discourse. See Jones, *Dostoevsky after Bakhtin*, 191.

23. Faulkner, *Absalom! Absalom!*, 127.

24. Cole, *No Color Is My Kind*, xiii.

25. See *The Strange Demise of Jim Crow*; *Life Stories*; *Still Life: The Humanity of Anatomy*; and *Stroke: Conversations and Explanations*.

Cole was a young old man who was starting to think personally about what it means to grow old.

Cole's work style was profoundly dialogic, in the sense that he constantly needed someone to be listening, responding to, challenging, and encouraging him. We started to explore scholarly work about men and old age; memoirs and essays by old men (Cicero, Malcolm Cowley, Donald Hall, and Roger Angell); and more of Philip Roth's fiction.[26] We watched popular films whose main characters were aging men played by Hollywood stars who were themselves aging—Harrison Ford, Sylvestor Stallone, Clint Eastwood, and Tommy Lee Jones. In particular, we looked for models of masculinity that didn't insist on dialogue as debate, as a zero-sum combat that produced one winner and one loser. Cole was always willing to examine the personal stakes of these academic interests, and he encouraged me to do the same. I often wondered why I was interested in the shape and the structure of stories. My relationship with my dad, like Cole's relationship with Bert Cole, was often combative. I knew that my dad wanted the best for my brother and me, but he craved control (did I also crave control?) and he always needed to be right (did I always need to be right?) Despite myself, I noticed my dad's values nesting inside me: an attraction to competition, the perverse thrill of bullying the bully. Sometimes, craving and hating power at the same time, I felt like Frodo clutching the One Ring. Maybe that's why I found a dialogic sensibility so compelling, and so difficult: it requires humility and vulnerability—qualities that are especially hard to come by for American men raised on a diet of flamboyant gunslingers and stoic Rambos.

Most of all, Cole and I were captivated by the film adaptation of Cormac McCarthy's novel *No Country for Old Men*, whose main character, the aging Sheriff Ed Tom Bell, is faced with the overwhelming violence and terror of the Mexican drug trade.[27] At the outset of the story, Bell's moral world seems to be intact. He believes in Truth with a capital T and has no doubts about right and wrong or which side he is on. In short, Bell is the quintessential small-town sheriff: honorable, old-fashioned, and set in his ways. The man who throws Bell's life into uncertainty, Anton Chigurh, appears from the start as a model of ruthlessness and efficiency. He methodically pursues Llewellyn Moss, a young welder who, on a hunting trip in the desert, stumbles upon a botched drug deal and a briefcase

26. Cole and Saxton, "'Old Age Isn't a Battle; It's a Massacre,'" 285–94.

27. McCarthy, *No Country for Old Men*. For some of my previous work on this material, see Saxton and Cole, "*No Country for Old Men*."

filled with just over two million dollars. Moss picks up the briefcase, takes it back to his trailer, and plans to make a new life with his wife, Carla Jean. As Chigurh hunts Moss and the money, Bell helplessly trails the action and ponders the implications of their bloody conflict.

By the end of the plot, Bell is overwhelmed. Chigurh has escaped with the money. Moss and his wife are dead. The peace in Terrell County has been shattered. Bitter and bewildered, Bell retires from his post as sheriff, no longer certain of who he is or where he fits in the world:

> I always thought I could at least someway put things right and I guess I just dont feel that way no more . . . . I'm bein asked to stand for something that I dont have the same belief in it I once did . . . . Now I've seen it held to the light . . . . I've been forced look at it again and forced to look at myself. For better or worse I do not know . . . . I never had them sorts of doubts before.[28]

Not surprisingly, most critics consider Bell a failure, albeit a good man and a sympathetic failure. Bell not only fails to catch Chigurh; he also fails to "be a man," to live up to the masculine expectations of a sheriff and a productive member of society. Cole and I disagreed. In our view, Bell's feeling of defeat is not, in the end, a failure: it's the beginning of a transformation that leads not to superpowers but rather to humility and uncertainty.[29]

To make our case, we took a closer look at how Bell's approach to conversation changes over the course of the novel. For most of his life, Bell, playing the role of the taciturn cowboy, gives in to the temptation to shut out other voices. He is, as Bakhtin puts it, "deaf to the other's response."[30] Bell recalls, for example, meeting a woman in Corpus Christi who worried that her daughter would one day be denied the right to have an abortion. "Well mam," he replies, "I don't think you got any worries about the way the country is headed. The way I see it going I don't have much doubt but what she'll be able to have an abortion. I'm goin to say that not only will she be able to have an abortion, she'll be able to have you put to sleep. Which pretty much ended the conversation."[31] The way in which Bell recalls the woman's insistent talking ("she kept on, kept

---

28. McCarthy, *No Country for Old Men*, 206.
29. Saxton and Cole, "*No Country for Old Men*," 97–116.
30. Bakhtin, *Problems*, 292.
31. McCarthy, *No Country*, 117.

on") suggests that her point of view is a mere annoyance.[32] Bell rules out in advance the possibility that the woman's perspective could change any of his own thinking. He also refuses to discuss the subjects that are most troubling to him: his daughter ("We lost a girl but I wont talk about that") and his military background ("I won't talk about the war neither").[33] As Bakhtin conceives it and McCarthy practices it, dialogue doesn't only occur between voices, but also *within* them: we can no more escape from dialogue, even in discussions with ourselves, than a character like Bell can forget the voice of his daughter. Bell's lonely "microdialogues," as Bakhtin calls them, plague Bell because they don't give others the chance to offer help.[34] For much of the novel, he conforms to a kind of "monologic masculinity" that limits the range of topics deemed appropriate for men and women to discuss, hews to a narrow definition of what counts as work and success, and demands precise boundaries of manhood.[35] But after Bell's views are "held to the light," he realizes that his own perspective is insufficient to account for what he has seen, which opens him to a different kind of conversation.

By embracing a more flexible understanding of what it means to be a man, Bell adopts a kind of "dialogic masculinity"[36] through conversations with at least two men on death row, Moss's father, Carla Jean, his uncle Ellis, and, most importantly, his wife. On the one hand, this search for dialogue is quite literal, as he drives along the West Texas roads in his weathered police cruiser. On the other, it is a metaphorical journey into Bell's consciousness, where he grapples with himself, past and present, and questions his role in a society where, it seems, he no longer has a home.

Although he can't offer a solution, Bell's search implies that there may be numerous ways of being an old man, not a one-size-fits-all image to which one must conform. By the novel's end, Bell seems to understand that any new scripts for late-life masculinity must begin and end with self-knowledge. As he puts it: "it's a life's work to see yourself for what you really are and even then you might be wrong."[37]

32. McCarthy, *No Country*, 206.
33. McCarthy, *No Country*, 90, 195.
34. Bakhtin, *Problems*, 220.
35. Campbell and Finney, eds., *Country Boys*, 28.
36. Campbell and Finney, eds., *Country Boys*, 28.
37. McCarthy, *No Country*, 295.

FROM *NO COUNTRY FOR OLD MEN* TO *OLD MAN COUNTRY*

In 2010, Cole embarked on an ambitious project—the first textbook in medical humanities, coauthored with Nathan Carlin and Ron Carson[38]— and our "old man studies" went on pause. Ever the dialogic thinker, Cole ensured that the textbook was collaborative in every respect. Cole and I coauthored the history and medicine section, Carlin wrote the religion and medicine section, Carson wrote the literature and medicine section, and the philosophy and medicine section was divvied up evenly. In the course of writing the book, Cole, Carlin, and Carson engaged each other in numerous day-long meetings and conference calls, critiquing and revising each other's work. As the book neared publication in 2014, Cole scrutinized each chapter and made editorial suggestions to help unify the book. From a disciplinary perspective, I would suggest that the vibrancy of Cole's style—manifested in both his writing and in his collaborative approach—is characteristic of medical humanities as a whole. The qualities that bioethics would dismiss—being too soft, too emotional, too open-ended—are indispensable to medical humanities.[39]

Participating in the textbook project was eye-opening. It was heartening to see Cole, Carlin, and Carson at the height of their powers, steadfastly supporting each other as both friends and colleagues. The textbook project also made it crystal clear that academia wasn't for me. Perusing arcane scholarship about health and disease was making my eyes bleed,[40] and the seven years I'd spent in grad school had left me deeply conflicted about university life. I had arrived in the English department as a burned-out jock who was eager to abandon the competitive grind of college basketball. Outside seminar, my classmates, a tight-knit cohort of seven, gathered for drinks and hosted pot lucks and, at the end of our first semester, held a mock awards ceremony with categories like Most Likely To Save the Planet and Most Likely to Be an Academic Superstar. Booze and banter were useful distractions from unsettling questions: Who would finish the program? Who would get a job? "A job," of course,

---

38. Cole, Carlin, and Carson, *Medical Humanities.*

39. "The difference between bioethics and medical humanities," in Larry Churchill's words during Cole's Festschrift conference, "is that medical humanities will open itself up to conversations with the dead." See also Friedman, "Precarious Position of the Medical Humanities in the Medical School Curriculum," 320–22.

40. Boorse, "Health as a Theoretical Concept."

meant a tenure-track position at a research institution. Anything less was failure. The savagery of the humanities job market, which seemed to be shrinking by the year, demanded robotic efficiency and monkish asceticism. One of the Victorianists admitted that he felt guilty whenever he had sex with his wife because he was squandering time that might have been devoted to research. Hearing this story, and dozens of others, it occurred to me that America's cultures of sports and the academy are fundamentally the same. They're obsessed with competition. Lurking beneath platitudes about team-building and community are questions of social worth: who will survive, who will excel, who will *win*.⁴¹

As I approached my program's finish line, the happiness that I shared with the success stories, with the "winners," was often tainted with elements of sadness. Someone's good news reminded me of the hippy Romanticist, marooned on medical leave, or the gentle modernist whose advisor threw her under the bus after eight years of toil. Eight years, and nothing to show for it—except for stress-related hernias that required surgery. As a rule, you were expected to avoid talking about these "losers." (Was it a coincidence that they were usually women and people of color?) Stay silent, wait a while, and eventually they would slip softly out of sight, to God knows where.

I had started to slip away myself, to my favorite city. In my eyes, New Orleans had everything that Houston lacked: improvisation, soul, and tasty beignets. It was also the birthplace of poker, a game that I was increasingly using to escape from my problems. One summer evening, during a long frustrating session at the downtown casino, I brooded on a central paradox of American life: we're often forced to compete against the people closest to us.⁴² A few hours later, riding the Megabus home to Houston, I had grim clarity about my role in academia: The game was rigged to pit us against each other, and I didn't want to play.

In 2014 I told Cole that I would be leaving my McGovern Center postdoc one year early to tell the story of poker in New Orleans. At first, he was confused and upset, and he tried to talk sense into me. I wouldn't budge. Over the next few months, as he prompted me to explain myself, his attitude shifted from disappointment to tentative acceptance, and eventually to enthusiastic support. The week before I left Houston, we went out for one last dinner and then Cole dropped me at my apartment.

---

41. See Burt, "Against Winning."

42. As the actor Walter Matthau put it, "Poker exemplifies the worst aspects of capitalism that have made our country so great," as quoted in Alvarez, *Risky Business*, 126.

We hugged each other and started to cry. Our relationship had evolved from a research partnership to a mentorship to a deep friendship, and neither of us wanted to give up the hour or so that we spent together each week. As it would turn out, we didn't stop: to my surprise, Cole wanted to keep working together. I don't know why. Maybe he saw some of his younger, more foolish self in me. Maybe he was motivated by a fatherly financial impulse—to set aside fifteen-gees-a-year to support a wayward writer—or maybe his appetite for conversation was simply too strong. In any case, we kept going. Although the setting would change—a Skype call replaced the round brown table—our enthusiasm for discussing literature and life didn't. Now, with a more flexible schedule, Cole was eager to return to the subject of what it means to grow old.

No Country for Old Men ends with a powerful dream that never fails to move Cole to tears. It's a cold snowy night, and Ed Tom Bell is on horseback riding with his father through a mountain pass. His father moves on ahead and out of sight. Somewhere in the cold and the dark, he fixes a fire to warm and light his son's way. Bell can only follow behind, knowing that he'll always arrive a bit too late but knowing, too, that his father has gone ahead to comfort and protect him. Then he wakes up.[43]

Using one fictional small-town sheriff as a springboard, *Old Man Country* paints a panoramic portrait of American men living in the Fourth Age. Although most of the book explores how twelve men face (or faced) the challenges of living a good old age, a crucial part of Cole's braided narrative involved his efforts to make peace with his father's suicide and with his stepfather's domineering and difficult personality. Burton, who died at twenty-seven, never found a way to live his whole life. Bert, who lived into deep old age, never found a way to share his life and love. "In writing this book," Cole declared, "I am looking for what my fathers couldn't find."[44]

Old Man Country also showcases Cole's remarkable versatility: his expertise in cultural history and gerontology; his knack for interviewing and active listening; his persistence; and his love of experimentation and creativity. He always likes to play all the roles—a risky tactic, to say the least. "Everything is always on the verge of failure," Cole told me once, when we were talking about his many projects. "There's no other way I can do it."[45] Now, as he embarked on yet another project, he pushed his

43. McCarthy, *No Country*, 295.
44. Cole, *Old Man Country*, 4.
45. Cole, interviewed by Saxton, New Orleans, Louisiana, October 30, 2023.

boundaries even further. Not satisfied with being a scholar, a journalist, a film critic, a memoirist, a psychoanalyst, an imp, a ghostwriter, and a spiritual seeker, Cole decided to turn himself into an interview subject. Tom Cole would interview Tom Cole. "Thanks for the chance to interview you," Cole began. "I understand that you are not an easy man to find."[46]

"Yes, I'm not always available to myself let alone to others," Cole answered. "It's good to take the time and see if you can find a way into the self/spirit who motivates and powers the book project."

Cole asked himself many of the same questions that he posed to Paul Volcker, Walter Wink, Denton Cooley, and the other subjects of *Old Man Country*. What do you look forward to? What are you afraid of? How do you think about your legacy? What do you regret? What should old men be contributing to the world today?[47] When asked what he did when he woke up in the morning, Cole answered that he usually rolled over and hugged the love of his life, Thelma Jean, hoping that she wouldn't get up too quickly (she almost always hurried away for her forty-five-minute walk). These days, in 2017, he was recovering from back surgery, so he usually stayed in bed and recited the Modeh Ani prayer (first in Hebrew, then in English) and thanked God for restoring his soul. He'd recently become more aware of the prayer's roteness, and of his tendency to get distracted when he was reciting it. So he repeated the prayer over and over, usually in Hebrew, trying to clear his mind and receive the calm waters of the (holy?) spirit. After he finished, sometimes he would turn on his iPhone and scroll through the New York Times or his email. Then he would get up and make breakfast. Coffee, which was becoming increasingly important to his alertness throughout the day, was easily found on the bottom left side of the freezer. "But this is probably more detail than you want," Cole told Cole. "I'm not sure what you are after."[48]

They kept talking. Cole discussed the frustration of managing a body that didn't work the way that it had used to. During the last few months, he'd worked hard in physical therapy and was recovering some strength in his legs and glutes; his stamina was returning as well. "Does this mean you want to avoid aging?" Cole asked. "To get old without aging?"

"That's what's confusing," Cole answered.

46. Cole, interviewed by Cole, Houston, Texas, June 24, 2017.
47. Cole, *Old Man Country*, 13.
48. Cole, interviewed by Cole, Houston, Texas, June 24, 2017.

Yes and No ... or No and Yes. I don't want to feel weak, bent over, unable to function well. Is this fear of aging? I don't want to look like an old man. But I do want to become an old man. I've had three surgeries in three years, and for the first time I think my strength is coming back—at least for a while. I want to make the most of it. I will adapt to whatever comes. I will keep trying to grow internally. Life is not a zero-sum game that conforms (or not) to my wishes. I hear the birds more often. I see the beauty of the clouds, the sunset, the bayou, the sky, beautiful women and men on the street. People who are not beautiful are more interesting to me now. I've read that this happens to some people and it sounded like a cliché. It is real, though I think it takes cultivation and awareness. Have I answered your question?

"Half way," Cole answered. "Are you afraid of becoming frail or appearing frail? Are you afraid of dying?"

"Yes and yes. Yet I feel increasingly equipped to handle what comes my way. I do not want a stroke, or a heart attack, or a diagnosis of cancer, or a fall. I think what makes these things emotionally manageable is loving and being loved. There is a calm well-being when I take in Thelma Jean's love."[49]

A few weeks later, I had my own opportunity to interview Cole. For a while the *Old Man Country* research had been a slog, and Cole was looking for a jumpstart, but I'm pretty sure that the interview was as much for me as it was for him. I had spent the last three years immersed in my little poker project: doing interviews, jotting down notes, visiting the Historic New Orleans Collection, reporting at the World Series of Poker, hanging around seedy underground cardrooms, studying game theory, and spending thousands of hours inside a casino environment whose logic—efficiency, exploitation, and extraction—could give the academic industrial complex a run for its money. I liked to play all the roles, too, and I was paying a steep price for it. Fortunately I had the great benefit of Cole's steadfast presence. He was skeptical when he needed to be and supportive when he needed to be, just as Carson had been when Cole was in the throes of writing *No Color Is My Kind*.[50] Interviewing Cole would perhaps teach me something, and it would also feed my own need for dialogue. Like Cole, I had come to believe that thinking isn't

---

49. Cole, interviewed by Cole, Houston, Texas, June 24, 2017.
50. Cole, *No Color Is My Kind*, 177.

something that one person can do alone: it takes two people to have a thought.

At our usual meeting time—a weekday late afternoon—I loaded Skype and found a wise old man smiling at me from his Houston office.[51] I unmuted myself and asked if the sound was working.

"Yeah, that's better," Cole said. "That's good."

I had been meaning to ask Cole something about stories. Years earlier, Cole believed that you can stitch together broken strands of your past and unify fractured pieces of your psyche. He believed that stories can heal. But his experience with Eldrewey had convinced him that the healing potential of stories was, in his words, "an illusion."[52] Good storytelling was no match for serious biological mental illness—at least in Eldrewey's case. "What do you believe now?" I asked. "Do you think that stories can heal?"

"Good question," Cole answered. "Especially since that's what I'm doing with these guys, for the book."

"And with yourself."

"Right. That's the quagmire: deciding what comes next. As you know, I'm stuck. I'm in a blind alley. And I'm frustrated by not having the time to think about it, although I think I made a breakthrough in the last couple of days."

Cole turned over the figurine of a bearded sage in his hands, seemingly lost in thought. Then he looked me straight in the eyes. "So what do I think about stories and the psyche and healing? Now, I think much more dialogically. None of us writes our stories by ourselves. None of us lives our stories by ourselves. We're always in a relationship. So I bring this dialogic thinking to these old men because I think of our meetings as an opportunity: a mutual opportunity of listening and telling, in which each of us has the potential to grow."

Playful and out-of-the-box interviews are another tool in Cole's vast intellectual toolkit. They're also, to repeat myself one last time, a wonderful example of Bakhtinian dialogism and alterity. For Bakhtin, alterity is implicit in every creative act, which involves a first stage of identification with the other and a reverse movement whereby the writer returns to his own position: "one must become another in relation to himself, must look at himself through the eyes of another."[53] This moment of empathy is at the heart of Bakhtin's understanding of aesthetic activity, which

---

51. Cole, interviewed by Saxton, New Orleans, Louisiana, July 26, 2017.
52. Cole, interviewed by Saxton, New Orleans, Louisiana, July 26, 2017.
53. Bakhtin, *Art and Answerability*, 15.

depends upon one person's accurately imagining what is really happening to and in the other. Both within the world of creation and outside it—in life itself—Bakhtin asserts that one must find one's own voice and hear the voice of the other. We're accountable, then, for any response given to others in the course of (co-)authoring our lives, a condition that he calls "answerability."[54]

HOMECOMING

It's never easy to settle on a last word. But it's worth remembering—or believing—that nothing is absolutely dead.[55] Every meaning will have its homecoming festival, and every ghost will tell its story.

"Dear Dad," Cole wrote one December afternoon,

> Today I was lying on the couch of my therapist/analyst Catherine Stephenson, and that ancient grief broke again. It seemed strange to be so undone by the waters of grief again. Or maybe it was the first time I cried so hard I couldn't stop. I don't remember how it started but I was, as always it seems, talking about what it must have been like for me after you died and Jackie went to live with her parents. I remembered the line from *Shadowlands* when C.S. Lewis is sitting by a lake with his grandson after his American wife has died. He says something like: "The pain now is part of the happiness then." It was hard to get through saying it. I knew I was crying for you. For the first time I asked, Why couldn't you have stayed longer? Why couldn't you? I don't really want you to go through, yet again, the reasons you killed yourself. Not sure what I want, except that you had stayed longer.[56]

"Dear Tom," Burton replied,

> I am always around. I am inside you. I am always here, even if "here" is a spiritual place, not a physical one. I don't know why the dam burst again. Maybe your reservoir of grief was/ is bottomless. But I don't believe that. Yes, the deep wound that you suffered when I died and Jackie disappeared will not ever

---

54. Bakhtin, *Art and Answerability*, 2.
55. Bakhtin, *Speech Genres and Other Late Essays*, 170.
56. Cole, letter to Burton Michel, December 14, 2017.

be healed. I am sorry for that. But you and I both know that you found me and finished your active grieving and the years of depression more than 15 years ago. So what happened today? I wish I knew. You are not depressed. You are split open. I know Catherine said that some orthodox priests used to consider spontaneous tears as mystical outtakes to God, or something like that. That's above my pay grade. I never got beyond rejecting the prayers and beliefs of orthodox Judaism. They seemed like magical gibberish that poured out of my father's mouth.

I suppose the best one can say now is that being split open is real, that it takes courage to be real. I think you are tired now. Let's call it a night. Just turn to me when you need me. I'm not going anywhere. Love, Dad.[57]

---

57. Burton Michel, letter to Cole, December 14, 2017.

5

Worthy to be Recorded
Justice, Relationships, and Documentary Filmmaking

CRAIG KLUGMAN

"We are important and our lives are important, magnificent really, and their details are worthy to be recorded."—NATALIE GOLDBERG

FOR DECADES, FILMMAKERS HAVE created movies about patients and doctors. For example, *End Game* is a forty-minute film that follows dying patients at UCSF Medical Center and the Zen Project.[1] The 2016 feature, *Extremis*, follows geriatrician-palliative care physician Jessica Zitter through caring for several hospice patients.[2] In 2020, documentary filmmaker Ken Browne released a thirty-minute video where he interviewed doctors who are also writers.[3] Few health humanities scholars, however, have undertaken the creation of documentary films themselves as a scholarly and artistic enterprise.

Back in the mid-1990s, as an aspiring journalist, I worked on two documentaries as an intern at KQED (a PBS affiliate) in San Francisco.

1. Epstein and Friedman, *End Game*.
2. Krauss, *Extremis*.
3. Browne, *Why Doctors Write*.

One film told a story of urban development at the cost of affordable housing, and the other video looked at a community-based mentoring program aimed at helping Black teenagers enroll in college. Later, as a scholar, I produced two creative nonfiction films, *Advance Directives* (2010) that showed the conversations and aftermath of those who underwent advance care planning and those who did not, as well as *A Cure for Dying* (2012) which showed a father leaving hospice care when his children begged him to enroll in an experimental drug trial.

Whereas my first efforts were part of my training to be a journalist, I would never have developed the second two films without the inspiration of people like Thomas Cole. During my doctoral work at the University of Texas Medical Branch, Cole was directing the graduate program while creating two of his movies—*Life Stories* and *Still Life*, which featured some of my classmates as well as people in the community whom I became privileged to know.

From 1998 through 2007, Cole was involved with the production of four documentary films (see Table 1). *The Strange Demise of Jim Crow* (1998) showed on PBS stations across the country (and can still occasionally be found on Houston television). This compelling documentary shows how Houston peacefully integrated in the 1960s beginning with student sit-ins. Through negotiations between white community leaders and Black business leadership, desegregation of hotels, movie theaters, and restaurants happened quietly, without violence and by design was never covered in the media.[4] In 2001, Cole was the producer and interviewer on *Still Life: The Humanity of Anatomy*, a documentary that follows medical students learning anatomy through their "first patient" (i.e., cadaver). The film also discusses why someone would donate their body to science.[5] In the same year, *Life Stories: Aging and the Human Spirit* appeared on PBS stations, showcasing a writing program for seniors run by the Institute for the Medical Humanities in Galveston, Texas, Cole's academic home.[6] This video was "the first project to document on videotape the rewards that autobiographical writing can bring when it is undertaken with a small group of people who come to trust each other over time."[7] The fourth film, *Stroke: Conversations and Questions* (2007) is actually two videos: (1) *Living After Stroke: Conversations with Couples*

4. Berman, *The Strange Demise of Jim Crow*.
5. ttwēak, *Still Life*.
6. Ankele and Macksoud, *Life Stories*.
7. Woodward, "Magical Moments in a Beloved Community," 429.

features interviews with couples exploring how they redefine their sense of self and their relationship after a stroke; (2) *Stroke: Early Recognition & Treatment* is a public service video with neurologists and patients talking about signs and symptoms of as well as prevention and recovery from a stroke.[8]

TABLE 1: THOMAS COLE FILMOGRAPHY

Title	Release Year	Cole Credit	Time	Distributor
The Strange Demise of Jim Crow	1998	Producer; Interviewer	56 minutes	California Newsreel; PBS
Life Stories: Aging and the Human Spirit	2001	Consultant; Group facilitator; Interviewer	60 minutes	Old Dog Documentaries; PBS
Still Life: The Humanity of Anatomy	2001	Producer; Interviewer	27 minutes	Fanlight Productions
Stroke: Conversations & Explanations	2007	Co-producer & interviewer–Part I; Consultant–Part II	47 minutes (combined)	Terra Nova Films

While each video is distinct, covering different topics and appealing to diverse audiences, several common themes wend their way through all four of the movies: the construction of filmic reality, the documentarian's relationship to their subjects, identity creation, and social justice. All four also raise the question of legacy, how we change the world and will be remembered for our brief careers whether that is integrating restaurants, donating one's body to science, telling a life story, or teaching others how to thrive in adversity.

WHAT IS A DOCUMENTARY?

John Grierson who is the "father of English documentaries" called these videos "creative treatment of actuality."[9] The first public showing of what were called "actuality films" was in Paris in 1895, where moviegoers saw 10 short films (less than fifty seconds each). Among the topics were beachgoers bathing in the sea, a baby eating, and workers leaving a

8. ttwēak, *Stroke*.
9. Grierson, "The Documentary Producer."

factory.¹⁰ These slice-of-life films captured actual events as they occurred. The first full-length documentary film was a controversial 1922 work known as *Nanook of the North*.¹¹ In this piece, independent American filmmaker Robert Flaherty tried to show viewers a way of living that was unfamiliar to most.

Broadly, a documentary is defined as a moving image with sounds, speech, and sometimes text compiled to inform viewers about a real-world topic, people, or place.¹² The goal is to bring to light real stories that have been hidden or overlooked using a variety of filming techniques. According to the Academy of Motion Pictures Arts & Sciences, a documentary is a "nonfiction motion picture dealing creatively with cultural, artistic, historical, social, scientific, economic, or other subjects. It may be photographed in actual occurrence, or may employ partial reenactment, stock footage, stills, animation, stop-motion, or other techniques, as long as the emphasis is on fact and not on fiction."¹³

FILMIC REALITY

Documentaries are often thought of as pictures of a real world (thus the early term "actuality films"). However, these videos are not objective, definitive CCTV footage of events that happened. Documentaries are less MRI and more abstract painting: "Documentary film speaks about situations and events involving real people (social actors) who present themselves within a framework. This frame conveys a plausible perspective on the lives, situations, and events portrayed. The distinct point of view of the filmmaker shapes the film into a way of understanding the historical world directly rather than through fictional allegory."¹⁴ These films tell stories about real events in the real world through a singular perspective, often using real people playing some version of themselves (or actors portraying real people). While facts and evidence offered in the film will be verifiable, the movie offers the perspective and interpretations of the documentarian.

10. Lattanzio, "On This Day in 1895."
11. Flaherty, *Nanook of the North*.
12. Nichols, *Introduction to Documentary*, 7.
13. "91st Academy Awards Special Rules for the Documentary Awards."
14. Nichols, *Introduction to Documentary*, 10.

Consider that a documentarian chooses the topic, whom to interview, what parts of the story to cover, and what material to include and exclude. They narrate and write chyron text (words at the bottom of the screen that give the viewer context and information. For example, the name and title of an interviewed expert). The documentarian then edits the film (chooses what parts of what interviews, images, sounds, to include), adds a soundtrack, and develops a marketing campaign that sells the movie by telling the audience what to expect.

For example, *Nanook of the North* is less a slice of an unfamiliar life than a documentarian's creation of what he thought that life should look like. There are claims that many of the scenes were set up and that the documentarian scripted the story and the characters (even assigning them fictional names). For instance, a whale hunt was staged even though the Inuit no longer conducted such activities. Filming in an igloo was dark, so the crew constructed an igloo with one wall removed to make filming easier.[15] "While posing, through on-screen text and its style of filming, as something incidentally capturing reality, Flaherty went through great pains to stage what was being seen on-screen."[16]

According to Kate de Medeiros, who was involved with the *Life Stories* documentary, "There's a lay person assumption that a documentary is the truth as opposed to an argument."[17] Building the argument requires the use of techniques not commonly found in fictional films that provide context and explanation for the viewer. (1) "Voice-of-god" commentary: The omniscient narrator speaks over the visuals, explaining what is happening. In *The Strange Demise*, one sees pictures of buildings, businesses, and the student sit-ins while the narrator explains the historic events that occurred. (2) Interviews with "social actors in their everyday roles and activities."[18] In *Life Stories*, the viewer sees a group of seniors in a writing group, seated around a table as they share their work. (3) B-roll: The viewer sees cutaways from interviews and other scenes that illustrate complicated points using still images, recreations, historical footage, reenactments, cartoons, illustrations, or other visuals. For instance, in *Life Stories*, while writers read their work, the viewer sees photos and images of their past. This technique holds viewer interest during long sections of dialogue and can hide when two incongruent sections of an interview are

15. Menand, "Nanook and Me."
16. Laman, "'Nanook of the North' at 100."
17. Kate de Medeiros, interviewed by Craig M. Klugman, February 6, 2023.
18. Nichols, *Introduction to Documentary*, 15.

spliced together (like a bandage over a cut). In *Stroke,* two segments of an interview were spliced together, and the splice was visually hidden by showing images of medical paperwork and aurally hidden by inserting an audio patch of background noise across the two segments. Other times, cutaways are a financial choice since it is cheaper to have one camera crew than two on a shoot. When I conducted television interviews as a journalist, the viewer would see the subject answer questions and then would see a cutaway of me nodding my head or even asking a question before returning to the interviewee on screen. When one considers that there was only one camera on the shoot, how is this accomplished? The answer is that the filming of me took place after the interview was over. The camera person moves the camera from behind me to be behind the interviewee (proof of one camera is that you don't see the camera behind either speaker) and records my brief performance. When edited together, the viewer feels like they are watching me react in real-time to the subject, but that is a convenient fiction.

Thus, documentarians face ethical choices when constructing their filmic argument: How to edit and arrange the film to get their point of view across and yet stay true to the events and people they are portraying. Filmmakers have an obligation to their subjects (who are or were real people), to the communities that permitted the recording, and to the viewer who wants to trust the accuracy and veracity of the documentarian.[19] In addition, they have a duty to the funders to be sure that the movie is financially viable by not going over budget and meeting deadlines while also being true to their artistic vision. A 2009 survey of documentary filmmakers showed that the creators are well-aware of these moral dimensions of their art.[20]

The deliberate choices and playing with reality can be seen in the creation of *Life Stories.* This film shows the "Share Your Life Story" writing workshops developed by Cole and then-graduate student, Kate de Medeiros.[21] The movie "documents a day in the life of a group of senior citizens in Galveston, Texas, who gather twice a month to 're-member' their lives through poems and stories."[22] The film offers "honesty" through a carefully constructed "reality."

19. Aufderheide, Jaszi, and Chandra, "Honest Truths."
20. Aufderheide, Jaszi, and Chandra, "Honest Truths."
21. de Medeiros, "Beyond the Memoir."
22. "Films—*Life Stories.*"

The movie opens with a view of one of the subjects, Ellie Porter, sitting in front of greenery, with the sun shining on her. She is scribbling with a pencil onto a notepad. She looks down at the paper. One hears light jaunty string quartet music, composed specifically for the film. The view quickly moves to waves crashing on the Galveston seawall and the words "Galveston, Texas" appear on the screen. Within moments, the viewer is transported to a great height, looking down on Old Red, the oldest and most iconic building at the University of Texas Medical Branch, which in 2001 was also the home of the Institute for the Medical Humanities where Cole's office was located. Rain is falling and two people carrying umbrellas converge together—one walking down a long flight of steps and the other wearing a raincoat, coming across a red-bricked plaza. Kate de Medeiros offers the first spoken words of the film, layered over this imagery. "I was walking back from a meeting one day and Tom stopped me and said that he had this great idea for a class and would I be interested in helping him do an autobiographical group for older adults."[23] The figures walk off and the view shifts to Cole sitting in front of a wooden balcony banister with the words "Dr. Thomas R. Cole, Institute for the Medical Humanities," on the lower third of the screen.

While a lovely beginning to the video, right from the start the scene is constructed. The use of the light music tells the viewer that they should feel hopeful, light-hearted, and comfortable. The image of Porter gives a preview of what the film will be about, people writing. She was likely instructed not to look at the camera (staring into the camera breaks the Fourth Wall and is called "flashing"—it breaks the mystique that we are direct observers of events). The sunshine on Porter and on the crashing waves suggests serenity and peace, of shedding light on something. As for that meeting in front of Old Red that begins the dialogue? It never happened. While one of the figures does appear to be Cole walking down the stairs, we never see the face of the second character. Because the viewer hears the voice of de Medeiros, one assumes that she is the second person. But de Medeiros was actually in Washington D.C. at the time and her voice was recorded later. The movie's pretense of showing a single one-day session of the writing group is also a conceit: In reality, filming took place over two days and participants were told to wear the same clothes both days.[24]

23. Ankele and Macksoud, "Life Stories."
24. Kate de Medeiros, interviewed by Craig M. Klugman, February 6, 2023.

In another sequence, the same instrumental strings cover a montage of group members leaving their homes and work, and arriving at a university-owned house, "Open Gates." Voiceovers and chyron text introduce the characters, explaining why they were attending. Quickly, they are seated around a table writing, pencils on paper. However, this was not a regular writing group: Cole and de Medeiros invited these individuals to participate in the film because they would be interesting characters. They were all members of writing groups, but the collective the viewer sees is composed of people from three different cohorts. Even the location is an illusion: The real writing groups met in public buildings, including inside the Fish Tales restaurant, not on campus at all.[25]

Before the members share their writing, Cole reads a quote from a writing expert, Natalie Goldberg:

> One of the main aims in writing practice is to learn to trust your own mind and body; to grow patient and nonaggressive. Art lives in the Big World. One poem or story doesn't matter one way or the other. It's the process of writing and life that matters . . . We must continue to open and trust in our own voice and process. Ultimately, if the process is good, the end will be good.[26]

Cole introduces Goldberg's rules of writing to the film group: "Keep your hand moving, don't cross out, don't worry about spelling, punctuation or grammar, lose control, don't think, go for the jugular"[27] instructions that were not part of the real writing groups.

In the movie, Cole is the facilitator who gives the group participants a series of tasks including writing their obituary and drafting a letter to a deceased loved one. The actual program, however, was structured around exploring writing genres and met for 90-minutes per session over 8 weeks.[28] The filmed portrayal butts up against the real program about 26 minutes into the video, when Cole talks about life writing for healing and catharsis, sometimes through tears. Several members push back against that saying that it is not about crying or therapy. Cole tells the viewer that writing is about reconciling the past and, at one point, Porter says, "This is crossing into therapy," which was not part of the real group.

25. Rimer, "Turning to Autobiography for Emotional Growth in Old Age."
26. See epigraph; also Goldberg, *Writing Down the Bones*, 12.
27. Goldberg, *Writing Down the Bones*, 8.
28. de Medeiros, "Beyond the Memoir."; interviewed by Craig M. Klugman, February 6, 2023.

Also, the genre-based assignments in the actual program did not include these two exercises.

Consider that while the viewer sees images of people writing, sharing their writing in a small seminar room, and being their "authentic selves," that out of frame, they are surrounded by a film crew. For those who have not been on a live shoot before, they would see a camera on a tripod (or a dolly if capturing people walking), bright lights set up around the room, and possibly a boom mic (a large microphone on the end of a pole) held above the group (just outside of the camera frame) to capture sound. In addition to equipment, there would be a camera person, sound engineer who is monitoring the audio, a boom operator, the director, and probably an assistant running errands. And that would be a small crew. Given the modest size of the seminar room seen in *Life Stories*, the participants were conscious of being filmed and as Heisenberg said about particles, people behave differently when being observed.

In a way, by making the choices of who should be in the film, where they should meet, and what their writing tasks would be, the filmmaker seeks to show a "best of all worlds" version of reality: "His [Cole's] purpose was to tell a really compelling story, and it's one that often rings very powerfully with people."[29] After all, this is not a fly-on-the-wall perspective but is deliberate storytelling. As the Honest Truths survey concluded, documentarians manipulate facts, sequences, and meanings to be more effective storytellers and help viewers grasp the larger truths and themes of the story.[30]

RELATIONSHIPS

At the core of each of these films is the notion of relationships. *Stroke* looks at how marriages are changed when one partner has a sudden organic alteration to who they were. The viewer hears couples talking about how the healthy partner must take on new roles in the family. When a sick partner needs significant care, the marriage must adapt. Instead of being husband or wife, the caregiver can end up feeling like a parent or a nurse.

Still Life explores the relationship between a medical student and their cadaver by interweaving student interviews, speaking with a future

---

29. de Medeiros, "Beyond the Memoir."
30. Aufderheide, Jaszi, and Chandra, "Honest Truths."

body donor, and displaying images of the burial-at-sea that occurs once dissection is done. Cole sees making the video as a chance for both future donors (who are also future patients) and future physicians to establish and find comfort in relating to death.

> This is about becoming more alive and more vital and more human and more compassionate by going into our relationship with death and our relationship with the dead and not putting up with our first reaction which is 'I don't want to go there.' You got to go there because it's who we are. And it can make a huge difference to the extent that you can generate the inner strength to explore these issues for yourself and your ability to live fully. To live compassionately.[31]

Similarly, death is an important aspect of medicine. Students need to learn how to handle their reaction and to assist patients in confronting their inevitable ends.

The film carefully crafts the student-cadaver relationship. The students learn general anatomy as well as gain insights into the life of their specific donors—one student comments on the cadaver's painted nails—and about their own views of death. In the climax, the donor meets current medical students, although as one reviewer notes, the emotional payoff that the audience has been primed for does not materialize. "Despite a build-up of alternating sequences of medical student opinion and donor narration that holds the promise of a formal intersection of science and humanism, the recorded encounter between the students and the donor is reduced to a handshake in a lab."[32]

Most movies use music to elicit emotion in the viewer.[33] But *Still Life* has no background music throughout which makes it hard for the viewer to feel the import of that handshake. The main sound is a buoy bell during flashes to the burial-at-sea that appears several times in the film, asking "for whom the bell tolls." For the students, the handshake is all that was possible because they have been trained to view a body with emotional detachment and a medical gaze.[34] The relationship between a medical student and their cadaver (or even future donor) is by necessity a transactional one that encourages objective engagement. Because

---

31. ttwēak, *Still Life*.

32. Greenberg, "Review *Still Life*," 87.

33. If you doubt this, watch a very sad or scary scene from a film with the sound turned off—it loses the impact.

34. Foucault, *The Birth of the Clinic*.

it is through the process of doing something horrific, disassembling a human body, that a person learns to objectify the body, to view it as an "it." In the work of Martin Buber, an "I-It" relationship is how modern humans relate to the world and often to each other. In this framework, a person views the other (anything outside of ourselves whether things or people) as things to be analyzed, classified, and explained.[35] We are distant observers.

The more interesting relationship throughout these films, though, is that between the documentarian and their subjects. When I asked Cole what themes he saw throughout his movies, he answered, "That they are conducted within the frame of I-Thou. Otherwise, they don't work. . . . You have to love the people you interview."[36] This relationship is one of encountering another person (or object) through directness, mutuality, honesty, longevity, and present-ness. This bonding is an active, participatory connection that changes both people involved.[37] In *Still Life*, many of the medical students were Cole's own students (one student was an MD-PhD student in medical humanities; a second medical student was the girlfriend of another MD-PhD student) and the future donor, Bob Harvey, was a UTMB employee and was also in *Life Stories*. The film's aim is to show medical students how to develop this deep relationship with their cadaver, to subjectivize it rather than objectify. From this position, the documentarian and the people in the film are changed by the process. The video they create together is an expression of their encountering each other. As Cole wrote to me, "If you open your heart and they open their heart, something happens that you wouldn't get at if you had kept a strict journalistic style."[38]

Cole's "I-Thou" relationship with his subjects is seen most prominently in *The Strange Demise of Jim Crow*. As creator, executive producer, and interviewer, Cole built this story on the success of his 1997 book, *No Color Is My Kind*. As the book relates, Cole was teaching in a psychiatric case conference in 1984 when he first learned about Stearns, who was a patient in the hospital. Stearns wanted to write his memoir, a desire that the psychiatry trainees took as a symptom of mental illness, but that Cole viewed as an opportunity. The two men began to meet with Cole interviewing Stearns and helping him to put together a manuscript. The

35. Buber, *I and Thou*.
36. Interview with Thomas R. Cole, February 3, 2023.
37. Buber, *I and Thou*.
38. Thomas R. Cole, email, February 3, 2023.

University of Texas Press acknowledged the importance of the history in the book but rejected it since the manuscript lacked "coherence and verified claims."[39] With the publisher's encouragement, Cole took it upon himself to write Stearns's story, turning an autobiography into a biography. The book became the seed that led to the larger story of Houston's desegregation told in *The Strange Demise*. The core of both book and film, is the I-Thou relationship that Cole developed with Stearns first and then with the other people he interviews.

IDENTITY

During his interview for *Stroke* part I—*Living After Stroke: Conversations with Couples*, Blair Justice says, "The old Blair is not gone, just hiding somewhere. And the new Blair is still emerging." Blair expresses that he is figuring out who he is, someone that has similarities to who he was before the stroke but is also somewhat different. Identity is the third theme that runs throughout these films.

Identity is one's sense of self—who a person believes themselves to be. A closer look delves into different types of identity including personal (psychological and physical), professional, and social. In terms of personal identity, how could anyone know that Blair before the stroke is the same person as Blair after the stroke? Philosopher Derek Parfit suggests identity is about unity over time.[40] One's sense of psychological connectedness to who they were in the past depends on holding memories of experience that occurred to that past-self. Since memories can fade over time or be erased as in a stroke, one's identity is also about knowing that one used to hold those memories. Personal identity is a deliberate act of narrative self-creation. This process is evident in *Life Story* where members of the writing group are coming to terms with their past by composing letters to a deceased loved one, writing about an abusive relationship, or even stating how they want to be remembered by crafting their obituary. They reconcile memories with the need for present healing.

Physicality is the second element of personal identity and comes from the fact that we inhabit a single body over a lifespan. That body may change over time due to diet, exercise, disease, aging, or even what one

---

39. Cole, *No Color Is My Kind*, xiii.

40. In fact, the word "identity" derives from notions of "sameness." See "Identity," in *Oxford English Dictionary*; Derek Parfit, "Personal Identity."

WORTHY TO BE RECORDED   103

wears but it is still recognized and accepted as a part of oneself.[41] Consider another interviewee from *Living After Stroke: Conversations with Couples*. As a result of his stroke, Robert Lake finds his lack of physical ability has changed how he views himself. "I feel sometimes as if I did die because the person that I was, I can't be. All those things that were part of a life that I can no longer do, gone away. So that person is gone. I'm now this dependent person instead of an independent person. I'm a person who is an object of care rather than a person who could take care." Clearly, post-stroke Robert is the same psychological person as pre-stroke Robert since he maintains many of the memories, but his altered physical abilities make him feel like a different person, forcing him to evolve his identity.

Another sense of identity is that of professional identity. For example, the first event a new medical student experiences is the White Coat ceremony where they don this symbol of their profession for the first time. By adopting new clothing, they [reversibly] alter their body and thus begin identifying as doctors. In many ways medical school is more than learning new skills and knowledge, it is about learning how to professionally identify as a doctor through specific didactic lessons and a prolonged clinical apprenticeship where they observe others in the role. Professional identity is "a representation of self, achieved in stages over time during which the characteristics, values, and norms of the medical profession are internalized, resulting in an individual thinking, acting, and feeling like a physician."[42] *Still Life* opens with a clip from the 1951 film, *People Will Talk*, where Dr. Noah Praetorius (played by Cary Grant) introduces medical students to the anatomy lab, a step in their process of becoming physicians.[43] The medical students in Cole's video explain their connection to the cadavers, overcoming their fear that they might be causing pain by cutting into the cadaver and learning to view it as an object. As student Eugene Gicheru says in the film, "The more that I think about that this was a living person, the more I shut it out."

41. There are several disorders, however, when one might reject parts of themselves: In gender body dysmorphia a person's gender identity does not match their physical body. General body dysmorphia can find a thin person seeing themselves as overweight, or a muscular person seeing themselves as too skinny. Body integrity disorder is a condition where one feels that a part of their body belongs to someone else and often, they want that part removed. In phantom limb syndrome, a person has sensations from a part of their body that has been amputated.

42. Cruess et al., "Reframing Medical Education," 1447.

43. Mankewicz, *People Will Talk*.

The Strange Demise created an opportunity for the interviewees to revisit memories of how they changed a city and to take on the identities that history has bestowed on them as activists and heroes (or villains for a few characters). Although decades passed between the events described in the film and the actual filming—a span of history when their bodies got older and their roles in society changed—the act of remembering creates the psychological connectedness that allows them to reclaim a part of themselves that was, for most, in the past. For Stearns particularly, his relationship with Cole allows him to reclaim his memories that allowed him to regain his identity and humanity that was stripped away from him when Stearns became a psychiatric patient. After all, the psychiatrists did not believe he had lived a life worthy of a memoir. As Cole writes, "By imposing a kind of retrospective order on the unpredictable events of a life, personal narratives assist in the achievement of identity."[44] The act of storytelling whether in words or images is part of identity formation and re-formation.

SOCIAL JUSTICE

"Out of the public view, white and [B]lack businessmen secretly worked out a plan to desegregate Houston's movie theaters and restaurants," said Lorenzo Thomas, narrator on *The Strange Demise of Jim Crow*. The viewer learns that students from Texas Southern University had threatened to block the parade to honor astronaut Gordon Cooper's trip to space unless desegregation happened. Because of quiet negotiations, the parade went on as planned, Houston desegregated, and nary a word was written in the local media. Cole's video brought to life a deliberately marginalized episode in Houston history, but a segment of the past that was important for the furthering of social justice.

The original actuality documentaries were simply about capturing a slice of life or a moment in time. Even they, however, took perspectives by choosing to show people vacationing at the beach, workers leaving a factory, even a baby. Focusing on those topics showed they were important and were how people should live their lives—where they work, where they vacation, and what they value. All documentaries move a person to thought or action, sometimes through deliberate choices and sometimes unintentionally. An intentional perspective could serve to further social

44. Cole, *No Color Is My Kind*, 2.

justice or to sow divisiveness. Some films are political propaganda meant to put forth a particular viewpoint that benefits a singular individual or party. For example. *Triumph of the Will* was a 1935 nationalist Nazi propaganda film meant to convince Germans of their greatness under Hitler and the dangers of the Jewish population.[45] More recently, the misinformation film *Plandemic* (2020) sought to convince people that COVID-19 was created by liberal elites to control populations and that masks actually activated the virus, rather than prevented spread. None of their claims are true, but it rapidly spread these conspiracy theories into the public discussion.[46]

Most documentary films, however, serve to further social justice.[47] Social justice seeks to improve access to political, social, and economic prospects for marginalized and vulnerable populations. It is one of the pillars of health humanities and is commonly the goal of many documentary films, to shed light on injustice.[48] The films aim to make viewers aware of people, places, and movements or encourage people to take action to improve belonging, equity, and inclusiveness. According to health humanist Therese Jones, documentaries "serve as accessible texts for the analysis and discussion of individual experiences of illness and disability or as evocative illustrations of issues such as access to care or end of life."[49] Rather than trying to stoke hate, division, or spread information, health humanities documentaries take a critical lens to analyze and understand equity and justice issues in health and well-being and provides space for reflection and discussion of these issues.[50]

Documentaries accomplish this goal by recentering narratives to focus on marginalized ideas, topics, events, and people.[51] Consider *Stroke* which looks not at the medical rehabilitation of the patients, but rather on their relationships with their partners. Or *Still Life*, which focuses on the relationship between medical students and their cadavers, a process that is usually kept out of the public eye. By making a hero of Bob Harvey,

45. Riefenstahl, *Triumph of the Will.*
46. Kearney, Chiang, and Massey, "The Twitter Origins."
47. Chattoo, "Oscars So White."
48. Aufderheide, Jaszi, and Chandra, "Honest Truths"; Klugman and Lamb, "Introduction."
49. Jones, "Moving Pictures," 283.
50. Kumagai and Wear, "'Making Strange.'"
51. Blackie and Lamb, "Courting Discomfort in an Undergraduate Health Humanities Classroom"; Gutierrez and DasGupta, "The Space That Difference Makes."

the future donor, Cole shows the importance and nobility of their gift to medicine. Documentaries bring forth voices of the powerless, such as the students featured in *The Strange Demise* whose stories were largely untold before then. All four videos create material and space for these difficult and necessary conversations.

Armed with the goal of social justice, a documentarian edits their work to achieve this aim. The filmmaker puts forth a persuasive viewpoint through their filmic choices and balances that with maintaining trust with the audience, interviewees, and portrayed events. Therese Jones summarizes this tension, "In essence, documentarians make endless choices, and each choice is an expression of a point of view. Moreover, because the documentary tradition is driven by a desire for social justice yet relies on the impression of authenticity, there is often an inherent conflict between persuading and informing, advocating and entertaining."[52] Providing a viewpoint in a documentary is expected, but that cannot be at the sacrifice of the film's integrity. Also, consider that if the presentation is too biased, it may prevent people from seeking out the movie in the first place. That these films have the power to move people to act, to think, and to speak means this power can be used for good or for nefarious means such as *Triumph of the Will* and *Plandemic*. Jones suggests that they can and should only be used for good means—improving visibility, access, and giving voice to the historically excluded. Thus, a health humanities documentary should aim to bend the arc toward social justice. After all, if the film tries to diminish or silence people then its aim is not to improve health.

How much can one film or even a body of work move the needle on justice? Such work can illuminate injustices, but there are few times where a movie itself leads to a change in policy or law. Even the infamous, Academy Award winning *An Inconvenient Truth* through which Al Gore made clear the dangers of climate change did not have an immediate effect on the carbon economy. As documentarian Frederick Wiseman[53] says:

> When I first started out, I had a rather naive and pretentious view that there was some kind of one-to-one connection between a film and social change. But now, while I like to think there might be a connection, I think there is no real way of knowing.

52. Jones, "Another Kind of DNR."
53. For full disclosure, I was part of an improv group called "The Frederick Wiseman Experience."

> People have all kinds of sources of different information, and it's totally presumptuous to assume that any documentary, or any one work of any sort, is going to be that important. Which is not to say I don't hope it has an effect, but I think if it does, it's elliptical, subterranean, circuitous and certainly not measurable.[54]

Cole's film then was unlikely to immediately change anyone's life, but it does promote inclusiveness and diversity when people come together peacefully and focus on their common interests, which in the case of *The Strange Demise* was ensuring that private enterprises flourished. Twenty-five years after its release, this video has poignancy today when the U.S. is seeking a way to reconcile its past racial sins alongside calls for true adoption of justice, equality, diversity, inclusiveness, and belonging. As Wiseman says, you never know when your film will be important or who it may influence, but the documentarian has to believe that it does.

DIVERSITY IN FILM

In terms of telling the story of desegregation in Houston, Cole—a New England-born, Jewish male filmmaker—might be a surprising choice. However, studies show that the vast majority of Oscar nominated documentaries are social justice stories directed and produced by white males.[55] Recall that *Nanook of the North* remains controversial since it is a white man's view of Inuit (specifically Itivimuit) life. In the last decade, female-identifying persons and people of color have been represented in documentary films in greater numbers but still far below their proportion of the U.S. population.[56] Does the filmmaker have an obligation to ensure diversity in representation? Should they be limited to only telling their stories and not those of others?

Strange Demise is the clearest film where issues of race can be viewed in part because of its topic. Both Black and white people are interview subjects and together they tell two sides of this story. Cole even won the 2018 Center for Healing & Racism Annual Juneteenth Ally Award, a recognition that he immediately gave to the Stearns family.[57] However,

---

54. Poppy, "Frederick Wiseman."
55. Chattoo, "Oscars So White."
56. Chattoo et al., "Diversity on U.S. Public and Commercial TV."
57. Thomas R. Cole email, September 10, 2023; "Annual Juneteenth Ally Award Recipients."

Cole faced a lot of resistance in creating the film from the students who had started the sit-in movement as well as the National Association for the Advancement of Colored People (NAACP) who did not trust an outsider to tell the story. In addition, most of the people (Black and white) involved with the desegregation movement were reluctant to speak with him because of the agreed upon media blackout that was foundational to the peaceful desegregation.[58]

Cole's other films did not focus on diversity, but still should be examined under this lens. In *Life Stories*—about the senior life project—there are a mix of the binary genders, no one with a disability, and the characters are all white appearing seniors. Granted, race was not raised by the narrator nor by the participants. However, given that Galveston Island in 2000 (film was released in 2001) was 15.4 percent Black and 17.9 percent Latine/Hispanic, the lack of characters from these populations stands out. *Stroke* has white, Black, and Latine couples among its interviewees but they are all heterosexual couples. There are disabled individuals but no same-sex or nonbinary couples. Lastly, *Still Life* does have racial diversity (white, Jewish, Black, Latine) in its subjects but only two female identifying persons (excluding the female cadaver) appear in the entire film out of 10 interviewees. Those two subjects appear in a total of 1:06 minutes of screentime in the 26:36-minute-long film. Is this a reflection of who was a medical student and body donor at the time? While I could not find demographics from 2000, in 2022, UTMB's medical class was 60 percent female, and nationally most willed body donors are male.[59] Proportional representation of on-screen subjects may not be the definitive answer of how to ensure representation in film since it does not look at the production staff, but it is one potential metric.

Some people may argue that it is unfair and even inappropriate to conduct a diversity analysis in these films. After all, I am writing in 2023, in the era of #MeToo and #OscarSoWhite. Can critics apply modern diversity standards to films created when people ignored these issues? Can a white, Connecticut, Jewish man tell the story of Texas racial relations? In some ways, he can be more objective because he does not have a vested connection to what happened, and he brought his skills as an experienced historian. On the other hand, one can ask if he was appropriating this story. Working at the turn of the millennium, Cole believed that

58. Thomas R. Cole email, September 10, 2023.
59. "Data Reference Card Details"; Asad, Anteby, and Garip, "Who donates their bodies to science."

history belongs to no one, and it is the trained scholar who can unearth them and tell them.[60] However, it is important that the documentarian have permission of the subjects of the story, as Cole did from Mr. Stearns in the book and as he eventually received from the other subjects in the film. One must also be aware of the privacy of subjects and how far they want the story told. The filmmaker needs to protect the subject as their involvement or sharing of the story could have a negative effect such as bringing scorn and stigma (or positively, celebration and heroism) and may have implications for their employment and relationships. As most health humanities scholars sit in a position of privilege (income, prestige, and a public voice) they should co-write the narrative with the subject and not impose their perspective.[61] After all, the filmmaker is borrowing the story that the subject lived. Today, a filmmaker might respond that we need to train people in these communities to be historians and documentarians to enable them to tell their own stories.

LOCATING THE DOCUMENTARIAN

The literary scholar Wayne Booth suggests that in any text, a reader develops a relationship with the *implied author* of a particular work and with the *imagined author* who created a body of work but not necessarily with the *real-life author*.[62] The same can be said for documentarians. One can examine who they are in a single work, in their body of work, or as the actual person. Cole does not appear at all in *Stroke* and thus, is an absent documentarian, whose hand is not seen, letting the interviewee's personal experiences and the medical science speak for itself. Similarly, Cole is not a character in *The Strange Demise*, except in one instance, where he asks a probing question of the subject. Although the viewer never sees him, the filmmaker tips his hand as shaper of the work. The Cole here is a historian who wants to tell a story important to his adopted city and that comes out of the I-Thou relationship he built with Stearns (who is not in the video).

Life Stories features a Cole who is a teacher, guiding his students in a process of self-reflection and discovery. He is a character in the movie, directing the action with his assignments and engaging with the members

60. Thomas R. Cole, email September 10, 2023.
61. Ray, "Who Gets to Tell Our Stories."
62. Booth, *The Company We Keep*.

of the writing group. In *Still Life*, Cole is both filmmaker and character. One sees the professor and scholar who shares his specific point of view: "It can make a huge difference to the extent that you can generate the inner strength to explore these issues for yourself and your ability to live fully. To live compassionately."[63] And that perspective also shows how Cole the filmmaker crafted the video. The work comes out of his interest in the topic and could not have happened without his existing relationships with students and the donor. The Cole here is an expert in empathy and humanity, showing the intimate relationship between a medical student and their first patient. The implied filmmaker in this work is also closest to the real-life scholar.

As an occasional filmmaker myself and as someone who has come to know Cole over the last twenty-five years, first as his student and later as his colleague, I have gotten to know the real documentarian. The Cole in this body of work comes across not as an expert filmmaker—as the quality varies dramatically across the different pieces—or as master of a genre, but rather as an educator and scholar. Quality refers to the technical aspects of the film: the writing, vision of cinematography, clarity of the sound, incorporation of B-roll, integrity of the dupes (copies), narrative of the overall story, and more. The quality of a film is often related to the budget. A larger budget allows for a bigger and more experienced crew (producers, writers, directors, sound engineers, boom operator, gaffers, cinematographers, lighting engineers, video editors, hair and make up, sets, food services, artists, dupers, and actors). Even background sound costs money to gain rights, one reason that *Still Life* likely has no background music. Many low budget films try to get students or other less experienced people whom they can pay with promises of a reel—copies of the film to demonstrate their talents.

Strange Demise has the highest production quality of all the films. This film had grants from the National Endowment for the Humanities, Texas Humanities, seven foundations, UMTB's Institute for the Medical Humanities, and donations from sixty-two individuals. One sees good lighting, professional sets, excellent sound quality, background music, sound stage locations, lots of B-roll, and excellent editing. The same quality exists for *Stroke* which was funded by a foundation and two units within the University of Texas Houston. The camerawork is smooth and steady, the visuals are not grainy (product of actual film or low definition

63. ttwēak, *Still Life*.

capture). Similarly, *Life Stories* was funded by PBS, Sealy Center on Aging, and two foundations.

At the other end is *Still Life* which was funded by Project on Death in America, Texas Humanities, and three university units. In this film, one sees a lot of handheld camera and single camera shots, uneven sound across the film, no background music, real world locations (free-to-use university labs and offices, public spaces as opposed to sound stages or more controlled environments), less than ideal lighting (lots of shadows and bright spots), and a smaller cast of characters. While good storytelling, it clearly had a lower budget which translated into a smaller and less experienced crew, and a less polished product.

CLOSING CREDITS

In his latest book, Cole asks himself and his many subjects four questions: Am I still a man, do I still matter, what is the meaning of my life, and am I still loved?[64]

> I am pleased with my external accomplishments. They made my mother proud and my university see that it was getting its money's worth out of me. But the most gratifying work has always been the quiet work of interacting with students, mentoring younger colleagues, working with older people in community settings, and interviewing people for films and books. It has been deeply gratifying to help students and others grow intellectually, personally, and professionally.[65]

As a spiritual person and documentarian, Cole's films ask what legacy one leaves behind after their short time on Earth. Cole's films show that he has been seeking the approval of his family, the knowledge that he helped his students, and the hope that he has changed his community for the better. The four films have aged well and are still relevant today. Through these documentaries, Cole has created a trove of lessons that students will continue to absorb for decades to come.

---

64. Cole, *Old Man Country*.
65. Cole, *Old Man Country*, 166–67.

PART THREE

Cultural Studies—Literature and Film

6

Carrying the Fire
A Metaphor for Persistent Generativity in Cormac McCarthy's No Country for Old Men and The Road

Woods Nash

INTRODUCTION

CARRYING THE FIRE IS an image with a significant role in two novels by Cormac McCarthy. Not coincidentally, each novel also features an aging male protagonist. Both Sheriff Bell of *No Country for Old Men* and the unnamed man of *The Road* long to carry the fire through dark worlds of chaos and danger. In this chapter, I use the concept of generativity to explore the meaning of this central image. In these novels, both Bell and the man perform different kinds of generative work. Why, then, does only one of them succeed in carrying the fire? The reason, I will argue, is this: to carry the fire is to engage in a particular type of generative work—work that one both embraces and succeeds in passing along to another person who could outlive oneself.

Near the end of *No Country for Old Men*, Sheriff Bell retires, having concluded that he is no match for senseless violence. After decades in law enforcement, his faith in himself and in the worth of his work has wavered. Beyond his loving marriage and the dead daughter with whom he converses, Bell is left with little but the courage to question the kind of person he has become. In the novel's closing scene, Bell recalls two dreams he had after his father died. In one, he loses the money his father gave him. In the other, the world is dark and cold, and his father is on horseback, transporting fire in a horn. His father rides on, leaving Bell behind. Taken together, these dreams underscore his father's moral superiority and Bell's waning hope. He has no fire to carry—let alone to pass on to another.

In contrast with Bell, the man in *The Road* has a young son who is his father's reason for keeping them alive. As they travel together through perilous terrain, they speak of themselves as bearers of a symbolic flame. The man teaches his son to endure the harsh climate and to confront human cruelty. The boy learns these lessons while also surpassing his father in compassion. As the man dies, he exhorts his son to keep going, assuring him that he knows how to survive, will have good luck, and can sustain their dialogue. The boy continues to carry the fire.

Because I will seek to characterize Sheriff Bell and the man in relationship to generativity, it will be useful to discuss this concept here at the outset. Introduced by psychologist Erik Erikson in the mid-twentieth century, generativity is a special category of activity: a person's devoting energy to members of other generations. Initially, Erikson restricted the term to the nurturing work of biological parenthood, but, eventually, he acknowledged that it can also refer to other "forms of productivity and creativity" through which a person seeks to influence future generations.[1]

Following the work of Erikson and other theorists, Rubinstein and colleagues created a framework for understanding generativity in U.S. culture. Through a qualitative study, these scholars concluded that generative work tends to have up to four foci: people, groups, things, and activities.[2] Examples of such foci would be students, organizations, antiques, and playing tennis. These scholars also identified four temporal contexts through which persons' generative work tends to move: historical, familial, individual, and relational.[3] An example of one person's working

---

1. Rubinstein et al., "Extending the Framework of Generativity Theory Through Research," 549.

2. Rubinstein et al., "Extending the Framework of Generativity Theory Through Research," 555–56.

3. Rubinstein et al., "Extending the Framework of Generativity Theory Through Research," 556–58.

through all four temporal spheres would be a novelist's understanding her writing in connection with surrealism (historical), her grandparents' story of immigration (familial), her impact on a mentee writer (individual), and how her writing contributes to her marriage (relational).

In summary, generativity is work that is oriented, in part, away from oneself. Often in U.S. culture such work focuses on other people and is future-oriented. Through generativity, a person might outlive herself, so to speak, if her work is taken up by someone who survives her. However, despite a person's best efforts, her generative work might not succeed in influencing others. What's more, a person might come to regret her generative work or, for whatever reason, wish that it *not* endure. Our novelist, for example, has engaged in the generative work of trying to influence her mentee, but the mentee might not absorb her influence. Or the novelist, having come to disavow surrealism, might not want her mentee to channel her example. With such scenarios in mind, I introduce the term *persistent generativity* to refer to what a person has or achieves when they engage in generative work that they embrace and succeed in passing along to another person who could outlive them.

Sheriff Bell's generative work takes two forms: (1) trying to fulfill his official responsibilities to different groups of people; and (2) maintaining relationships with his wife and deceased daughter. Because Bell is not proud of how he has performed in the first type of work, he does not want it to survive him. And the second type of work, in its current form, cannot outlive him. Bell has no persistent generativity. In other words, he has no fire to carry.

WITHOUT FIRE TO CARRY: *NO COUNTRY FOR OLD MEN*

Bordered to the south by the Rio Grande river, Terrell County, Texas, is enormous and sparsely populated. In 1980, when the novel begins, Ed Tom Bell has served as county sheriff for more than thirty years. He won't last much longer. The drama is spurred on by other men. Llewellyn Moss, a former U.S. military sniper, is hunting antelope when he stumbles upon a drug deal gone wrong. He discovers corpses and a "load of bricksized parcels," but no money.[4] Scouring the nearby desert, Moss tracks down a dead man and a briefcase containing more than two million dollars.

---

4. McCarthy, *No Country for Old Men*, 13.

When he flees with the money, Moss is trailed by rival parties: gunmen from a Mexican cartel, and a rogue killer named Anton Chigurh. As the chase ranges through the borderlands, Sheriff Bell fails to keep up. More people die. Bell contacts Moss's wife, pleading with her to convince her husband to surrender to police protection. When she finally agrees to help, it's too late. Moss is killed by the cartel, and his wife is murdered by Chigurh. Bell is right to suspect that Chigurh has the money, but he refuses to pursue him any longer. Instead, Bell decides to retire.

My discussion of *No Country for Old Men* will explore Bell's moral psychology. I will focus only on McCarthy's novel, not on the award-winning film it inspired. In the novel, Bell's thirteen monologues offer insights about him that the film omits. Several of these details—such as Bell's reflections on his military service—are vital for an assessment of his character and the forms of generativity he experiences. Most of Bell's monologues precede his retirement, but the final few are spoken afterward, leaving us uncertain as to how much time his reflections span. Regardless, I seek to show that, over the course of the monologues, Bell undergoes an important change. He transitions from a man who seems confident of his moral commitments, the worth of his career in law enforcement, and the need to guard his own soul, to a person who shows more vulnerability—one with the courage to doubt his values and to acknowledge his personal and professional failures. Bell becomes someone who longs for—but has not yet found—a form of generative work that could bear meaning beyond the bounds of his own life.

Bell's faith in his profession, in his good moral standing, and in the security of his soul is expressed concisely in this excerpt from his fourth monologue.

> I was sheriff of this county when I was twenty-five. Hard to believe. My father was not a lawman. Jack was my grandfather. Me and him was sheriff at the same time, him in Plano and me here. I think he was pretty proud of that. I know I was. I was just back from the war. I had some medals and stuff and of course people had got wind of that. I campaigned pretty hard. You had to. I tried to be fair. . . . I dont recall that I ever give the good Lord all that much cause to smile on me. But he did.[5]

---

5. McCarthy, *No Country for Old Men*, 90–91. In the novel, Bell's monologues are presented in italics to signal a shift of narrative perspective and to set them apart chronologically from the rest of the story. However, in this essay, I do not italicize excerpts from the monologues because doing so would not add to their meaning.

Here, Bell speaks of his generative work as sheriff in two temporal contexts: historical and familial. In the same monologue, Bell mentions his gratitude for his wife, Loretta, and states his conviction that she is his moral better. Briefly, Bell also alludes to a painful loss: "Me and my wife has been married thirty-one years. No children. We lost a girl but I wont talk about that. . . . She's a better person than me, which I will admit to anybody that cares to listen. Not that that's sayin a whole lot. She's a better person than anybody I know. Period."[6]

In his early monologues, Bell does not portray himself as perfect.[7] Still, he holds a basic belief in his own decency and in the meaningfulness of his career:

> I was twenty-one when I went in the army and I was one of the oldest in our class at boot camp. Six months later I was in France shootin people with a rifle. I didnt even think it was all that peculiar at the time. Four years later I was sheriff of this county. I never doubted but what I was supposed to be neither. People anymore you talk about right and wrong they're liable to smile at you. But I never had a lot of doubts about things like that. In my thoughts about things like that. I hope I never do.[8]

Much of what Bell knows of right and wrong he learned, he says, from his father. As a young man, Bell's father traded horses; he also attended college but never completed a degree.[9] Apart from these details, we hear almost nothing about him. An important exception is Bell's praise for his father's moral example:

> My daddy always told me to just do the best you knew how and tell the truth. He said there was nothin to set a man's mind at ease like wakin up in the morning and not havin to decide who you were. And if you done somethin wrong just stand up and say you done it and say you're sorry and get on with it. Dont haul stuff around with you. [...] I might of strayed from all of

---

6. McCarthy, *No Country for Old Men*, 90–91.

7. Russell Hillier has a more biting view. In a broad assessment of Bell's personality, Hillier sums Bell up as "an inflexible, fastidious, and punctilious man." In my view, Hillier does not give Bell enough credit for the ways he does confront his feelings and, to borrow Hillier's phrase, "own up to his sense of defeat." Hillier, *Morality in Cormac McCarthy's Fiction*, 224–25.

8. McCarthy, *No Country*, 158–59.

9. McCarthy, *No Country*, 308.

that some as a younger man but when I got back on that road I pretty much decided not to quit it again and I didnt.[10]

Despite such self-assurance, cracks begin to appear in the edifice. For example, after saying he hopes he never doubts his ethics, Bell remarks: "On my better days I think that there is somethin I dont know or there is somethin that I'm leavin out. But them times are seldom."[11] One such doubt begins to arise in relationship to his military service in World War II—an experience that, like the death of his daughter, Bell is not yet ready to divulge. "I wont talk about the war neither. I was supposed to be a war hero and I lost a whole squad of men. Got decorated for it. They died and I got a medal. . . . There aint a day I dont remember it."[12] Apparently, during Bell's first campaign for sheriff—and through all the years and elections after—his losing "a whole squad of men" was a fact he failed to mention.

Before I begin to describe how Bell changes, one last point: his fear of what he's up against. Bell does not know the name Anton Chigurh, but he has witnessed the devastation wrought by this new visitor to his jurisdiction. Bell wants no part of it.

> Somewhere out there is a true and living prophet of destruction and I dont want to confront him. I know he's real. I have seen his work. I walked in front of those eyes once. I wont do it again. I wont push my chips forward and stand up and go out to meet him. It aint just bein older. I wish that it was. . . . I think it is more like what you are willin to become. And I think a man would have to put his soul at hazard. And I wont do that. I think now that maybe I never would.[13]

Here, in the novel's opening monologue, Bell expresses a profound terror of what an encounter with Chigurh might do to him: Bell could lose his soul. Readers soon learn why. Chigurh is depicted as an implacable force of evil. For example, after finding an officer murdered by Chigurh, a fellow sheriff reports to Bell: "I just have this feelin we're looking at somethin we really aint never seen before." Bell replies, "I got the same feelin."[14] Another character, Carson Wells, describes Chigurh to Moss:

10. McCarthy, *No Country*, 249.
11. McCarthy, *No Country*, 159.
12. McCarthy, *No Country*, 195.
13. McCarthy, *No Country*, 4.
14. McCarthy, *No Country*, 46.

"You cant make a deal with him. Let me say it again. Even if you gave him the money he'd still kill you. There's no one alive on this planet that's ever had even a cross word with him. They're all dead. These are not good odds. He's a peculiar man. You could even say that he has principles. Principles that transcend money or drugs or anything like that."[15] The scholar Lydia Cooper regards Chigurh as a villain who is both "God-like and devil-like" in his inexorability and in the utter annihilation he perpetrates.[16] Similarly, Manuel Broncano writes: "Chigurh is both messenger and executor of fate, the Grim Reaper whose irruption into the life of an individual means that that life has come to an end."[17] What Sheriff Bell fears, were he to pursue Chigurh, is something akin to spiritual destruction. Instead of chancing that fate, Bell ultimately resigns his post as sheriff.

Bell's moral shift hinges on his belated admission of his failures and guilt—an acknowledgment that began, as we've seen, with his passing mention of his time as a soldier. This moral change speeds up when Bell visits his Uncle Ellis, who was a deputy under Bell's grandfather. Their conversation, with the reminiscences of Bell's monologues, are part of his ongoing life review.[18] With Ellis, Bell unburdens himself of a long-kept secret. During World War II, Germans bombed a French farmhouse commandeered by Bell and his fellow soldiers. Bell was not the only survivor. When he came to, he took on the Germans with a machine gun and, somehow, survived. He was awarded the Bronze Star. For years, the story ended there. Now, however, Bell confesses that, after the battle, he "cut and run."[19] He left his buddies behind. Ellis tries to console him. "Maybe you ought to ease up on yourself some." But Bell demurs: "Maybe. But you go into battle it's a blood oath to look after the men with you and I dont know why I didnt. . . . If I was supposed to die over there doin what I'd give my word to do then that's what I should of done. You can tell it any way you want but that's the way it is. I should of done it and I didnt. And some part of me has never quit wishin I could go back." Then the clencher: "I didnt know you could steal your own life."[20]

---

15. McCarthy, *No Country*, 153.
16. Cooper, *No More Heroes*, 122–23.
17. Broncano, *Religion in Cormac McCarthy's Fiction*, 123.
18. Saxton and Cole, "*No Country for Old Men*," 111.
19. McCarthy, *No Country*, 276.
20. McCarthy, *No Country*, 278.

At last, Bell has spoken of the war. But there is one more layer to his sense of failure. Bell goes on to compare his cowardice to the courage and fidelity of Jack, his grandfather who was also a sheriff. Jack, he says, never would have abandoned his buddies. "He'd of set there till hell froze over and then stayed a while on the ice."[21] And this, Bell is sure, makes his grandfather the better man. In other words, had Jack known that Bell's career in law enforcement was built on a lie of heroism, Jack would have been far from proud to call his grandson his fellow sheriff. For Bell, this intergenerational rupture is important, and it is deepened, I will argue, by Bell's moral distance from his father and by the fact that Bell has no heir.

In the final monologue before his retirement, Bell draws a connection between his betrayal in battle and his unwillingness to chase Chigurh. When he failed in France, Bell was a young man, he assured himself, with plenty of life ahead to make up for the wrong:

> I said that I was twenty-one years old and I was entitled to one mistake, particularly if I could learn from it and become the sort of man I had it in mind to be. Well, I was wrong about all of that. Now I aim to quit and a good part of it is just knowin that I wont be called on to hunt this man. . . . So you could say to me that I aint changed a bit and I dont know that I would even have a argument about that. Thirty-six years. That's a painful thing to know.[22]

When death is almost certain—by remaining at the farmhouse that was under attack, or by continuing to chase Chigurh—one could argue that there is wisdom in quitting. Fleeing is Bell's best chance of survival. But that is not how Bell sees it. Just as he once violated his oath as a soldier by abandoning his buddies, he is now reneging on his promise to protect the people of Terrell County. He was not, as he puts it, "equal to" the task or a "bad enough dog" to keep criminals from coming into his yard.[23] For this reason, on his final day as sheriff, Bell has a potent sense of "defeat"—a feeling of "being beaten," which, alluding to the war, he has not experienced "in a long time."[24] Being a soldier and being sheriff are different kinds of generative activities Bell performed in service of different people and groups. But Bell is not proud of this work. He would not want others

---

21. McCarthy, *No Country*, 279.
22. McCarthy, *No Country*, 282.
23. McCarthy, *No Country*, 299.
24. McCarthy, *No Country*, 306.

CARRYING THE FIRE 123

to heed his example. Instead of fulfilling his oath to guard his comrades and fellow citizens, Bell twice reverts to mere self-preservation.

Despite this damning assessment, Bell is changing. Unlike the stubborn self-assurance of his past, Bell has begun to show vulnerability. As Benjamin Saxton and Thomas Cole point out, "Critics who dismiss Bell as a failure should consider the courage that it takes him . . . to question his most cherished values and to pursue conversations with urgency and honesty."[25] Bell concludes his confession to Ellis by saying he also intends to tell his wife, Loretta—a conversation that, given how much Bell admires her, would probably be very difficult for him. Worth noting, in this context, is that what I have called Bell's "monologues" are, in fact, a series of conversations he has with one or more unnamed persons. Yes, Bell can still sound bitter and recalcitrant, and readers never hear from his interlocutors; yet, at times, it is clear that Bell is responding to them.[26] Through dialogue, and in self-reflection, Bell claims to be trying hard to see himself for who he really is.[27]

In the first monologue after his retirement, Bell reveals another example of the significance of conversation. Earlier, as we saw, Bell refused to speak of his only child—a daughter who died many years ago. Now, he opens up: "I talk to my daughter," he begins. He goes on:

> She would be thirty now. That's all right. I dont care how that sounds. I like talkin to her. Call it superstition or whatever you want. I know that over the years I have give her the heart I always wanted for myself and that's all right. That's why I listen to her. I know I'll always get the best from her. It dont get mixed up with my own ignorance or my own meanness. . . . I listen to what she says and what she says makes good sense. I wish she'd say more of it. I can use all the help I can get.[28]

This passage is even more poignant in light of a discussion Bell and his wife once had. They were lamenting, Bell reports, the "pretty high" percentage of U.S. children being raised by grandparents because their parents "wouldnt raise em."[29] Readers might wonder if this social critique was informed by the couple's personal grief.

---

25. Saxton and Cole, "No Country for Old Men," 112.
26. For example, see McCarthy, No Country, 124.
27. McCarthy, No Country, 295.
28. McCarthy, No Country, 285.
29. McCarthy, No Country, 159.

Bell's revelation that he has invested his daughter with the heart he wishes he could have had is an expression, I believe, of his desire for a meaningful legacy. He is deeply sorry that he and Loretta did not have the chance to raise her and to help her become better than himself. He regrets that his life has broken the chain of his father's and grandfather's good moral character. In his final monologue, Bell returns in his thoughts to the French farmhouse where he broke his military oath. Recalling "a stone water trough in the weeds by the side of the house," he says:

> I dont know how long it had been there. A hundred years. Two hundred. You could see the chisel marks in the stone. It was hewed out of solid rock.... And I got to thinkin about the man that done that. That country had not had a time of peace much of any length at all that I knew of.... But this man had set down with a hammer and chisel and carved out a stone water trough to last ten thousand years. Why was that? What was it that he had faith in? It wasnt that nothin would change.... He had to know bettern that.... I have to say that the only thing I can think is that there was some sort of promise in his heart. And I dont have no intentions of carvin a stone water trough. But I would like to be able to make that kind of promise. I think that's what I would like most of all.[30]

As Bell thinks back to the first place he failed to keep his word, he shares his enduring longing for "faith" and the ability to make a lasting "promise" to the future. He wants to create something beautiful and useful that has the sturdiness to outlive him. He wants the kind of generativity that is like the passing of a torch to the next generation. But Bell's prospects are bleak. Chigurh was an omen of widespread moral disorder, Bell believes, leaving him unable to envision the future.[31] So, in this last monologue, Bell turns his thoughts to a different realm. The novel ends with his narrating two dreams he had decades ago, after his father died. Apparently, with this telling, Bell is trying to do his father "justice" by acknowledging his debt to the man who, he says, "never broke nothin in me."[32]

> I dont remember the first one all that well but it was about meetin him in town somewheres and he give me some money and I think I lost it. But the second one was like we was both back in older times and I was on horseback goin through the mountains

30. McCarthy, *No Country*, 307–8.
31. McCarthy, *No Country*, 283.
32. McCarthy, *No Country*, 308.

of a night. Goin through this pass in the mountains. It was cold and there was snow on the ground and he rode past me and kept on goin. Never said nothin. He just rode on past and he had this blanket wrapped around him and he had his head down and when he rode past I seen he was carryin fire in a horn the way people used to do and I could see the horn from the light inside of it. About the color of the moon. And in the dream I knew that he was goin on ahead and he was fixin to make a fire somewhere out there in all that dark and all that cold and I knew that whenever I got there he would be there.[33]

If the novel closed with these words, it might be reasonable to find a glint of optimism in its final image, as some scholars do. For example, in a messy reading of the second dream, Cooper contends that Bell possesses "the means to revivify hope in humanity's capacity to create, even in a world filled with evidence of humanity's capacity to destroy."[34]

Cooper's grandiose conclusion is unsupported—most obviously, perhaps, because it is Bell's father, not Bell, who is carrying the fire in the dream. Furthermore, as noted above, Bell has not yet kindled hope in his capacity for a new form of generative work—"to make that kind of promise" to the future, as he puts it—to say nothing of hope in all of humanity. The novel does not close with Bell's certainty that he still has time to resuscitate his life and, eventually, join his father by the campfire. No, as Bell's first dream suggests, he thinks he has "lost" something of worth his father imparted to him. The story ends with Bell's recognition that this dreamy destiny—reunion with his father at the fireside—is a delusion: "Then I woke up."[35] Bell has not become a participant in carrying the fire.

By recounting these dreams from years ago, Bell seems to make progress in what he calls "a life's work," which is the journey of seeing himself for who he really is.[36] In the end, Bell knows he's a man who has failed in war and in law enforcement. To return to the terms introduced by Rubinstein and colleagues, military service and law enforcement might have served, for Bell, as two activities in two spheres of generativity—historical and familial spheres, respectively—through which Bell, serving the public, could have outlived himself. That is, had he succeeded

33. McCarthy, *No Country*, 309.

34. Cooper summarizes this dream as one in which Bell "stood outside in the dark and cold world and saw his father in the distance building a fire." Cooper, *No More Heroes*, 131.

35. McCarthy, *No Country*, 309.

36. McCarthy, *No Country*, 295.

as soldier and sheriff, Bell might have linked past to future, offering his model to younger generations. But Bell's example, he suggests, is not one he would want others to adopt.

Nevertheless, at the end of the novel, Bell remains confident in his devotion to two relationships—to loving his wife, and to conversing with his dead daughter. These bonds constitute his ongoing work in the relational sphere of generativity. Curiously, while Bell says he has imagined for his daughter the heart he wishes he could have had, he also refers to his wife, in the present, as "my heart."[37] The repetition of this image emphasizes the fact that Bell's center is outside himself. These bonds are truly other-oriented commitments. Unfortunately, however, this is not the kind of generative work that could survive Bell. When he dies, these ties will die also.

More optimistically, Cole and Saxton suggest that, in retirement, Bell's marriage could become a source of greater meaning and even lead him to "a new way of thinking about aging masculinity."[38] Perhaps so. He and Loretta are looking forward to more time together. "If I didnt have her," Bell says of his wife, "I dont know what I would have."[39] Maybe Loretta will help him become a better person. Maybe their marriage could even become a model that younger couples will emulate—a torch that others will take up. Who knows. But as the curtain closes, this much is clear: Bell lacks a vision of how to make a "promise" that could outlive him. He is devoid of persistent generativity. For this reason, he has no fire to carry. The road ahead could be rough.

A LONG WAY TO MODEST HOPE: *THE ROAD*

In an elegant inversion of the closing dream from which Bell "woke up," McCarthy's next novel, *The Road*, opens with a father's awakening: "When he woke in the woods in the dark and the cold of the night he'd reach out to touch the child sleeping beside him. . . . In the dream from which he'd wakened he had wandered in a cave where the child led him by the hand. Their light playing over the wet flowstone walls."[40]

---

37. McCarthy, *No Country*, 300.
38. Cole and Saxton, "No Country for Old Men," 611.
39. McCarthy, *No Country*, 301, 305.
40. McCarthy, *Road*, 3.

While Bell rouses *from* a world turned dark and cold, the man awakens *to* such a world. In Bell's dream, his father recedes, bearing the light away. But in the man's dream, father and son stay joined, shining "their light" over cave walls—an early allusion to carrying the fire. Finally, for Bell, monstrous evil remains undefeated. But in *The Road*'s first dream, man and boy meet a grotesque creature, its "eyes dead white and sightless."[41] Fortunately, their presence frightens the beast away.

These juxtapositions—plus the common themes of father-son and fire/light—are strong suggestions, I believe, that it is fruitful to read the two novels together. For *The Road*'s two protagonists, could the above inversions of Bell's experience foretell some destiny better than Bell's? The odds seem insurmountable. Some unexplained catastrophe has rendered the world gray and cold. A blanket of ash occludes the sky. Gone are governments and currencies. In what was once the U.S., man and boy travel alone. They trek across the southern Appalachians and continue southeast toward the coast, where the weather might be warmer. No animals. Few plants. Almost everything dead or dying—including the man, of some unnamed illness. They push a shopping cart with blankets and other provisions. They scavenge empty shops and homes, searching for tools, lantern fuel, and canned goods. To keep warm at night, they often build campfires. Of the few other people they meet, most pose a violent threat. Ever-alert, father and son walk on, "each the other's world entire."[42] Sometimes, as if to revive their flagging spirits, they remind themselves that they are "carrying the fire."[43]

In *The Road*, I will argue, the image of carrying fire is a metaphor for the generative work of surviving and loving others. More specifically, the man's generative work has three immediate foci: a person (his son), things that aid their survival (e.g., clothing), and activities that express love (e.g., conversation, compassion, survival skills). Temporally speaking, this generative labor is entirely relational: the boy must learn to perform such work. As an Olympic torch is passed from one runner to the next, the man's generative work is the fire he is handing to his only child, who will survive him. In other words, carrying the fire is a metaphor for performing generative work that could outlive oneself. Finally, as they travel, man and boy sometimes allude to the fourth foci of this generative

---

41. McCarthy, *Road*, 3.
42. McCarthy, *Road*, 6.
43. McCarthy, *Road*, 83.

work: a group of fellow "good guys" who are also carrying the fire and whom father and son hope to locate and join.

The novel's first spoken words are those of the man, about his son: "If he is not the word of God God never spoke."[44] This statement, Beatrice Trotignon observes, "is reminiscent of the specific power assigned to divine language [in Judeo-Christian traditions], not only in the idea of the biblical text being the very words of God, but also in the way God is said in Genesis to create the world by spoken command, and is, of course, described as Logos itself in the New Testament."[45] Trotignon is alluding to the opening verses of John's gospel, where Jesus—whom Christians regard as God's divine Son—is called "the Word." She notes several other instances of the man's use of biblical language, even in conversation with the boy. For example, he tells his son, "My job is to take care of you. I was appointed to do that by God."[46]

Trotignon is also struck by the sacred resonances of the fire they carry, which she calls "a Promethean fire symbolizing hope and ethical behavior and which, in the Bible, is also a sign of God's covenant," as when Moses encounters God in a burning bush.[47] However, Trotignon seems unaware of explicit connections between fire (or light) and Jesus in Christian scripture. For example, in the same passage from John's gospel that describes Jesus as "the Word," we also find a reference to light: "In Him was life, and that life was the light of all mankind. The light shines in the darkness, and the darkness has not overcome it."[48] Later in John's gospel, Jesus declares, "I am the light of the world. Whoever follows me will never walk in darkness, but will have the light of life."[49] In these ways, by linking the image of carrying fire to Judeo-Christian theology (i.e., to the Son who establishes a new covenant between God and humanity), the novel hints that those who carry fire might enter, with others, into a special type of bond or communion. The bearer of fire can achieve self-transcendence by passing the torch to others. In *No Country*

---

44. McCarthy, *Road*, 5.
45. Trotignon, "Persisting Relic of Prayer," 199.
46. McCarthy, *Road*, 77.
47. Trotignon, "Persisting Relic of Prayer," 200.
48. John 1:4–5 (New International Version).

49. John 8:12 (New International Version). Also see Luke's gospel, where John the Baptist says of Jesus, "I baptize you with water. But one who is more powerful than I will come, the straps of whose sandals I am not worthy to untie. He will baptize you with the Holy Spirit and fire." Luke 3:16 (New International Version).

for Old Men, as we saw, Bell's dreams suggest that he is not carrying his father's fire, and—even if he were—Bell has no one to whom he could impart the flame. But in *The Road*, the man is teaching the boy to carry fire, and the boy proves worthy of the lesson.[50]

In one house they enter, under a locked hatch, they discover naked people, cowering together in the basement. Too frightened to help them, man and boy climb the stairs, just as the captors are returning to the house. Later, after a narrow escape, the boy realizes that the captives were being kept as food. He says, "We wouldn't ever eat anybody, would we?" "Of course not," his father assures him. "Because we're the good guys," the boy answers. "And we're carrying the fire," he adds. "Yes," his father says.[51]

In this passage, carrying fire is associated with being part of an abstract group of "good guys"—abstract because man and boy have not yet met any fellow members. Soon, being the good guys is connected, in turn, to three activities: surviving, showing compassion, and engaging in conversation—including with the dead. These activities inform the meaning of carrying fire.

Near another house, as the man walks through a field, he discovers a buried door. The boy is terrified, recalling the locked basement. But his father knows they're starving—that they can't afford not to open the door. He makes a lamp. "Hold your hand in front of the flame," he says. "Don't let it go out." Then, to stoke courage from his son, he adds, "This is what the good guys do. They keep trying. They don't give up."[52] The boy agrees. His father leads the way underground, where they find "everything": crates of canned goods, blankets, lanterns, mattress pads, and fresh clothes.[53] The boy hesitates. "Is it okay for us to take it?" he asks. "Yes. It is," his father says. "They would want us to. Just like we would want them to." "They were the good guys?" the boy wonders. "Yes. They were," says his father.[54] Before going to sleep, they enjoy several cans of

---

50. Luttrull was the first scholar to connect the image of carrying fire in these two novels with what he calls "their archetypal root: Prometheus, the Titan who stole fire from the gods." Luttrull, "Prometheus Hits *The Road*," 20. For a similar reading that evokes mythological "tricksters"—from Loki to Lucifer—see Yarbrough, "Tricksters and Lightbringers in McCarthy's Post-Appalachian Novels," 46–55. And for a Jungian reading of the same image, see Bortz, "Carrying the Fire," 28–42.
51. McCarthy, *Road*, 128–29.
52. McCarthy, *Road*, 137.
53. McCarthy, *Road*, 139–42.
54. McCarthy, *Road*, 139–40.

pears. Eventually, father and son will leave the bunker and take much with them—food, clothing, various tools—to aid their survival.

The next morning, still in the bunker, the man prepares an enormous breakfast: ham, buttered biscuits, eggs, coffee. Before eating, the boys asks, "Do you think we should thank the people? . . . The people who gave us all this." "Yes," the man says, "I guess we could do that."[55] The boy begins: "Dear people, thank you for all this food and stuff. We know you saved it for yourself and if you were here we wouldnt eat it no matter how hungry we were and we're sorry that you didnt get to eat it and we hope that you're safe in heaven with God."[56] The boy doesn't know it yet, but, as we will see, his prayer-like address to "the people" is preparing him to keep talking to his father, after the man dies.

Over the course of the story, much of the man's biblical language—and perhaps whatever faith he had retained—seems to fall away. This change is signaled early in the novel, as he sits with the boy by a fire, their hands held out to the flames.

> He tried to think of something to say but he could not. He'd had this feeling before, beyond the numbness and the dull despair. The world shrinking down about a raw core of parsible entities. The names of things slowly following those things into oblivion. Colors. The names of birds. Things to eat. Finally the names of things one believed to be true. More fragile than he would have thought. How much was gone already? The sacred idiom shorn of its referents and so of its reality. Drawing down like something trying to preserve heat. In time to wink out forever.[57]

For the man, this "feeling" seems to reach its culmination while he and the boy sort through the ruins of another house:

> In a drawer he found a candle No way to light it. He put it in his pocket. He walked out in the gray light and stood and he saw for a brief moment the absolute truth of the world. The cold relentless circling of the intestate earth. Darkness implacable. The blind dogs of the sun in their running. The crushing black vacuum of the universe. And somewhere two hunted animals trembling like groundfoxes in their cover. Borrowed time and borrowed world and borrowed eyes with which to sorrow it.[58]

55. McCarthy, *Road*, 145.
56. McCarthy, *Road*, 146.
57. McCarthy, *Road*, 88–89.
58. McCarthy, *Road*, 130.

"At the very least," Trotignon comments, "God is a reassuring trope" that helps the man keep going.[59] What persists for him, from the novel's first spoken words, is his tendency to see his son as an almost-sacred being and to preserve all he can for the boy. On the road, they meet an old man, a lone traveler, and the boy insists on sharing their food. His father relents. They give him a can of fruit, invite him to join them for the night, and sit with him by the fire. In a further show of compassion, they give him more to eat. "I've not seen a fire in a long time," the old man says, "I live like an animal.... When I saw that boy I thought that I had died." The man replies, "What if I said that he's a god?"[60]

In the morning, before parting ways with the old man, the boy wants to provide him with even more. But his father refuses to part with much. Hours later, the boy remains sullen. "Are you talking?" the man asks him. "Yes," says the boy, still pondering the old man's plight.[61] Here, as after other tumultuous experiences, the man coaxes his son to keep conversing. For example, after they reach the coast, someone seizes the chance to steal their possessions. Father and son track down the thief, and the man takes everything back—including, cruelly, the thief's own clothes. Later, father and son argue, and the child's compassion wins out. The man leaves the clothes for the thief to find, but the boy remains dissatisfied. That night, they hardly speak. "You have to talk to me," the man says in the morning. The boy replies, "I'm trying."[62] It's as if, Trotignon observes, the man senses that, in the novel's bleak world, meaning exists only in sustained dialogue.[63]

Even if the man has lost religious faith, he never loses faith in the boy.[64] Just days before dying, the man is weak and coughing relentlessly. He and the boy barely speak. As the father pushes their cart, the son walks ahead. Sometimes, the man "would raise his weeping eyes and

---

59. Trotignon, "Persisting Relic," 200.
60. McCarthy, Road, 172.
61. McCarthy, Road, 174–75.
62. McCarthy, Road, 261.
63. Trotignon, "Persisting Relic," 203.
64. Some scholars argue that the man retains a type of religious faith. For example, invoking a sacramental theology of the cross—that "the basic giving-over of God [in Jesus Christ] grounds all reality"—Matthew Potts points to the man's own self-giving, to his son, as central to the novel's ethics: "the dispossession of the self which constitutes the love between these two characters is profoundly theological and actually all that theology finally offers in the face of death and disaster." Potts, *Cormac McCarthy and the Signs of* Sacrament, 180–81.

see [his son] standing there in the road looking back at him from some unimaginable future, glowing in that waste like a tabernacle."[65] That the future has become "unimaginable" for the man is reminiscent of Sheriff Bell's inability to make sense of the moral disorder that has come to his door. However, the critical difference between these men is that, while Bell has no moral heir, the man has the boy to survive him and to go on carrying the fire.

The day before he dies, the man continues to associate light with the boy. He watches the child "come through the grass and kneel with the cup of water he'd fetched. There was light all about him. He took the cup and drank and lay back. . . . [The boy] took the cup and moved away and when he moved the light moved with him."[66] Later, when the child returns to his side, the man tries to reassure him. "You need to go on, he said. I cant go with you. You need to keep going. You dont know what might be down the road. We were always lucky. You'll be lucky again. . . . Do everything the way we did it. . . . You need to find the good guys. . . . You have to carry the fire."[67] But the boy lacks confidence, saying, "I dont know how to." Then he asks his father, "Is it real? The fire?" "Yes it is," the man says. "Where is it?" the boys wonders aloud. "I dont know where it is." And his father answers, "Yes you do. It's inside you. It was always there. I can see it."[68]

The child is unsure. If his father can't survive, he wants to die too. "You said you wouldnt ever leave me," he reminds him. "I know," the man answers. "I'm sorry. You have my whole heart. You always did. You're the best guy. You always were. If I'm not here you can still talk to me. You can talk to me and I'll talk to you. You'll see." Skeptical, the boy asks, "Will I hear you?" "Yes. You will," his father says. "You have to make it like talk that you imagine. And you'll hear me. You have to practice. Just dont give up. Okay?" "Okay," the boy promises.[69]

In this scene, carrying fire is, once again, linked to being one of the good guys, maintaining the will to survive, and conversing. Now it falls to the boy to sustain their loving bond by doing as his father taught him and by practicing a prayer-like dialogue. "The crucial thing," Trotignon remarks, "is that the father's promise of speaking back is one that can

65. McCarthy, *Road*, 273.
66. McCarthy, *Road*, 277.
67. McCarthy, *Road*, 274.
68. McCarthy, *Road*, 278–79.
69. McCarthy, *Road*, 279.

only be kept if the son keeps it for him, if the son proceeds to this strange ceremony of talking and listening to his own imaginary answers made up for his departed father."[70] While Sheriff Bell, as we saw, speaks to his dead daughter and imagines for her the heart he wanted for himself, the man gives the boy his "whole heart" and relies on him completely to preserve their shared ways and thoughts. In doing so, the man tries to issue to the future the kind of promise that Bell, remembering the stone trough, still longs to make.

As his father sleeps, the boy watches him. Their last night together. "He closed his eyes and talked to him and he kept his eyes closed and listened. Then he tried again."[71] Later, when the man wakes in the dark, coughing, the story comes full circle: "Old dreams encroached upon the waking world. The dripping was in the cave. The light was a candle which the boy bore in a ringstick of beaten copper. . . . In that cold corridor they had reached the point of no return which was measured from the first solely by the light they carried with them."[72]

Three days after the man dies, someone appears on the road: "a veteran of old skirmishes, bearded," a shotgun slung over his shoulder.[73] He's sorry, he says, that the boy's father died. He invites the boy to come with him. He's "one of the good guys," he assures the child, and has a family. He says they are also carrying the fire. "Okay then," the boy says.[74] Before going, he says goodbye to his father. "I'll talk to you every day," he whispers to his father's body. "And I wont forget. No matter what."[75] They leave and join the man's family, and the woman "put her arms around [the boy] and held him. Oh, she said, I am so glad to see you."[76] The passage continues: "She would talk to him sometimes about God. He tried to talk to God but the best thing was to talk to his father and he did talk to him and he didnt forget. The woman said that was all right. She said that the breath of God was his breath yet though it pass from man to man through all of time."[77] This final affirmation of the boy's dialogue with his father, coupled with the idea of breath passing from one person to

70. Trotignon, "Persisting Relic," 204–5.
71. McCarthy, *Road*, 280.
72. McCarthy, *Road*, 280.
73. McCarthy, *Road*, 281.
74. McCarthy, *Road*, 282–84.
75. McCarthy, *Road*, 286.
76. McCarthy, *Road*, 286.
77. McCarthy, *Road*, 286.

another, across time, reinforces the novel's suggestion that carrying fire is performing generative work that one affirms and that has the power to outlive oneself. In the end, the boy is carrying the fire only in a limited, potential sense: he knows how to survive and how to love—abilities the boy could develop further and pass on to others. He has not yet achieved persistent generativity. However, the family he has joined includes a girl—a hint that he might have the opportunity.

CONCLUSION

In this chapter, I have argued that to carry the fire is to engage in a specific kind of generative work: work that one embraces and succeeds in passing along to another who could outlive oneself. A person who performs such work achieves what I have called *persistent generativity*. In *No Country for Old Men*, Ed Tom Bell defends others as a soldier and as sheriff, and he maintains relationships with his wife and dead daughter. However, in the end, Bell no longer endorses the first form of generative work, and the second type cannot survive his death. He has no persistent generativity. Therefore, as Bell's two dreams suggest, he is not carrying the fire. In contrast, the man in *The Road* has a young son who could outlive him and is the sole focus of his father's generative work: imparting the abilities to survive and to love others. For man and boy, surviving and loving are the two practices that constitute the symbolic fire they carry. The man embraces these practices and teaches them to his son. The man achieves persistent generativity, and the boy bears their torch into the future.[78]

I close with a final observation. Meghna Datta Roy and Minati Panda argue that a person's potential for generativity depends profoundly on limits imposed by their social, cultural, and economic conditions.[79] In this light, *No Country for Old Men* and *The Road* might be read as cautionary tales. That is, these novels might offer us a glimpse of what happens to human beings' capacities for generativity when the social, cultural, and economic conditions that once facilitated so much generativity begin to erode or even collapse.

78. Also see Patton, "McCarthy's Fire," 131–43. Patton analyzes the image of carrying fire in these two novels. With my reading, I have tried to give the image more specificity than what Patton characterizes as "a metaphor for some kind of moral order" and "the guarantee of a future humanity." Patton, "McCarthy's Fire," 142.

79. Roy and Panda, "Is Generativity Erikson's Answer to Human Ageing in the Neoliberal World?", 101–57.

7

Older Women's Sexuality— in Life and in Film

Renee Flores

INTRODUCTION

Delilah, a 79-year-old female, presents with vaginal dryness. She had been seeing her obstetrics and gynecology physician but had not seen her in a while. She says that she had recurrent urinary tract infections and was told that this was because she had atrophy of the vaginal walls from lack of estrogen, which started after menopause. Her husband died ten years prior, and she has not been interested in dating. She has three grown children who live outside the home. She likes volunteering at the local community center.

Recently, Delilah met a widowed man. She says they have been meeting for coffee, which turned into a few lunches, and now he wants to take her to dinner. She is worried about where the relationship might go. When her husband's health started to decline, they rarely engaged in sex. It has been over 15 years since she has had vaginal intercourse. She says that it was a little painful in the later years after she went into menopause, which is when she started estrogen. This did help with pain and lubrication. She never thought she would find someone she would be interested in romantically after her husband died. However, she says that her friend brings "a spark" to her life and she wants to have sex with him.

Vicki, an 89-year-old female, came to my clinic based on the recommendation of her male friend. Her male friend, Robert, also my patient, came to see me for erectile dysfunction. Vicki and Robert met at a senior living facility. Vicki was widowed and had moved into the facility about two years prior. Robert was divorced and lived in the facility for about one year. Their relationship started as friends. They take the facility-sponsored shuttle to the grocery store and to the movies. They both liked to watch older movies, like *Breakfast at Tiffany's* and *Rebel Without a Cause*. They would take turns choosing romantic classic movies and popular action-packed movies. They spent intimate moments sharing life stories.

Their relationship evolved into a sexual relationship. If she stayed in his room overnight, she would make sure to get up early so that people at the facility would not get "the wrong idea" about her. When Robert started seeing me, he mentioned that Vicki complained that she had never had an orgasm. He wanted advice to help with this. When she came to see me, she said that she wanted to engage in sexual activity and enjoyed foreplay with hands, mouth, and vaginal intercourse. The fact that she had never had an orgasm bothered Robert more than her. Still, she would like to have one if possible; she had just given up on the idea when she was married.

Both of these women present with common scenarios that older adult women experience. Statistically, older women live longer than men, yet both may seek companionship and relationships, including intimacy and sexuality, throughout their lifespan. In this chapter, I will present some research on older women's sexuality and then turn to an analysis of two films—*Something's Gotta Give* and *Good Luck to You, Leo Grande*—as they depict and, in some ways, challenge ageism about older women's sexuality.

SEXUALITY AND AGING RESEARCH

Despite the aging population, the sexual behaviors and sexual functions of older people are not well understood. According to the CDC, overall life expectancy is 77. For white women, it is more than 81, and more than 78 for Black women in the United States.[1] In 2007 Lindau et al. published one of the first studies in the United States to assess the sexual function

---

1. Centers for Disease Control and Prevention, "Life Expectancy."

and behaviors of older adults. The survey sample consisted of 3,005 adults (response rate about 75 percent), aged fifty-seven to eighty-five years, 52 percent women, and 48 percent men. Among the study participants, 73 percent were fifty-seven to sixty-four years of age, 53 percent were sixty-five to seventy-four years of age, and 26 percent were seventy-five to eighty-five years of age. Among those who reported not being in a relationship, 22 percent of men and 4 percent of women reported sexual activity within the last year. Although the oldest group reported less sex, 54 percent reported having sex at least two to three times per month, and 23 percent reported having sex at least once a week or more. In all age groups, women reported significantly less sexual activity than men. Sexual activity was associated with self-reported health. Therefore, the "very good" health self-reporters also said more sexually active lifestyles, and vice versa.[2]

A more recent study published in 2016 suggested that 60 percent of men and 35 percent of women over sixty-five, and 19 percent of men and 32 percent of women over age eighty-five are still having frequent sex, reported as at least twice a month or more. In the eighty-five-plus group, 49 percent of men and 62 percent of women reported kissing/petting, and 17 percent of men and 7 percent of women reported masturbation.[3] The Lindau et. al study supports what has been published in the literature regarding sexual activity among older adults.

The disparity between men and women in sexual satisfaction—known as the orgasm gap, or pleasure gap—has been noted for decades. Beginning in the 1950s, Alfred Kinsey reported several observational studies on discrepancies in orgasm frequency in unmarried women and men living in the United States. This study looked at men and women born after 1910, aged fifteen to fifty-five years of age, and 36 percent of women reported that they had never had an orgasm, while 100 percent of men reported having orgasms previously. Regarding the frequency of orgasms (before marriage), women reported 223 orgasms compared to 1,500 orgasms reported by men.[4]

---

2. Lindau et al., "A Study of Sexuality and Health Among Older Adults in the United States."

3. Lee, Nazroo, O'Connor, Blake, and Pendleton, "Sexual Health and Well-Being Among Older Men and Women in England."

4. Kinsey, Pomeroy, Martin, and Gebhard, *Sexual Behavior in the Human Female*, 519.

More than forty years later, Laumann et al. assessed sexual practices in the United States in married and nonmarried relationships. This study found that amongst married couples, 28.6 percent of women and 75 percent of men reported always having an orgasm with their spouse. Comparing this to unmarried/short-term partners (defined as non-cohabiting relationships lasting less than one month), 43 percent of women and 80.5 percent reported always having an orgasm with their partner.[5]

A more recent study by Doring and Mohseni corroborates these earlier studies.[6] This is a systematic literature review published in Germany. A total of twenty-five publications were reviewed between 1982 to 2021, with a large sample size of 49,940 women and 48,329 men. They found that 30–60 percent of women and 70–100 percent of men report orgasm, a trend that continues to favor men having more orgasms than women.[7]

Research evaluating sexual encounters and experiences is still inadequate for older adults, as research studies tend to exclude older adults. One study examining perceptions about sexual pleasure for both men and women showed that men perceive sexual pleasure as a "higher sense of entitlement" for men than women.[8] These data continue to show that older adults are having sex with gender differences that do not favor a women's sexual standpoint. The pleasure gap remains in old age.

Aging and Body Image

Orli Langer-Most and Nieli Langer write: "Sexuality is a fundamental dimension of all human beings and refers to an individual's self-perception of being attractive as a sexual partner beyond the sexual urge and the sex act. Sexuality for older people often provides the opportunity to express physical passion, affection, loyalty, and esteem in the face of typical and extraordinary changes in functioning."[9] Yet the media still continues to represent *sexy* as something only attainable for youthful adults. It may be challenging to feel comfortable about aging in a culture where older women are rarely seen, and those who are seen are celebrated primarily

---

5. Laumann, Gagnon, Michael, and Michaels, "Social Organization of Sexuality Sexual Practices in the United States," 130.

6. Döring and Mohseni, "Gender Orgasm Gap."

7. Döring and Mohseni, "Gender Orgasm Gap," 74.

8. Klein and Conley, "Role of Gendered Entitlement in Understanding Inequality in the Bedroom," 1047.

9. Langer-Most, "Aging and Sexuality," 286–87.

for their "youthful" good looks. In an interview about the movie *Good Luck to You, Leo Grande*, one of the films to be analyzed below, it is noted that:

> Thompson is keenly aware of how subversive it is for a woman her age to dare to be nude, especially in a medium whose foundational grammar is based on the display of women's bodies. "Impossible bodies," Thompson notes, "either because they naturally belong to the very young women who are in the films, or [they're] bodies of old women who do nothing but restrict what they eat and go to the gym." Thompson says she has been spared the worst of Hollywood's obsession with looks; most of the characters she has played aren't distinguished by their faces or bodies; when she was sent a script describing a character as a beauty, she says, "I'd just not continue to read it."[10]

In western society, "old" connotes "incompetence, misery, lethargy, unattractiveness, asexuality, and poor health," whereas "young" connotes "competence, happiness, vitality, attractiveness, sexuality, and good health."[11] Research has shown that facelifts are becoming more routine as the social pressures for women to sustain a youthful appearance are increasing.[12] In any case, although women generally have higher body dissatisfaction at all ages, studies show that women tend to shift their focus to health and body function as they age, so eighty-five-plus women may become more comfortable with body image.[13]

Common conditions of aging that can impact sexuality include energy and activity levels, medical conditions, and medications. Arthritis is commonly encountered in late mid-life women, causing frustration, concern, and hindrance in sexual activity. Hypertension and diabetes mellitus can cause chronic physical changes that decrease sexual function, and the treatment for these illnesses heightens sexual dysfunction.[14] Multiple studies have shown an association between poor health and sexual

---

10. Hornaday, "Emma Thompson Wants Us to Like Our Bodies."
11. Gerike, "On Gray Hair and Oppressed Brains," 68.
12. Bordo, *Unbearable Weight*, 25–26.
13. Grogan, "Age, Ethnicity, Social Class, and Sexuality," 149.
14. Pearlman, "Late Mid-Life Astonishment: Disruptions to Identity and Self-Esteem," 8; Addis, Ireland, Vittinghoff, Lin, Stuenkel, and Hulley, "Sexual Activity and Function in Postmenopausal Women with Heart Disease," 124.

dysfunction. Age alone is not an indicator of sexual problems; medical and physical health are linked to sexual dysfunction.[15]

Lindau et al. reported at least one sexual problem for both men and women in approximately half of its respondents. Maintaining (90 percent) or achieving (37 percent) an erection was the most common.[16] Waite et al. reported that 28 percent of men aged fifty-seven to sixty-four and sixty-five to seventy-four and 24 percent of men aged seventy-five to eighty-five reported erectile problems. Another typical concern for men included the inability to climax. Forty-four percent of women aged fifty-seven to sixty-four; 38 percent of women aged sixty-five to seventy-four; and 49 percent of women aged seventy-five to eighty-five state that lack of interest in sex is the most common sexual problem, followed by inability to climax, as well as issues with vaginal lubricant (not correlated with age).[17] Dyspareunia is also common because of vaginal atrophy after menopause, which causes painful intercourse, even after treatment because of the psychological anticipation of penetration. Another disorder that may present after menopause is hypoactive sexual desire disorder (HSDD), which causes distress secondary to loss of libido. Both dyspareunia and HSDD are linked to sexual dissatisfaction. However, aging and menopause are not.[18]

Since older women are viewed as not sexually active, common sexually transmitted infections (STIs) are often not diagnosed or treated. According to the CDC, in older adults aged sixty-five and older, rates of syphilis, gonorrhea, and chlamydia increased by nearly 50 percent in recent years.[19] This is likely because of the inconsistent use of condoms. Waite et al. reported that 2 percent of women aged fifty-seven to sixty-four, 5 percent aged sixty-five to seventy-four, and 3 percent aged seventy-five to eighty-five used a condom during vaginal intercourse.[20]

Aging women's responses to changes in physical and health status are also affected by relationship status. In partnered women, psychosocial

---

15. Lindau et al., "Study of Sexuality and Health among Older Adults in the United States," 772.

16. Lindau et al., "Study of Sexuality and Health among Older Adults in the United States," 769.

17. Waite, Laumann, Das, and Schumm, "Sexuality," i62.

18. Thomas, Hess, and Thurston, "Correlates of Sexual Activity and Satisfaction in Midlife and Older Women," 340; Gentili and Godschalk, "Chapter 57: Sexuality," 572.

19. Center for Disease Control, "Sexually Transmitted Disease Surveillance."

20. Waite, Laumann, Das, and Schumm, "Sexuality," i59.

factors (such as relationship satisfaction, the importance of sex, and communication with her partner) are related to sexual pleasure. Although age is not associated with sexual satisfaction,[21] age seems to impact sexual activity through the physical decline of the partner's health rather than waning interest.[22] Partnered heterosexual women tend to have more insecurities about their partner leaving for a younger woman, consistent with heterosexual marriage and divorce patterns. Single heterosexual and lesbian older adults are also insecure about more youthful women, which is secondary to media influences.[23] Lack of or loss of a partner is more common as people age, particularly women. Lindau et al. reported that in the age group seventy-five to eighty-five years of age, 78 percent of men compared to 40 percent reported having a spouse or other intimate partner.[24]

Notwithstanding the continuation of sexual activity throughout the ages and the high prevalence of sexual problems, women are more likely than men to discuss sexuality with physicians. Studies report that women's reluctance to convey sexual concerns, age differences between the woman patient and the physician, and "negative societal attitudes about women's sexuality and sexuality at older ages may also inhibit such discussions."[25] Sixty-six percent of women did not discuss their sexual problems with a clinician because of the embarrassment of bringing it up. Physicians also lack the training and education to address women's sexual dysfunctions.[26]

Still, research shows that women are having sex throughout the ages, despite the negative biases toward aging women. Openly recognizing some physiological changes as normal and countering the negative stereotypes and anti-aging attitudes, older women may become more comfortable seeking out sexual health specialists, talking to their doctors, and approaching sexuality as a quality of life metric. Representations of

21. Thomas, Hess, and Thurston, "Correlates of Sexual Activity and Satisfaction in Midlife and Older Women," 340.

22. Waite, Laumann, Das, and Schumm, "Sexuality," 163.

23. Pearlman, "Late Mid-Life Astonishment: Disruptions to Identity and Self-Esteem," 6.

24. Lindau et al., "A Study of Sexuality and Health among Older Adults in the United States," 772.

25. Lindau et al., "A Study of Sexuality and Health among Older Adults in the United States," 772.

26. Bauer, Haesler, and Fetherstonhaugh, "Let's Talk About Sex," 1247; Langer-Most, "Aging and Sexuality," 287.

older women having sex may contribute to a culture shift in this regard. I now turn to two recent such films.

TWO FILMS

Something's Gotta Give: Plot Summary

Something's Gotta Give highlights the life of a thriving New York playwright, Erica (Diane Keaton). Divorced, she is self-sufficient, with a beautiful beachfront second home in the Hamptons. On a weekend away, she runs into her daughter's new male friend, Harry, in his boxers getting food in the kitchen. Harry Sanborn (Jack Nicholson) dates women under 30 and is spending the weekend with Erica's daughter, Marin (Amanda Peet). After accidentally running into each other (uncomfortably), they all decide to spend the weekend together as "adults amicably."

While at dinner, Erica asks Harry about his past relationships. She remembers reading an article about him titled "The Escape Artist." Harry had been labeled the "famous bachelor," as he had never been married yet previously engaged to Diane Sawyer. Erica says she is impressed that he dated Diane Sawyer, and Harry says, "Yeah. Women your age love that about me."

After the dinner, Marin and Harry start to engage in foreplay for the first time when Harry has a heart attack. Rushed to the hospital, Harry is stabilized by cardiologist Dr. Julian Mercer (Keanu Reeves). Julian, a massive fan of Erica's plays, flirts with Erica as Harry recovers. Harry cannot return home because of his heart condition, so Marin volunteers Erica's Hampton home for rehabilitation. During his rehabilitation, Harry unintentionally runs into Erica naked on her way to take a shower.

Although reluctant to notice Erica, given her idiosyncrasies, their similar ages, and commonalities, an unexpected friendship emerges. Julian makes a house call to visit Harry (to get to know Erica better). Harry later engages in an intimate and sexual relationship with Erica despite this age difference. With a fallout, Harry returns to his home when he recovers, returning to his prior dating habits. However, he views relationships differently since his time with Erica. Erica is sad about the relationship's ending and writes a play about Harry.

Zoe (Erica's sister) runs into Julian at the farmer's market and invites him to Erica's. Erica and Julian start dating. For her birthday, Erica and Julian go to Paris. Harry decides to surprise her and sees her there with

Julian. The three have dinner, and Harry parts ways while Erica and Julian return to the hotel. Harry walks to a bridge in Paris, and it starts to snow, and he turns around, and Erica is there. The film ends with Erica, Harry, Marin, and her new family at a restaurant.

Good Luck to You, Leo Grande: Plot Summary

Dressed in business attire, Nancy Stokes (Emma Thompson) has booked a hotel room and is awaiting the arrival of her male escort. As Leo (Daryl McCormack) arrives in the room, he asks permission to kiss Nancy on the cheek and compliments her on the perfume she is wearing. Leo asks for some fizz to help with the mood. He compliments her again, toasting "to a very fine vintage."

But Nancy is nervous. She asks him about his trade in the escort business, and she is concerned about him being hired without wanting to complete the contract. He asks about her desires, and she says she wants to have sex with him that night. She is worried about being a disappointment to him. He grabs her and kisses her on the mouth.

She talks about not liking surprises, and wants to have sex now to "get it over with." She opens the discussion about never hiring an escort service before. She talks about past sexual disappointments and how she has never experienced an orgasm. Nancy says that after the death of her husband two years ago she has decided she will never fake an orgasm again. Leo would be the second man she had ever had sex with. She starts to have second thoughts about hiring Leo. Nancy starts to open up about her two children and her disappointment. She discusses her only sexual experience, which was with her husband, talking about how oral sex was "demeaning" for both of them, per her husband. Eventually, Nancy does become comfortable having sex with Leo.

Although Nancy mentioned she would only hire Leo once, she arranged a second meeting. This time, she comes with a list of sexual activities she wants to try. She then meets with Leo regularly, becomes curious about who he is, and discovers his real name. Nancy mentions that she wants to get to know him better because of their sexual relationship and to help him resolve the conflicts with his mother. Leo gets upset and asks Nancy not to contact him anymore.

She contacts him to meet up one last time, and they meet at a restaurant. Nancy apologizes to Leo for her actions. Meanwhile, she runs into a formal student. The student tells Leo she is uptight and discloses that Nancy called the girls in their school "sluts" for wearing short skirts. In revealing her newfound sexuality and pleasure, Nancy tells the student that Leo is a sex worker and shares the importance of sex and pleasure. Afterward, Leo and Nancy go upstairs for their last sexual rendezvous. She still does not have an orgasm with their sexual encounter, but she self-pleasures and reaches orgasm. The movie's final scene shows Nancy standing naked in front of the mirror: a full-frontal nude.

ANALYSIS OF FILMS

Ageism affecting older people and sexism affecting women are commonly associated with discrimination.[27] For example, the representation of older women in media is less than men, accounting for nearly 70 percent of all older adult actors; men appear twice as often as women: "Women face double jeopardy of representation on TV—discriminated based on both their age and gender."[28] Studies report that 93 percent of older adults aged fifty to eighty reported age-specific ageism and discrimination, which women stated slightly more than older men.[29] The top two ageist messages conveyed were "I hear, see, or read jokes about old age, aging, or older adults, and "I hear, see, or read things suggesting that older adults and aging are unattractive or undesirable."[30]

Indeed, older adults who reported watching four or more hours of television (or internet browsing or reading magazines) reported more ageism than those with less media exposure. Ageism is associated with poor physical health, chronic health conditions, poor mental health, and poor mental health outcomes.[31] The power of media to impact behaviors, thoughts, and attitudes is particularly evidenced by research and advertisements. Women's aging bodies are viewed as less attractive than young-looking ones, which, again, is prominent on television programs and films,[32] and also featured on magazine covers and social media. The lack of popularity of shows that promote positivity in the sexual lives

27. Lamb, "Not Your Grandmother's Ageism," 66.
28. Markov, "Diversity and Age Stereotypes," 2757
29. Allen et al., "Experiences of Everyday Ageism," 6.
30. Allen et al., "Experiences of Everyday Ageism," 3.
31. Allen et al., "Experiences of Everyday Ageism," 6.
32. Jones and Batchelor, *Aging Heroes*, 68; Grogan, "Age, Ethnicity, Social Class, and Sexuality," 146.

of older adults narrows the possibilities for imagining and relating to romance and intimacy in later life. Recurrent messages center around sentiments such as this one: "I want someone young to love me. I want someone young and fresh and new to be attracted to me. I don't want a forty-five-year-old woman who looks great for her age, young for her age. No matter how great she looks, she's still forty-five."[33]

Another study examined the feminist/young adults' perception of older adult sexual expression confronting ageism. Although there have been mild shifts of ageism and stereotypes of older women as asexual, there continues to be a pretense about sexual pleasure. The belief is that sexuality is associated with something "dirty," sexual satisfaction of her partner, always spontaneous and natural, and must end in sexual intercourse.[34]

In the film *Something's Gotta Give*, while Erica, Zoe (Erica's sister), Harry, and Marin are having dinner together, Harry and Erica discuss Diane Sawyer because Harry was once engaged to her. Erica is enthralled with her intelligence and career accomplishments, while Harry chatted about her great legs. The difference in views leads to an uncomfortable conversation:

> Zoe: Come on. This is really fascinating what is going on at this table.
>
> Marin: Zoe teaches women's studies at Columbia.
>
> Harry: Okay. So, this is gonna hurt.
>
> Zoe: No. Look, let's take you and Erica for example. Harry, you have been around the block a few times. Am I right? What are you, around 60?
>
> Harry: Hand motions—63.
>
> Zoe: 63! Never married, which, as we know, if you were a woman, would be a curse. You'd an old maid, a spinster. Blah, blah, blah. So instead of pitying you, they write articles about you. Celebrate your never marrying. You're elusive and ungettable, a real catch. Then, there's my gorgeous sister here.
>
> Erica: No, wait. What?

---

33. Gordon, as cited in Gerike, "On Gray Hair and Oppressed Brains," 39.

34. Hartmann, Philippsohn, Heiser, and Rüffer-Hesse, "Low Sexual Desire in Midlife and Older Women," 730.

Zoe: Look, please. No, this is interesting. Look at her. She is so accomplished. The most successful female playwright since who? Lillian Hellman? She's over 50, divorced, and she sits in night after night after night because the available guys her age want something. (Looking at Marin) Forgive me for saying this honey, but they want somebody that looks like Marin.[35]

Film scenes like these reinforce the stereotypes of older women feeling unwanted and unattractive. Older women are perceived as less sexual than younger women and older men. Movies like *Something's Gotta Give* lend popularity to older men dating younger women, and not vice versa. *Something's Gotta Give* challenges this typical media depiction by pairing a younger man with an older woman (Erica dates Julian), but in the end she chooses a man her age, favoring societal norms. Until the recent release of *Good Luck to You, Leo Grande*, films exclusively match young women and older men in film.

Double standards for men are more common in media. Men in their sixties often have younger love interests, like Jack Nicholson in *Something's Gotta Give*. Research has shown that about five percent of men over 65 are pictured on television, which is more common than older women. Older woman's bodies are not often exposed on television, except in hospitalized settings, and have traditionally been depicted negatively, i.e., "incapacitated, incompetent, pathetic, and the subject of ridicule."[36] Hollywood casts with aging actresses in the 1990s rarely had grey or white hair. Contrary to men (almost all age-appropriately grey), most women dyed their hair shades of red, blonde, or brunette. Older-looking actresses and "older gray-haired models" for fashion were generally not accepted. The grey-haired women endorsed ageism and sexism discrimination in the job markets of Hollywood by concealing their hair with dye.[37]

Generally, the stereotypical roles in Hollywood for older women have leadership roles as the adoring grandmother, awful stepmother, and aged female boss. Older adult women in sexual roles are played by women with youthful appearances who usually have had plastic surgery. Cher, for example, "looks much younger at forty-six that she did at forty, as most actresses of her generation, for whom face-lifts are virtually routine."[38]

35. Meyers, *Something's Gotta Give*.
36. Grogan, "Age, Ethnicity, Social Class, and Sexuality," 146.
37. Gerike, "On Gray Hair and Oppressed Brains," 39.
38. Bordo, "Unbearable Weight," 25.

Actresses undergoing cosmetic surgery in Hollywood continue to flood the media, planting cultural expectations of what aging women's bodies *should* look like "in which the surface of the female body ceases to age physically as the body grows chronologically older."[39]

In *Something's Gotta Give*, when Harry is released from the hospital, he stays with Erica in the Hamptons because he has not been cleared to go back home to New York City. Erica stays up late working on a play, and Harry is also up late as well, for they both are having trouble sleeping. She undresses and is on her way to take a shower when Harry gets confused, trying to get to the kitchen.

> Erica: AHHHH! (naked)
>
> Harry: OH! Holy!
>
> Erica: AHHH! NOOO! NOO! NOO! (runs off)
>
> Harry: Oh God! (covering his eyes) Oh, wow! Oh, I'm sorry. Oh, God, am I sorry.
>
> Erica: What are you doing?!?...
>
> Harry: I didn't really see anything. Just...Just your tits.[40]

Although Harry emphasizes the point of not wanting to see *an older woman* naked, the film industry ventured to show her (Erica) naked. Like in *Something's Gotta Give*, society favors the relationship between Harry and Marin over Erica and Julian, an older man and younger woman, versus an older woman and younger man, respectively. The message from the media is consistent. Men in Hollywood reflect aging with a "sexy and heroic image, whereas women" reach a judgment of being "invisible" with aging.[41]

Television media heavily influence women's sexual behaviors. An analysis of television media, consisting of twenty-five primetime programs focusing on representations of heteronormative sexuality and gender, was portrayed six hundred and sixty-two times in the fifty-one hours of television recorded programming. The data from this study showed that men represented on television value women based on their appearance, are persistently consumed by thoughts of sexual fantasies, are initiators of sex, and openly talk about sex. Conversely, the study showed that women on television were judged by their sexual behaviors.

39. Bordo, "Unbearable Weight," 25.
40. Meyers, *Something's Gotta Give*.
41. Jones, "Aging Heroes," 182.

For instance, how a woman dressed would portray a "good girl" versus a "bad girl," yet were also encouraged to use their bodies to attract good-looking, wealthy men. Women *should* use their smiles, flirt, and act ditsy to gain a man's attention. This heteronormative message integrates romantic and sexual experiences that play out as "real men pursue sex" and "good girls set sexual limits."[42] One of the critical points that this study outlines for women's sexuality is that women "walk the precarious line between making themselves sexually available to men and being appropriately demure-the tension at the heart of femininity."[43]

In *Good Luck to You, Leo Grande*, towards the end of the film, Nancy says: "It is a very powerful thing, sexual fulfillment. It makes you feel . . . well, it made me feel invincible . . . . I have felt more alive and powerful this last month than I can ever remember."[44] Such a depiction is rare. Indeed, in my literature review, I found one film analysis performed in the United States, which reviewed thirteen films (released from 2002 to 2008). In this analysis, the author reported that midlife women's sexuality is subdued, and relationships were depicted as "age-appropriate." The study also suggests that women's sexuality is valued and essential; and that women *should* place their sexual desire, pleasure, and emotional needs before a man's. As suggested in this discussion, these films indicate that more films are still needed to depict women's sexuality in a positive light.[45]

An older woman heroine at the center of sexuality captures the prominent themes of films like *Something's Gotta Give* and *Good Luck to You, Leo Grande*. *Something's Gotta Give* was one of the first movies that "defends [women's] desirability for the first time in Hollywood films... [advocating] for a new way of thinking about age and desire."[46] In the movie *Good Luck to You, Leo Grande*, Nancy pushes the boundaries of the sexual norms by not only hiring a younger male sex work but also bringing a list of sexual activities she would like to perform, showing a shift in the less passive role portrayed in other movies:

> Leo: You don't have to do any of this

---

42. Kim, Sorsoli, Collins, Zylbergold, Schooler, and Tolman, "From Sex to Sexuality," 146.
43. Timmermans, and Van den Bulck, "Casual Sexual Scripts on the Screen, 1482.
44. Hyde, *Good Luck to You, Leo Grande*.
45. Weitz, "Changing the Scripts," 30.
46. Sims, "Genre, Fame, and Gender," 209.

Nancy: No, I know. I . . . I want to be a woman of the world. There are nuns out there with more sexual experience than me. It's embarrassing.

At one point early in the movie, she does have the stereotypical insecurities of moral dilemma, body image, and inability to perform oral sex well. However, by the movie's end, she gains more confidence, gets over the moral encompass of being a previous religious education teacher, and stands naked in the mirror. This is one of two movies that has not used a body double to show an older woman's nude body. When Emma Thompson was interviewed about this scene, standing in a hotel room naked at sixty-two years old, looking at the lines and folds of her body, "It's a neutral gaze. It's not approval—'Oh my God, I look great.' And it's not, 'Oh my God, I look horrible.' It's, 'That's my body. And I know that it can bring me joy.'"[47]

CONCLUSION

The films discussed in this chapter depict white older women in heteronormative relationships, and thus the discussion is limited in this way. A quantitative study analysis examining older adults in American primetime television series (between 2004–2018) revealed that out of 33 different series, 112 episodes, 2,003 characters, only 133 were older adults, concluding small shifts toward more representation of older adults as well as 85+ adults, lesbian, gay, bisexual, and transgender (LGBT) persons, people with disabilities, and some ethnic minorities.[48] Even though reflective dimensions gain strides toward older women expressing sexuality, people of color and underrepresented minorities, and people in the LGBT community, there continues to be a lack of representation in television. To date, only one television series, *Grace and Frankie*, has ventured into portrayals of characters with sexualities and identities of older gay couples, and one television series with a transgender older woman, *Transparent*. However, the series was produced for streaming, not primetime television programming.[49]

So, the heterosexual script is pervasively normalized, and our culture still seems uncomfortable with sexuality in older adults, particularly

47. Hornaday, "Emma Thompson Wants Us to Like Our Bodies."
48. Markov, "Diversity and Age Stereotypes," 2760.
49. Markov, "Diversity and Age Stereotypes," 2749.

for miscegenation couples and the non-cisgender communities. Gender socialization[50] within the media and television for women in recent years seem to be changing, shifting toward positive sexual identity. The sexual content of media has been increasingly more liberal with the integration of "new sexual selves" caused by media's influence on family dynamics and malleability.[51] In one of the scenes in *Good Luck to You, Leo Grande*, Nancy talks with Leo, stating that sex "was her only freedom"[52] she had ever had.

In the last two years, only three mainstream movies have featured older women and sex. To date, two films released in 2023 showcase women and sexuality: *80 for Brady* and *Book Club 2*, which also "indicate [positive] paths ... in later life."[53] It is liberating to have two movies released in two years that showcase older women seeking men for their sexual desires—this is both stimulating and humanizing for women of all ages. Socialization of healthy sexual practices is significant throughout the lifespan, yet still has an opportunity to reflect the 39 million people that are 65 years and older, 2.7 million LGBT adults aged 50 and older, and 1.1 million LGBT 65+ living in the United States.[54] Aging and its effects on sexuality and older women should be normalized in the media so that women, like the women who visit their doctors and those who come to my clinic, are more comfortable exploring sexuality with all the impressions that life brings, which include the pressures of society and media. It is my hope that women will stand in the mirror and experience aging acceptance as well as connection—both with themselves and their partners.[55]

---

50. Gender socialization is the process of teaching individuals how to behave under the social expectations (from parents, teachers, schools, friends, television/film) of their gender roles. See Eddens, "Gender Stereotypes."

51. Gagnon and Simon, *Sexual Conduct*, 224.

52. Hyde, *Good Luck to You, Leo Grande*.

53. Cole, Carlin, and Carson, *Medical Humanities*, 158.

54. See "Understanding Issues Facing LGBT Older Adults," https://www.lgbtmap.org/policy-and-issue-analysis/understanding-issues-facing-lgbt-older-adults.

55. Pearlman, "Late Mid-Life Astonishment: Disruptions to Identity and Self-Esteem," 6.

PART FOUR

Religion, Spirituality, and the Anthropocene

8

The Fourth Age as a "Feared" Old Age
Issues for Understanding Spirituality and Religion in Later Life

PAUL HIGGS

INTRODUCTION

IN *OLD MAN COUNTRY*[1] Thomas Cole recounts discussing old age with Daniel Callahan, the former director of the Hastings Center and author of *Setting Limits: Medical Goals in an Aging Society*.[2] In his late eighties, and with a host of illnesses including emphysema, asthma, and mobility problems, Callahan felt that he had accomplished everything he wished to achieve and was ambivalent about living for much longer. As if echoing themes from his seminal work on the interplay between increasing life expectancy and the cultural importance of extending it, Callahan questions the value of a life defined by corporeal limitations. Cole describes this as "entering the Fourth Age" and reflects on the continuing significance of Callahan's bioethical framing of later life. Cole's interview with Callahan therefore acts as a point of entry in thinking about how the conceptual figurations of the Third and Fourth Ages as developed by Chris Gilleard and myself connect with the bioethical dilemmas thrown up by

1. Cole, *Old Man Country*.
2. Callahan, *Setting Limits*.

the apparent irreconcilability of these challenges to a unitary notion of old age. In particular, I wish to look at the idea of the "completed self" as an extension of Third Age culture, and the valorization of individual choice and agency in avoiding the travails of "deep old age." While choosing voluntary euthanasia as a means to avoid a personally unwanted old age is comparatively rare position across Europe and North America, in the Netherlands it has become the subject of parliamentary debate and in a number of other countries it has been the focus of discussions about the right to choose when to end one's life. Such developments chime, I contend, with important elements of Third Age culture that prioritize choice and autonomy over acceptance and set up challenges for the place of aging in contemporary western societies.

Although debates about these issues may be framed in terms of secular bioethics, much of the battleground is occupied by religious thinking about the meaning of life at all stages. Hence, a key part of this contribution is also concerned with how ideas of the Third Age and Fourth Age impact on contemporary Christianity and its relationship to the valorization of individual agency and choice. In Cole's interview with Callahan, it is interesting to note that Callahan himself was opposed to the notion of voluntary euthanasia becoming an accepted part of public policy in healthcare even though such choice could be justified in bioethical terms. In the same chapter Cole also made a point of interviewing Sidney Callahan, Daniel's wife who was a public intellectual in her own right. She had a different take on living with the disabilities of old age. Drawing on decades of Catholic social activism she emphasized a more holistic approach to these corporeal limitations utilising the resources of theology, community, and communication. The contrasts between these two individuals may be instructive, both in terms of how the coordinates of later life are being constructed and how older embedded religious worldviews are being challenged and maybe reconstructed.

THE THIRD AGE

Before discussing the issues surrounding notions of the completed life, it is important to outline what I believe to be the context of contemporary later life and why I think that the terms Third Age and Fourth Age are so important in these and many other debates. There is ample evidence to support the argument that the social and cultural changes within western society have made the unitary category of old age problematic. We know that the institutionalization of the life course in the late nineteenth and the early to mid-twentieth century gave rise to our contemporary understanding of old age in terms of retirement. However, for most of that period, the nature of old age was still associated with infirmity, decline, and death. Only a minority of the male population reached retirement age, and the older population were viewed as a problem for the state and its welfare services. The latter part of the twentieth century, however, witnessed dramatic shifts in both morbidity and mortality for the retired population and a decline in poverty rates as pension systems started to mature. Retirement for many meant a period of relatively healthy post-work life. Such a retirement became a normative expectation for many people living in North America, Europe, and Australasia—a period that could last not just years but decades. In summary, the social space of later life has become substantially removed from the worlds of old age experienced by previous generations and which had provided the coordinates for the moral understanding of growing old.

In what follows I will be drawing on the "Cultures of Aging"[3] approach as a lens to understand the impact of what I see as the generationally-based cultures of the Third Age and their assumptions regarding the "natural" nature of aging.[4] These assumptions have been transformed by the emphasis on agency, choice, and lifestyle that is emblematic of the cultural field of the Third Age. Often the emphasis on an "ageless" later life creates a cultural and social distance from those identified as frail, dependent, or simply old. This category which represents a feared "real" old age is seen to constitute a key element in the social imaginary of a Fourth Age.[5]

The current idea of the Third Age can be attributed to the late Cambridge historian, Peter Laslett, in his book *A Fresh Map of Life*.[6] Using demography to underpin how old age had been transformed at both a social and an individual level, Laslett's work highlighted the distinction between a fit, healthy, and productive later life and an old age that was dogged by ill health, incapacity, and dependency. Feeling that old age was treated as a residual category of social and health policy, he believed that the possibilities of improved health and greater longevity could allow the

3. Gilleard and Higgs, *Cultures of Ageing*.
4. Jones and Higgs, "Natural, the Normal and the Normative."
5. Higgs and Gilleard, "Frailty, Abjection and the 'Othering' of the Fourth Age."
6. Laslett, *A Fresh Map of Life*

Third Age to be viewed as a veritable "crown of life" where older individuals, freed from the responsibilities of work and family, could pursue their own interests in ways that benefited the communities in which they lived. Laslett's tone was very much exhortatory; identifying the Third Age as a self-selected time to achieve personal fulfilment and personal cultivation. He believed that in the circumstances of the Third Age, people needed to be encouraged to become more self-aware of this need for agency. This voluntarist aspect of Laslett's vision can be seen in organizations such as the University of the Third Age (U3A), which take this combination of self-development and cultural awareness as their *raison d'etre*.[7] This focus may explain why Laslett's vision of the Third Age received a muted response in the UK with many writers seeing it as only relating to the relatively affluent retirement opportunities of middle-class men[8]. In the USA, on the other hand, the idea meshed with more positive ideas of aging such as productive aging and wasn't considered so controversial that it couldn't be incorporated into views of various models of "successful aging."

In a series of books starting with *Cultures of Ageing: Self, Citizen and the Body*, Chris Gilleard and I have rethought the concept of the Third Age so that it less reliant on being understood as a personalized set of choices and instead is presented in terms of the interconnections between social processes, material resources, and cultural dynamics. Drawing upon Pierre Bourdieu's cultural sociology and Karl Mannheim's sociology of generations, we have argued that the Third Age is primarily a generational cultural field, with varying levels of participation by individuals in later life. This field is marked out by the entry into later life of a particular consumer-oriented post-Second World War generation.[9] Much has been written about the seismic importance of this baby boomer generation and its transformation of society and its institutions. Of equal importance has been the transformation of mass culture and embedded notions of normativity. These changes have challenged patterns of social authority as well as the understanding of personal relationships and the family. The rise of youth culture in the 1960s created a widely felt "generational schism," one which emphasized the rejection of that deemed "old" in favor of what was consciously "new." Chris Gilleard and I have argued that it is this schism that has provided the foundations for the

7. Laslett, "The Third Age, the Fourth Age and the Future."
8. Bury, "Ageing, Gender and Sociological Theory."
9. Gilleard and Higgs, *Contexts of Ageing*.

emergence of the Third Age.[10] The aging of the baby boomer cohort has shaped a distinctive cultural field, whose parameters of personal choice and individualized lifestyle have sustained the pursuit of "distinction" into later life. For this retired generation there is a virtue in continuing to make purposeful choices about how they wish to live and what they think the choices should be. In the process, the emerging later lifestyles of this generation are a continuation of the rejection of the institutionalized structures of the life course particularly as they relate to a restricting and potentially dependent old age.

THE FOURTH AGE

Thus far, we have only looked at the accentuation of the positive within the cultures of the Third Age, but even in Laslett's conception of the Third Age there was an old age that acted as a limit to the Third Age—one that was defined by ill-health, incapacity, and dependency. This idea of the Fourth Age compresses all the disabilities and dependencies of old age into a "compression of morbidity" which marks a terminal decline leading to death. Less prosaically the gerontologist Paul Baltes also saw a distinction between the openness of the Third Age and the negative realities he saw as typifying the Fourth Age. As a lifespan developmental psychologist researching aging in the 1970s and 1980s, he was keen to refute the idea of mental decline in later life and argued for the continuing plasticity of cognitive function in people in their fifties, sixties and seventies. Much later he became interested in the loss of that plasticity in cognitive function at much older ages and saw that the plasticity and potential present at earlier parts of later life was replaced by processes of decline that could not be mitigated even by comprehensive social intervention.[11]

Having discussed the importance of the "new aging" brought about by the contemporary cultures of aging, Chris Gilleard and I have also noted the importance of this "feared old age" in acting as a boundary or "event horizon" for the Third Age.[12] For us the Fourth Age is not a cultural field but rather a "social imaginary,"[13] mediated by the cultural

10. Gilleard and Higgs, "The Third Age."
11. Baltes and Smith, "New Frontiers in the Future of Aging."
12. Higgs and Gilleard, *Rethinking Old Age*.
13. Chris Gilleard and I have borrowed the concept of the social imaginary to

representations of the dependency and decline of the "really old" and the attendant practices of social and health policy. The social imaginary of the Fourth Age projects particular aspects of incapacitating old age as a terminal destination, a location stripped of the capacities that allow others to articulate choice and autonomy. Infamously we have used the metaphor of a cosmological "black hole" to explain society's lack of comprehension about how lives dominated by cognitive decline, frailty, and abjection can have any meaning let alone desirability. Consequently, one of the dilemmas for people as they grow older is negotiating what we have called the "event horizon" between being able to participate in the cultures of the Third Age as an agentic individual and being deemed too "confused" or "frail" to manage this successfully. This "risk" may then trigger the intervention of social and health care services with the concomitant consequence that the older person becomes truly a "subject" of the discourses of the Fourth Age.[14]

THE COMPLETED LIFE

Given Paul Baltes relatively pessimistic assessment about late later life, it is not surprising that he believed that the principal task in the Fourth Age was the maintenance of dignity in life and that furthermore such an imperative could involve the setting of self-chosen limits to life.[15] This reflected research that he had conducted on popular expectations of aging and longevity. Not only was there evidence that many respondents believed that the ideal lifespan should conclude around the ages of 80–84, but also most of those studied expressed a wish to have control over their own death. Chris Gilleard in commenting on Baltes concludes:

---

describe the Fourth Age to highlight the way that it is separate from the cultures of the Third Age in which individuals can participate to varying degrees, according to their circumstances. The social imaginary has been described by Charles Taylor as "the ways people imagine their social existence, how they fit together with others . . . and the deeper normative notions and images that underlie these expectations." See Taylor, *Modern Social Imaginaries*, 23. Consequently, in relation to the Fourth Age imaginary, it frames how old age and those deemed to be frail, abject, lacking autonomy and needing extensive care are viewed by those who are not defined as exhibiting these markers. In the context of the Third Age, it embodies the long-established belief that old age presents a distressing prospect for all who do not die before old age sets in and which places the person 'outside' of the pleasures, activities and rewards of everyday life. See Gilleard and Higgs, "The Fourth Age and the Concept of a 'Social Imaginary.'"

14. Gilleard and Higgs, "Aging without Agency."
15. Baltes "Facing our Limits."

"His research suggested there may be an amount of life that exceeds the desire for life. The right to life, liberty, and longevity may need matching by another right—to an ending, to limits."[16] In a similar vein, the influential physician Ezekiel J. Emanuel's article in *Atlantic* magazine "Why I Hope to Die at 75" expressed the view encapsulated in his title; that life until seventy-five allowed an individual to attain all that a "complete life" would aspire to, whereas life after seventy-five was progressively marked by trends towards "faltering and declining" and that it would be better to avoid rather than extend.[17]

While neither Baltes and Emanuel were advocates of voluntary euthanasia, movements surrounding the "right-to-die" have become significant in countries from Australia to the United States. Often constructed in relation to issues of the intolerable suffering that can result from incurable medical conditions, it is also the case that such movements are part of broader social movements espousing individual autonomy. Different nations have adapted to calls for the right-to-die in different ways often adopting a piecemeal approach meaning that such rights can differ considerably depending on the legal situation in differing jurisdictions. However, most of the debate about voluntary euthanasia has been conducted around the opportunity for individuals to be released from the consequences of medical conditions, calls for the validity of a "completed life" as an acceptable reason for such actions have surfaced in countries such as the Netherlands. The Dutch civil society group *Uit Vrije Wil* (Of Free Will) proposed that the emancipation and self-determination of older citizens could only be seen to be achieved if they were allowed to decide about the conditions of their own deaths. In particular, the initiative cited wide-spread fear by many older people of ending life in a care home, consequently, older people should be free to be able consider their life "completed" before this point arrives and that they therefore should be able to request euthanasia on these grounds.

Since the original initiative began in 2010 with a petition containing 116,871 signatures demanding the legalization of assisted suicide in cases where an individual claims to have lived a "completed life," there have been parliamentary consultations and two proposed legal changes to the euthanasia laws in the Netherlands. As yet these legal challenges have not been successful.[18] As Bernhard Weicht and Bernhard Forchtner have

16. Gilleard, "Finitude, Choice and the Right to Die," 1243.
17. Emanuel, "Why I Hope to Die at 75."
18. "Completed Life Euthanasia Proposal Needs for Safeguards against Misuse."

pointed out: "The initiative that started the debate on the possibilities and conditions of the completed life a decade ago has thus managed to inspire and shape the political discourse profoundly."[19] This discourse can be understood within the framework of conflicts between the different cultures of later life presented in the Third and Fourth Ages. The capacity to be able to choose is seen as a cornerstone of Third Age culture and this can be extended to the idea of the "good death" and the adoption of the significance of what can be termed as "deathstyles." Commentators on the completed life initiative such as Els van Wijngaarden point out that in countries with legalized euthanasia the choice implicit in the organized death can lead to the acceptance of the completed life.[20] Moreover, as Weicht and Forchtner's study of the coverage of the completed life debate in Dutch newspapers discovered the resistance to the initiative split what they called [the] liberals from the religious. The former saw their motivations centering around autonomy while the latter saw the issue in terms of human worth. This division relates to much more than just the persistence of religious views in Dutch civil society, rather it shines a light on one of the ways that the re-ordering of the unitary notion of old age into the more dualistic formulations of later life has led to cultural turbulence. In essence the potential for "ageless aging" which can be seen in many aspects of the Third Age not only leads to a distancing from the Fourth Age but also potentially the conclusion that it can be seen as a life not worth living. In this it sets up challenges for the role of Christianity in contemporary democratic societies which is increasingly given the role of defending the notion of old age as the Fourth Age imaginary; whether or not they wish this to be the case.

TRANSFORMING RELIGION AND SPIRITUALITY IN LATER LIFE

In discussing the relevance of the Third and Fourth Ages on thinking about the role of religion in contemporary society, we cannot avoid the long-term rise of secularization across significant parts of the globe. Max Weber's notion of the progressive "disenchantment" of the modern world with religion is probably the best-known of the explanations of

---

19. Weicht and Forchtner, "Negotiating Euthanasia."
20. Van Wijngaarden, Goossensen, and Leget, "The Social–Political Challenges."

the secularization process.[21] While never fully disappearing, the role of religion in mediating much of modern western life has become less influential in society as faith has moved from the public to the private sphere and/or disappeared altogether. This approach seems to describe the fate of the mainstream Christian denominations in Europe and North America concerned as they are with declining congregations and generational disaffiliation.[22] Although the situation in Europe is viewed as more severe than in North America, it is the case that even there the ostensible high levels of religiosity may a much more volatile "faith" market with a corresponding high level of "churn" as individuals and families move from one church or denomination to another. These observations have led to a generally accepted view that within Europe and North America the processes of secularization are quite advanced and that it is irreversible. Consequently, Christian religious belief and practice is seen to be increasingly confined to older cohorts whose practices were set down in societies with very different cultural coordinates.[23] From this, the debate regarding the completed life is one that puts Christianity seemingly at odds with important aspects of the cultures of the Third Age; namely a desire to keep old age at a distance, a feared yet avoidable possibility rather than a necessary component of a completed life. In this rendition, the only meaning that can be attached to old age is that of "unsuccessful" aging and the only option for believers is to accept that their faith endorses acceptance of decline and dependency.

Writers such as John Vincent[24] illustrate this dichotomy, challenging contemporary culture's promotion of "medical immortality," which he argues robs old age of its dignity and its proper place in society. Instead, he calls for an acceptance of the Fourth Age as representing the "real" nature of old age which can be better understood in terms of the "valued symbolic meanings" of religion than through the technological imperatives of the painless "good death." He writes:

> In the Fourth Age older people lose control of their bodies to the medical professionals. Life at this stage is circumscribed by the postponement of death. However, medical knowledge is structured around the preservation of life and the avoidance of death,

21. Jenkins, "Disenchantment, Enchantment and Re-enchantment."
22. Bullivant, *Mass Exodus*.
23. The decline of the Sunday School in the lives of recent cohorts of children is one aspect of this noted by Peter Coleman. Coleman, *Belief and Ageing*, 13.
24. Vincent, *Old Age*.

and involves a sense of failure (and the possibility of accusations of negligence) if life is not preserved . . . . The good death is thought of in bodily terms, not human terms. It is constructed in the right dosage of medication; it is not constructed out of human relationships and symbols that transcend individuals and their bodies.[25]

The rise of secularism in the global west is however a much more complicated project than it is often presented. Not only has religion not disappeared from even western Europe, but there is the possibility that in fact there has been to various degrees a "reenchantment" of the world going on. The German sociologist Jurgen Habermas[26] argues that we live in a "post-secular" world, given that religious affiliation and practice are now more conspicuous than they have been for centuries. Likewise, Zygmunt Bauman[27] has made much of the argument that the attractiveness of the post-modern has its origins in a cultural dissatisfaction with the answers to the problems of contemporary society thrown up by secularized modernity.

This reenchantment takes many forms, but there are aspects of it that also fit into the generational habitus that gave rise to the emergence of the Third Age. The institutionalization of the modern life course can be viewed as a necessary outcome of a rationalized worldview where the government of life is seen as an essential task of the nation state. Rebellion against the institutions and ascriptions of the old order was as much a crucial part of the generational ferment of the 1960s as was its rejection of political consensus. A notable feature of what became seen as the counter-culture was that it also accepted the possibility of different interpretations of what came to be termed spirituality;[28] these often accentuated a lack of systematic doctrine as well as a key role for sensual experience in everyday life.

The distinction between spirituality and religion may be a relatively recent phenomenon as far as the study of religion may be concerned, but in practice the term spirituality is generally used to point to something more personal and private than established religion. As Ellor and McFadden see it, spirituality represents a new kind of hermeneutic.[29] Others

25. Vincent, *Old Age*, 159.
26. Habermas, *An Awareness of What is Missing*.
27. Bauman, *Mortality, Immortality, and Other Life Strategies*.
28. Häberlen, *Beauty is in the Street*.
29. Ellor and McFadden, "Perceptions of the Roles of Religion and Spirituality."

have seen it as the "secularization of spirituality" where spirituality is seen in terms of its capacity to provide sources of meaning and purpose.[30] This is placed in contradistinction to the nature of religion which is often identified as a social and political tool leading to intolerance and divisiveness. While the opposition between spirituality and religion can be made much too stark, with other figures such as Grace Davie coining terms such as "believing not belonging"[31] and "vicarious religion"[32] to point to the more complex relation between religious and spiritual belief, the contrast illustrates the way in which the baby-boomer cohorts have reworked the cultural parameters of what has previously been a key dimension of social life. Bryan Turner has noted the importance of generation in producing what he calls "low-intensity religion"; a form of practice that is individualistic, highly subjective as well as post-institutional.[33] This has been picked up by a number of researchers who have seen more person-centred forms of spirituality leading back to a new conception of religion.

Elizabeth MacKinlay,[34] an Australian Anglican directly addresses the issue of generational change and the significance of the baby-boomer cohorts. She acknowledges that this group emphasizes matters of autonomy, control, and material benefit, but she interprets them as representing the spiritual tasks of aging which the Third Age's promotion of "successful" aging throws up but is unable to address. For MacKinlay, these tasks focus on the self and on personal transcendence. Here she is reflecting themes of "gero-transcendance" developed by Lars Tornstam[35] out of Erik Erikson's theory of stages of psychological development where the last stage of life is marked by the achievement of ego integrity and wisdom. For Tornstam, the achievement of this wisdom lies in the individual shifting concerns from materialistic concerns to more cosmic and transcendental ones where they see their selves as part of a greater universe.[36] The loss of a societal meaning of old age has been a recurring theme in work on this area, work that acknowledges that such issues become of individual interest as people reach their sixties and seventies,

30. Matthews, "Religion and the Secularization of Spirituality."
31. Davie, *Religion in Britain since 1945*.
32. Davie, "Vicarious Religion."
33. Turner, *Religion and Modern Society*.
34. MacKinlay, "Baby Boomers Ageing Well?"
35. Tornstam, "Gerotranscendence."
36. This process can be extended to other faiths, as MacKinlay illustrates in a later work. See MacKinlay "Ageing and Spirituality across Faiths and Cultures."

but which also accepts that old age offers fewer attractions when people are impacted by issues of frailty and dementia.

Consequently, while some are seeking to reimagine the theology of old age by considering what older people are for and others are implementing programs for integrating healthy aging into spiritual development, there seems to be an uncertainty about how aging as old age can be incorporated into contemporary religious practice. One solution seems to be to redefine the public roles of clergy as carrying out generic spiritual work rather than being representatives of denominational interests. In the UK, where there has been a long tradition of Anglican chaplains in National Health Service hospitals and other health care settings, many chaplains are now incorporated into a non-clinical occupational group associated with the delivery of "spiritual care" and graded accordingly. Once again it would seem that secular shifts have transformed the role of religion in the image of the generational habitus of the baby boomers and their progression through the life course.

CHRISTIANITY AND THE FOURTH AGE

How does the problem of the completed life relate to this overview of religion and the Third and Fourth Age? One conclusion is that religion, while not disappearing into a secularized void, has had to adapt many of its assumptions, particularly around individual autonomy and choice. The emphasis on spiritual development and discernment has already made theological strictures seemingly anachronistic particularly in areas such as assisted dying. While this option has been legislated for in many countries, under the concept of "unbearable suffering," it has always been opposed by the major Christian churches from the papal encyclical *Evangelium Vitae* down. If unbearable suffering is not considered a good enough reason to accept an individual's end-of-life choice, then it is unlikely the fears of a Fourth Age would be sufficient cause. Many practitioners in palliative care would contend that their work in providing appropriate end-of-life care can provide a different experience of this terminal phase removing much of the fear of dying in old age.[37] However, even this is unlikely to remove the shadows of the Fourth Age imaginary as it is not something that can be easily refuted or disproved. The fear will remain and the reluctance to embrace it will continue. A consequence of

---

37. Back, Park, Greer, et al., "Clinician Roles in Early Integrated Palliative Care."

these deep roots is that religion *qua* religion is continually pushed back to embracing the Fourth Age ["the dying of the light"] rather than resisting it. Such a position runs counter to the times. After all, for a generation who hoped they "would die before they got old," the potential abjection of a dependent old age is something that cannot be easily contemplated, let alone accommodated. For all the engagement with charitable work carried out by many members of Christian communities, they are as equally likely to avoid getting too close to the social imaginary of the Fourth Age unless they become personally involved with it. This then creates a dilemma for Christianity in the western world.[38] The great irony is that their congregations are aging and contain many people affected by the gravitational pull of the Fourth Age. This, however, may offer opportunities for religion to engage with the social imaginary of the Fourth Age, rather than only offering a vision of an unwanted old age of pain and loss.

Often forgotten in summaries of our work on the Fourth Age is that one of its vectors is the "imperative to care."[39] This imperative can be realized in many different ways and is, given its associations with dependency, part of the feared future represented by the Fourth Age. However, it is also an imperative that needs to be carried out in order that respect for the older person as a person is to be maintained, not just at an instrumental level but also at a cultural one too. The spiritual tasks of aging are challenged by the often co-existence of profound physical and cognitive dependency associated with needing such care. Here, the notions of transcendence, meaning, forgiveness, and gratitude which are often seen as important objectives in the provision of care do not easily extend to life with severe dementia.[40] What is also required is an acceptance of the potential non-reciprocity between those cared for and those who do the caring. Much of what orientates care policy assumes that dignity for the cared for will result in positive results for the staff.[41] This may never occur and may lead to frustration in the social relationships that take place in nursing homes and other forms of congregate care. A more appropriate starting point might be a cultivation of a "selfless" care which accepts that

38. I am aware that much of this chapter focuses on the situation of Australasia, western Europe, and North America. How these issues impact on Christianity in the Global South with its multiplicity of cultures and levels of religiosity is something that is beyond my knowledge. Equally, a lack of familiarity with religions other than Christianity makes the possibility of comment on them unwise.

39. Higgs and Gilleard, *Personhood, Identity and Care in Advanced Old Age*.

40. Tornstam, "Gerotranscendence."

41. Noddings, "The Language of Care Ethics."

the imperative to care is as much a calling as it is an exchange. This can build on the historical legacies of care that have existed in the Christian past as well as in other faith traditions.

Religion is not just a matter of theological and moral orientation. It is almost synonymous with forms of religious practice, the organization of time as well as the performance of rituals. These religious practices can help negotiate the existential challenges of what Malcolm Johnson has called "biographical pain" where long-buried issues that individuals had always intended to "put right" can be addressed and forgiveness achieved.[42] Moreover, it is often the case that institutionalized religion has more resources available to explore the nature of frailty and dependency than secularized medicine. Not only does religion have centuries of experience regarding the end of people's lives; it also has ways of explaining what is occurring to older people's bodies. While it may be the case that individual spiritual beliefs can also draw on these resources, the absence of the embeddedness and ritual of collective belief limits the full impact of these capacities. Given this, the pastoral role of religion may be one of its greatest strengths as it provides succour to its adherents. Even with regard to dementia, participation in well-practiced rituals and prayers constitutes a form of engagement that can be helpful for those with the condition as well as those caring for them. Julian Hughes[43] sees that a theological approach may also permit different views of bodily transcendence and personhood; ones that acknowledge that responding to rituals and familiar prayers of individuals severely affected by dementia is an affirming behavior. As a result, it might be argued that there is an important continuing role for religion in situating responses to the problems posed by the Fourth Age imaginary. These might include developing different discourses around the moral worth of persons, the importance of compassion as well as the potential for the mobilization of the idea of pity in contemporary debates around social policy. This may not make the social imaginary of the Fourth Age disappear, but it can raise the possibility of a "more than human" response to the various situations activating its imaginary.

---

42. Johnson, "Spirituality, Biographical Review and Biographical Pain at the End of Life in Old Age."

43. Hughes, "A Situated Embodied View of the Person with Dementia."

CONCLUSION

I began this chapter by considering the paradox that faced Daniel Callahan as he came to the realization that his own life was constrained by the limitations of old age and that according to his own thinking such a life had little purpose. He was opposed to voluntary euthanasia but also expressed the view that continuing to live had little purpose. Although he was not a baby boomer, his dilemma illustrated some of the points regarding the position of old age in modern society that have become apparent in both arguments for voluntary euthanasia and more recently the idea of the "completed life." These points regarding the importance of autonomy and choice, in the generational habitus of post-war cohorts, have along with a rejection of the ascribed positions of old age led to the emergence of both the cultures of the Third Age and the social imaginary of the Fourth Age. This in conjunction with the diminishing the role of Christianity in western society and the growth of a more individualised spirituality have presented challenges to the role of religion in situating later life. This is not however a simple tale of the triumph of secularization over religious belief, rather as we have seen it represents different dimensions of post-secularity. Christianity, as it relates to later life, has adopted different responses to these challenges including taking a more active interest in personal spiritual development. These may help churches relate to Third Age culture, but they are still left with the knotty problem of the vicissitudes of aging itself which require different responses and resources. Here, instead of being left with the residual category of deep old age as a marker of its own irrelevance, Christianity can look to its own traditions to see that those enveloped in the Fourth Age gain the recognition of their own worth as persons worthy of being cared for. This invocation of the role of religion emerges from Sidney Callahan's interview with Cole where she tells him that Dan lacks the spiritual and psychological resources to find meaning or comfort in the midst of physical decline. Something that she has been able to utilize in her own life as she grows older.

9

Aging in the Anthropocene
Notes on Death, Meaning, and Intergenerational Justice Inspired by Thomas Cole

LARRY CHURCHILL

"In rebuilding a moral economy for an extended life course, we must not only attend to questions of justice within and between different stages of life, we must also forge a new sense of the meanings and purposes of the last half of life."[1] —THOMAS COLE

THE SOCIAL AND SPIRITUAL ANCHORING OF LIFE'S MEANINGS

In his fascinating series of lectures, *Death and the Afterlife*, Samuel Scheffler argues that we place more value in the continuation of human life after our own deaths than in our own afterlife. Imagine, he says, that "the earth would be completely destroyed thirty days after your death in a collision with a giant asteroid."[2] He invites us to reflect on how many of our most important life projects we do not expect to complete before death but rely on others to take up and push forward. Harry Frankfurt, in one of the accompanying commentaries, puts it this way: "if people thought

---

1. Cole, *Journey of Life*, 237.
2. Scheffler, *Death and the Afterlife*, 18.

that mankind did not have a future their ability to lead value-laden lives would be serious eroded."[3]

I strongly suspect that Scheffler and Frankfurt are right, with the obvious caveat that one could always find some egoists who, in David Hume's words, prefer the destruction of the world to the scratching of their finger.[4] My more serious claim, discussed by neither Scheffler nor his four commentators, is that this is an age-dependent valuation. At least this is true for me. The reasons for this are likely numerous, but I will highlight a few.

One reason is that as I age I am less invested in my personal survival generally. Aging has taught me that I was not designed for an indefinite period. My knees and hips are less flexible, my gait less confident, my eyes more troubled by early signs of cataracts and glaucoma. Everything works less well than it once did. I am not tempted to think—as I pretended throughout my forty's—that I am just a little over twenty-five! It was a fantasy then, and it is unimaginable now. My younger brother has been dead for four years, and more than a third of my high school class is gone.

Another factor that makes me less concerned about a personal afterlife is that I have no clear conviction about what it would look like, unless I take Mark Twain's advice: "Heaven for climate, Hell for company."[5] It has been a long time since I believed that there is a deity who tallies our actions and intentions, or measures our faith, to reward the righteous in an afterlife. While I do claim a spiritual life, it has been sheared of specific beliefs about what follows death. My chief problem with organized, standard-brand religion is the preponderance of belief systems, including afterlife beliefs, and the dearth of compassionate practices. Most established religions police what kinds of experiences can count as "spiritual" or "sacred." Yet spiritual experiences and expressions seem polymorphous and without obvious limits. Consider the wide range of human activities that have been reported as conduits for the sacred—praying, meditating, and singing, but also dancing, eating, and a variety

3. Scheffler, *Death and the Afterlife*, 139.
4. Hume, *Treatise of Human Nature*, 416. The full quotation is: "Tis not contrary to reason to prefer the destruction of the whole world to the scratching of my finger." Here Hume is emphasizing the cool, dispassionate nature of reason, which he considered unable to move us on moral questions, in contrast to the passions, which he considered the distinctive source of morality. While I do not agree with Hume on all points, I do argue that motives such as biophilia and a deep regard for Earth—essential to our well-being—do spring from a source other than a calculating, efficient reasoning process.
5. Twain, *Wit and Wisdom of Mark Twain*, 28.

of sexual activities, to name only a few. Religions go wrong when they systematize and thereby restrict what can count as holy. Consequently, most of what is now on offer as afterlife beliefs seem like a consumerist version of spirituality that depend on a vanity about human importance I do not share. The homo sapiens track record on compassion for humans different from us, not to mention our regard for other life forms, is, at best, very spotty. Making the case for our spiritual importance or moral superiority would be a very steep climb.

The closest I can come to belief in an afterlife is a sense that I am part of a sacred universe. An incarnational theology means that I could be part of some sacred whole I can intuit but have yet to really understand. By an incarnational theology, I am not referring to any doctrine, but simply to the observation that physical beings of all sorts can bear a sacred imprint. I owe this sense of a sacredness more to the psychology of Abraham Maslow and the poetry of Walt Whitman, among others, than to any theological doctrine.

Maslow is better known for his "hierarchy of needs," but he also was a brilliant observer of human spiritual life, which he describes as centered in "peak experiences."[6] Such experiences entail the sense that the world is sublimely beautiful, where ego-concerns fall away, and others are seen as intrinsically valuable. The universe itself is perceived as a place where I belong, and have always belonged, a vast interconnected network where evil is reconciled. This kind of experience issues in feelings of awe and wonder, and responses of gratitude, reverence, and worship. I am attracted to this description because this is how it has sometimes been for me, especially when I was out in nature rather than at my desk.

Whitman has been a touchstone for me since my youth, and his lyrical mysticism captures something most theological doctrines do not. In *Leaves of Grass*, he writes:

> Why should I wish to see God better than this day?
> I see something of God each hour of the twenty-four, and each moment then,
> In the faces of men and women I see God, and in my own face in the glass;
> I find letters from God dropped in the street, and every one is signed by God's name,
> And I leave them where they are,
> For I know that others will punctually come forever and ever.[7]

6. Maslow, *Religions, Values and Peak Experiences*, 91–96.
7. Whitman, *Leaves of Grass*, 74.

One of the marks of a truly spiritual life was put forward by Paul Ricoeur, expressed by Oliver Abel, in his "Introduction" to Ricoeur's posthumously published *Living Up to Death*. Living a spiritual life means renunciation of all ego concerns and getting beyond every consideration of rewards, punishments, or retribution.[8] Virtue truly is, as the Stoics have long taught, its own reward. Anticipating an afterlife payoff for virtue only diminishes its value.

But there is also something more going on with my conviction than my afterlife is less important than the future of others who will follow me. Aging persons always reach a transition or decision point about whether they have had enough. But enough of *what*? Enough of putting one's own personal survival and flourishing high on the list? Enough life for a sense of fulfillment or completion, or enough suffering and dependence, if a person's disabilities are large and progressive? There are many variables in this calculus, and clearly it is as individualized as we are.

A baseball analogy may be helpful here. For me this is a sense that I've had my innings, my times at bat, my swings at the pitches that life throws. Some trips to the plate were hits, some were easy outs, a few walks, and occasionally I was hit by a wild pitch. But whatever my batting average, I've had enough turns. Wanting more times at bat to improve my average seems both immature and foolhardy. Others deserve their time to shine. And, besides, I can't read the curve ball or slider very well anymore, and being anxious for a hit makes me prone to swing at pitches outside the strike zone. It is time to relinquish my place in the lineup. I am still OK to sit in the dugout and cheer, and even to give advice: "Don't get suckered by the high fastball." I could pinch-hit in an emergency, but don't put me in the starting lineup. I'm done. Striving for more youthful or middle-age fulfillment distracts me from developing the deeper meanings of elder life.

In my late seventies, my life has been very fortunate by almost any reckoning; I wake up most mornings with some surprise that I am still here and functioning reasonably well. My most common feeling is one of gratitude,[9] and my most common hope is that those I love will also have long, satisfying lives. My death tomorrow would be sad for some who know me, but in no sense a tragedy. The tragedy would be to not die in a timely way and to live too long, especially if my continued life were a substantial burden for me or those caring for me. Once diminishment

---

8. Ricoeur, *Living Up to Death*, xiv.
9. Sacks, *Gratitude*.

and decline are expected and accepted events in life, I think most elders deep down harbor fears of living into a time when they are "all but dead," or "as good as dead," precisely because our lives can then serve no larger purpose. I have seen this is my work in hospitals, and in my own family. The 20th century life-extending-but-not-restorative technologies have given a new poignancy to Solon's ancient dictum, "No man should be called happy till his death."[10]

MEANING IN AGING

The question is sometimes posed whether the meaning of life as we age is discovered or invented. Can we find it, or is it up to us to make it? Yet this question poses traps that must be identified and avoided.

The first trap comes from the assumption that there must be some singular meaning to aging—i.e., *the* meaning of aging—typically imagined as a higher wisdom available for those who persist with the quest after the usual sources for meaning have atrophied. The question should be posed in a plural mode. What *meanings* can attend old age? The search for a singular and essentialist meaning runs contrary to experience and typically ends in dogmatism.

The second trap lies in the either/or form of the question. My experience is one of both/and. In childhood and my early adult years, a meaning structure was there in the customs and rhythms of my family of origin. Then, within my family of generativity, I had choices about whether to modulate or adapt those customs and practices, complicated by the fact that my spouse had brought her own. So, discovery was layered with rediscovery and appraisal, and invention comes in through adaptation of what one thinks is best at the time in a cultural context quite different from that of my childhood. Note that any new and on-going meanings are the work of several people, both in the sense of participation by spouses and friends, and in the sense of influences of the ever-changing cultural ethos.

The layering of meanings that results might be described as a palimpsest, or a document erased and written over, but with some of the original writing still visible. As life continues, my sources of meaning change again as new issues emerge and their resolutions are enacted in

10. Ovid, as quoted in Montaigne, *Complete Essays of Montaigne*, 54. The original source is likely Herodotus, and it seems to be a common sentiment in ancient Greece. It also appears in Sophocles's *Oedipus Rex*.

middle age, with their significance folded into the existing patterns of writing. Entering old age, with child rearing and career behind me, still more issues and resolutions are recorded on the text, with both loss and gain. I have lost the satisfactions of clear and persistent everyday reassurances that I am someone of importance, doing something worthwhile, that I am seen and heard, and that my intentions and aims are understood and shared by those around me, whether adult children, extended family, colleagues, students, or institutions. But the gain is also substantial. In large measure, meaning in life now comes not from *what* I do, but from *who* I am. In one sense this is freeing, since I no longer worry much about meeting any exterior standard, and the internal measures seem truer, if more humbling. Yet this internal metric of self and meanings can also be more challenging. So, while I still need the recognition and support of others for whatever I now take my life to be about, most days I am called upon to be my own judge. Can I live up to my own ideals for a worthwhile way of living in later life?

MEANING IN AGING-AND-DEATH

The better question is one that includes the dimension that is implicit in my aging, namely, my finitude, my limited lifespan. How do I discover-and-invent my meanings for aging and death?[11] This more holistic approach is the one expressed in this quotation from Thomas Cole: "Aging is a moral and spiritual frontier because its unknowns, terrors, and mysteries cannot be successfully crossed without humility and self-knowledge, without love and compassion, without *acceptance of physical decline and mortality*, and a sense of the sacred."[12] Note the way here that in surveying the "moral and spiritual frontier," Cole brings mortality into play, as accompanying physical decline. This should alert us to the idea that meaning in aging and meaning in death are a package, best explored together.

In *Sunday Morning*, poet Wallace Stevens says, "Death is the mother of beauty."[13] The same could be said of meaning; death has many children in the sense that awareness of death heightens the sense of transience and

---

11. A more developed version of this thesis of aging-and-death as a unit of meaning can be found in Churchill, "Accepting and Embracing Our Mortality."
12. Cole, *Journey of Life*, 243, emphasis added.
13. Stevens, "Sunday Morning," 66–70.

fragility of everything—and gives it a new luster. Knowing that we will eventually lose everything we value and love makes what time we have more precious. This understanding is as old as Homer. In *The Odyssey* we see Odysseus forgoing immortal life with the goddess Kalypso with the hopes of returning to Ithaca and a mortal life with the aging Penelope.[14] The reason for his choice is wrapped up in the meaning-making processes of a mortal life that are not available to timeless deities. Eternal life presents an endless number of occasions of good and bad decisions, for love and happiness.[15] Unlike mortal beings, Kalypso cannot know the longing for something fragile and passing. She does not share this human vulnerability, or the joys and sorrows that attend it. Martha Nussbaum has expressed this well: "The peculiar beauty of *human* excellence just is its vulnerability."[16] The possibilities for meaning in old age arise with the realization of finitude. As the Psalmist put it, "Teach us to number our days that we can get a heart of wisdom."[17] The meaning possible in old age that was not available before lies precisely in the nearness to death, in the more frequent reminders that we are only here for a while, and that the days that are left have a depth that previously we had not noticed. This depth could be some stunning new insight into the nature of God, or ourselves, but more often, in my experience, this insight is simply in the quotidian rhythms, in the realization that the ordinary things we have always had are something miraculous, gifts we could not have earned. Instead of a puzzling search for meaning in old age, meaning often arrives at our front door, dressed in the garb of the everyday. But first we must relinquish the sources of meaning we are prone to hold onto, those carefully curated meanings of youth and middle age that served us so well, but that in old age become impediments.

So, to add to Cole's thesis, it is not just the acceptance of decline and death, but the *embrace* of decline and death that makes for meaning in old age. Still, it would be a mistake to think that accepting and even embracing one's death is a stopping point; I suspect it is only the beginning, as we start to wonder what kind of life we are leaving behind for others. If the survival of humanity matters to us, as Scheffler claims, we will be naturally led to wonder what kind of life the survivors will have. As I write in 2023, the realistic picture is a very sobering one.

14. Homer, *Odyssey*, 93–94.
15. Churchill, "Odysseus's Bed; Agamemnon's Bath," 1–13.
16. Nussbaum, *Fragility of Goodness*, 2.
17. Ps 90:12, New English Version.

What links the search for meaning in old age to the problems of climate change? In what follows, I will argue that one important source for meaning in old age is intergenerational fidelity and justice. Meaning can be found for elders by joining the fight for the planet, and for the future generations of humankind.

FROM THE IMAGINED CATASTROPHE TO THE REAL ONE

Scheffler's lectures seems oblivious to the fact that his imagined death of humanity in an asteroid strike bears an unnerving resemblance to the direst predictions about global warming. It is not an asteroid but the catastrophic heating and flooding of the Anthropocene[18] that could lead to near human extinction by the end of this century. I find it remarkable that the group of renowned philosophers who comment on Scheffler's work in 2015—the same year as the historic Paris Agreement on global warming—could studiously parse his logic for an imaginary world catastrophe and fail to even note the real-world catastrophe.

The Anthropocene can be described as the geological era in which humans, for the first time, play a substantial role in shaping Earth and its environment.[19] The exact beginning point is a matter of debate, but many scholars identify the Industrial Revolution as the period during which human actions began to take a serious toll on environmental integrity.

The scientific evidence that human production of greenhouse gases (GHGs)—most prominently, carbon dioxide, methane, and nitrous

---

18. The term "Anthropocene"—despite its wide usage, is sometimes criticized as a descriptor of the current era of global warming because it is thought to imply that humans are still the center of the universe. Others object because they sense in this term a reaffirmation of traditional male dominance. I intend Anthropocene as gender inclusive, where anthropos refers to humans, not only men. I also retain this term because it properly asserts that humans are the major cause of current, severe climate degradation, and because only humans can fix it. A term like androgynocene might better denote gender inclusiveness, but such a new term would require its own explanation. Perhaps Anthropocene serves another useful purpose. It has been and remains predominantly males who are pulling the levers of political and economic power, and a toxic masculinity—dominance of nature, lack of respect for interdependencies, and disregard for the well-being of future generations, minorities and the poor—is a major contributing force to the crisis we are now experiencing.

19. For a more complete analysis of the issues of global warming, its cultural and social causes and the potential remedies, see King, Henderson, and Churchill, *Bioethics Reenvisioned*, 110–36.

oxide—cause global warming is beyond question. GHG concentrations are causing polar ice to melt, permafrost regions to shrink, oceans to warm and rise, and hurricanes, typhoons, and similar storms to increase in number and intensity. Flooding and fires world-wide are at unprecedented numbers. All the while, tropic rainforests, the great reservoirs holding carbon from the atmosphere, are being depleted at a record pace.

The effects of this profligacy toward our natural resources will be almost beyond imagination. The Paris Agreement of 2015 is an aspiration to keep global warming to below 1.5 degrees Celsius (C) above preindustrial levels. The most recent report from the Intergovernmental Panel on Climate Change (IPCC) is that, to meet this goal, carbon poisoning of the atmosphere most be cut in half by 2050. No country is on a pace to remotely approximate that goal. The most we can realistically hope for, even with very coordinated changes, is a 2-degree C rise in temperatures and a sea level rise of 3–6 feet, creating as many as three hundred million climate refugees. The massive displacements and death will be greatest among the poorest sectors of the world population, who have contributed the least to environmental pollution. Food and water shortages as well as the breakdown of economic and political systems will add to the deaths, as will the overwhelming of medical and public health systems. For example, 58 percent of all infectious diseases—including Lyme, West Nile, hantavirus, typhoid, influenza—have been worsened by climate hazards, such as warming, drought, wildfires, sea-level rise, and extreme rainfall and flooding.[20]

And as I alluded to, justice issues stream through the climate issues. While China is the largest polluter, the U.S. per capita carbon footprint is double that of China. The U.S., China, and the European union are currently responsible for 41.5 percent of all global emissions of GHGs.[21] If we look at the justice picture by socio-economic status, we see that from 1900 to 2020 the world's richest 10 percent were responsible for 52 percent of the global carbon emissions, while the poorest 10 percent were responsible for only 7 percent.[22] Yet this poorest 10 percent will be the first to die in floods, droughts, migration, and political and economic upheavals.

20. D'Angelo, "Climate Change is Supercharging Most Infectious Diseases."
21. EPA. "Global Greenhouse Gas Emissions Data."
22. Oxfam International, "Carbon Emissions of Richest 1 Percent More than Double the Emissions of the Poorest Half of Humanity."

Just how fast all this will happen is unknown since it is unclear whether the degradation of the climate will occur at a steady and predicable pace or in cascades of rapid change after critical tipping points are exceeded. Our modeling for the speed of climate change is far from precise; it could be compared to driving at night in the fog on an unknown road. But there is agreement that the likelihood is for more rapid degradation of the environment, that is, in leaps rather than a more predictable steady-state decline.[23] Still, humans have some control, and the changes that could lessen or even reverse global warming are well known. Keeping fossil fuels in the ground, switching to electric cars, building the power grids to run on solar and wind, promoting regenerative forms of food production, and greatly reducing beef consumption are key. Human adaptation and survival capacities—in the form of making these changes in the next decade—will be put to the test as never before. Yet even massive technological changes in how energy is produced will mean little if the cultural patterns of consumptive capitalism and habits of increasing rather than curtailing overall energy use persist. The answers are as much cultural, political, and ethical as they are technological.

In brief, it is no overstatement to say that different modes of thinking and living are now required to meet the challenges of the Anthropocene, and that neither the traditional tools of my field, bioethics, nor the usual way of thinking in ethics more generally will be adequate. Going forward into a time of degradation of human living conditions, with the accompanying social, political, and economic upheavals, a different set of primary values is needed. Instead of dominating nature for our own health and happiness, we must now learn to revere it, adjust our modes of living to its limits and rhythms, and forge a new emotional and moral bond with the Earth.

Neglected traditions of ethics now have new relevance. For example, Stoicism, especially late Roman Stoicism, promotes an ethical system built on living in accord with the natural order, of shaping our wants and desires according to nature's provisions and discerning, as Epictetus said, what is in our control and what is not.[24] Also important for our current era is the Stoic emphasis on the equality of persons and the essential solidarity of all humans. "We are all parts of a great body," Seneca wrote, and our companionship is "like a stone arch, which would collapse if the

---

23. Romm, *Climate Change*, 77–126.
24. Epictetus, *Art of Living*, 3.

stones did not support each other."[25] Stoicism is only one example, and there are a variety of Christian traditions rapidly revising their readings of *Genesis* and other sacred texts to emphasize stewardship of creation, rather than domination, as a fundamental duty. In addition to reviving older traditions, there is also the need for new concepts grounded in our experiences of appreciation for our animal nature and our linkage with all life. Here my chief candidate for an axial norm is biophilia.

Unlike the forms of familiar love—eros, agape, philia and storge—biophilia denotes an affection for and desire to relate to other living things. It is best described by the late Harvard entomologist E. O. Wilson as "the innately emotional affiliation of human beings to other living organisms. Innate means hereditary and hence part of ultimate human nature."[26] Wilson argues that other organisms are the collective matrix from which the human mind emerged and is permanently rooted. I have written elsewhere about the kinds of human experiences that need to be nurtured to develop the moral traits essential for a viable life in a more limited future.[27]

INTERGENERATIONAL JUSTICE: CAN ELDERS BECOME GOOD ANCESTORS?

In *The Journey of Life*, Cole writes: "In rebuilding a moral economy for an extended life course, we must . . . attend to questions of justice within and between different stages of life."[28] Whatever meaning can be found in old age, it must be found in a recognition that our current profligacy toward the environment threatens to leave a world greatly diminished by comparison to the one we inherited. My parent's generation that weathered the Great Depression and fought World War II is often called the "greatest generation." My age cohort is on a path to be the most destructive generation. As a beginning in rectifying this fate, we must become masters of long-term thinking, caring more for our progeny than our comforts and conveniences. The stakes could not be higher.

25. Fideler, *Breakfast with Seneca*, 143.
26. Wilson, "Biophilia and the Conservation Ethics," 31.
27. Schenck and Churchill, "Six Maxims for a Marginally Inhabitable Planet," 494–510.
28. Cole, *Journey of Life*, 237.

The patterns that predispose us to think about the near future are everywhere around us. Election cycles in politics, quarterly reports in business, and two-week or monthly compensation rhythms are just a few examples. Of course, many elders do think long-term about the wellbeing of their children and grandchildren, about their financial and spiritual legacies, but this is typically limited to those closest to us, a circle of family and a few friends. Thinking about the future of Earth as a habitable planet is not something that many of us routinely do. Some philosophers have argued that we are simply not equipped as humans to think this way, having been taught throughout our evolution that survival depends on noticing immediate threats, most of which are local rather than global.[29] The temporal displacement of cause and effect is also a new challenge for us, and the idea that things we cause, like release of GHGs, will not appear in their full destructive form of global over-heating until decades later is something foreign to most ethical systems in the west.[30]

No one has written more persuasively about the alternatives to short horizon thinking than Roman Krznaric in *The Good Ancestor*. The book's title is taken from Jonas Salk, who said whether we are good ancestors is the most important question we must ask ourselves.[31] Krznaric poses six "good ancestor conversations," which he calls "deep-time humility," "intergenerational justice," "legacy mindset," 'transcendent goal," "holistic forecasting," and "cathedral thinking."[32] Together they form a compelling case.

Deep-time humility refers to the realization that we have been present on Earth for a short time, and that we humans are a barely discernible blip in the history of living things. As Krznaric puts it: "Consider the earth's history as the old measure of an English yard, the distance from the king's nose to the tip of his outstretched hand. One stroke of a nail file on his middle finger erases human history."[33]

Intergenerational justice means weighing future lives as equally valuable or more valuable than our own, if for no other reason because futures lives will far outnumber present ones. At this juncture I want to disaffiliate what I am saying from the currently fashionable Oxford philosophy of "longtermism," which seems to rely heavily on a utilitarian

29. Gardiner, *Perfect Moral Storm*, 123.
30. Jonas, *The Imperative of Responsibility*.
31. Krznaric, *Good Ancestor*, 3.
32. Krznaric, *Good Ancestor*, 39–162.
33. Krznaric, *Good Ancestor*, 49.

calculus, with all the usual problems associated with utilitarianism. So, I am not claiming that future generations are the only thing that is valuable, but rather than we cannot in good faith ignore them. If cumulative generations of the dead throughout history number one hundred billion, and the currently living account for 7.7 billion, then future generations, even on the most modest predictions, will number in the tens of trillions.[34] We who are currently alive are a fleck of dust on the population apple.

The idea of embracing a transcendent goal means setting realistic goals that can be accomplished only in the future, transcending my personal lifespan, goals whose value will be recognized and taken up by those who survive me. Holistic forecasting means setting out in detail multiple futures and weighing their probabilities and desirability. Basically, will the future unfold as a cascade of continuous crises of food and water, political and economic instability and social collapse, or one of adaptation and survival? A middle course of modest adjustments in a business-as-usual approach is no longer a possibility.

Finally, cathedral thinking refers to the mindset of those who laid the cornerstone of the great cathedrals of Europe, knowing that it would take multiple generations to complete the task. What long-term projects will I embrace whose fruition is far longer than a single lifespan, or multiple lifespans? The best estimates of the time needed to turn around our degradation of the soil if we began today is twenty-five years, while the timeframe for reversing global warming stretches well into the next century. I will live to see none of this, but I can make a worthy start with the time I have left.

CONCLUSION

Near the end of *Old Man Country: My Search for Meaning Among the Elders*, Cole talks about his ambitions for his future, and how he will "pay the rent" as an elder, in part by becoming "an advocate for halting and reversing Climate Change."[35] I have taken him at his word in developing this essay and argued that this way of justifying and finding meaning in old age is the most important work we can do. But how? Again, the actions individuals can commit to undertake are well-known, if not always

---

34. Krznaric, *Good Ancestor*, 83.
35. Cole, *Old Man Country*, 167.

simple. A start is to know your carbon footprint. The average person in the U.S. generates roughly sixteen metric tons of carbon dioxide annually. The average person in China emits approximately eight metric tons.[36] A metric ton is the gas it takes to fill a sphere that is thirty-two feet in diameter. To keep global temperatures at 1.5 degrees C we would need to reduce that to less than 2 metric tons, which may seem impossible, but more feasible if energy sources move quickly toward renewables and cultural traditions of conservation can become more common.

Meanwhile, some commonsense measures include adopting a plant-based diet, reducing or eliminating air travel, buying locally with reusable bags, composting, driving a hybrid or electric vehicle, buying fewer clothes, purchasing carbon off-sets, and supporting clean energy political candidates locally and nationally. The task will be different for each of us, but we can take guidance from Arthur Ashe, the tennis champion who used his fame to work for racial justice nationally and globally: "Start where you are; use what you have; do what you can."

---

36. "CO2 Emissions per Capita."

Epilogue

CRAIG IRVINE

"No one cares how much you know until they know how much you care."
—ATTRIBUTED TO THEODORE ROOSEVELT

IN THE POEM "A Clearing," Denise Levertov invites us down an "enticing" driveway. Traveling through "the shade of its green tunnel," we arrive at a "clearing"—an "expanse of sky" enclosed by "big trees"—where one is "given a generous welcome" and "sheltered ... from the assaultive world." This is "paradise," Levertov writes, and paradise

> is a kind of poem; it has
> a poem's characteristics:
> inspiration; starting with the given;
> unexpected harmonies; revelations.
> It's rare among
> the worlds one finds
> at the end of enticing driveways.[1]

This book is a Levertovian clearing—an opening for inspiration, unexpected harmonies, and revelations in the forest of academic disciplines. As the introduction makes clear, Thomas Cole has been inviting students, teachers, and scholars into multi- and inter-disciplinary clearings for almost forty years. It is therefore fitting that this volume should represent a broad—though certainly not the full—range of the disciplines that Cole has "crossed" over the course of his career. He is a master of inspiration, of unexpected harmonies, of revelations. Time and again, he has had the

---

1. Levertov, *This Great Unknowing*, 54–55.

courage to risk defying the "disciplining" of thought by the academy's would-be gatekeepers. Having worked in the health humanities for many years, I can testify to the profound influence of Cole's "undisciplining" in the development of this field. Indeed, his contribution is incalculable: it is impossible to gauge the compass of the outward, rippling movement of the ideas, stories, images, and provocations in his books, articles, and films—a movement well represented in the chapters herein.

I would like to turn my attention, however, to what Cole accomplishes outside all disciplinary, inter-disciplinary, and cross-disciplinary boundaries: the *love* he bestows on countless students, friends, mentees, and colleagues. As Cole's friend, I have experienced this love firsthand. Thelma Jean Goodrich was already one of my very closest friends when Cole and she met in 2006. At that time, I knew and admired Cole's work in medical humanities, but we'd never been introduced. I trusted Goodrich, who is a keen judge of character, but having previously been disappointed, even repelled, by the arrogance and egocentricity of prominent scholars—even those who write eloquently about empathy—I approached my introduction to Cole with some trepidation.

In Cole's case, I need not have worried. "The most beautiful people we have known," writes Elizabeth Kubler-Ross, "are those who have known defeat, known suffering, known struggle, known loss, and have found their way out of the depths. These persons have an appreciation, a sensitivity, and an understanding of life that fills them with compassion, gentleness, and a deep loving concern. Beautiful people do not just happen."[2] Though my very first impression might have been of Cole's arresting physical presence—tall, strong, handsome—it wasn't long after we'd settled into the banquette at the restaurant that his compassion, his gentleness, his genuine, loving concern overwhelmed any trepidation I'd felt before meeting him.

As Kubler-Ross makes clear, it's not just having experienced the depths of suffering, struggle, and loss that fills one with compassion, gentleness, and deep loving concern, but having found one's way out of those depths. This finding requires the courage to face one's suffering, including one's own role in its perpetuation, with uncompromising honesty. Cole's honesty and courage were immediately, palpably apparent in the generosity and keenness of the attention he brought to our initial encounter. They have been reinforced in every subsequent meeting. He

---

2. Kubler-Ross, *Death*, 96.

cares. He is, I contend, constitutionally incapable of *not* caring—whether about his family, about his friends, about his work, the environment, or the world. I have personally benefited from the quality of this care, particularly when I've struggled to find my bearings in my own work—when I could not find my way to a clearing in the forest of "disciplining" pressures and personalities. It isn't so much the advice he gives, sage though it may be, as the care, born of his own suffering, with which he embodies it. If I were to qualify, or perhaps extend, Kubler-Ross's sentiment, it would be to insist that the journey out of the depths never really ends—in this life, at least. It is the abiding honesty and courage—the *loving care*—with which Cole faces life's challenges, life's depths, whether recurrent or new, that I most welcome in his advice, in his attention, in his compassion, gentleness, and deep concern.

I cannot help but think here of George Eliot's closing words about her heroine Dorothea at the end of *Middlemarch*. Dorothea was most certainly a character who found her way out of the depths—one of Kubler-Ross's "beautiful people." In the novels final paragraph, Eliot writes that

> Her finely touched spirit had still its fine issues, though they were not widely visible. Her full nature, like that river of which Cyrus broke the strength, spent itself in channels which had no great name on the earth. But the effect of her being on those around her was incalculably diffusive, for the growing good of the world is partly dependent on un-historic acts, and that things are not so ill with you and me as they might have been is half owing to the number who lived faithfully a hidden life and rest in unvisited tombs.[3]

While Cole has certainly not lived a "hidden life" and has indeed contributed in "widely visible" and even historic ways to the "channels" with "great names on the earth" to which he has turned his attention, I would insist that his greatest contributions are those he has bestowed as loving friend, husband, father and grandfather, mentee, counselor, and guide. With very few exceptions, all human beings ultimately rest in "unvisited tombs." Centuries, even decades after our deaths, no one will mourn at any of our graves. The single most important question we must all face is whether we, like Dorothea, have contributed to the "the growing good of the world." In this volume, we celebrate someone for whom we can most assuredly answer, *Yes*.

3. Eliot, *Middlemarch*, 811.

APPENDIX ESSAY

A Qualitative Evidence Synthesis of *Medical Humanities*

ANNELISE BERLER AND ISAAC S. CHUA

INTRODUCTION

THE FIELD OF MEDICAL humanities has a history that, like the subject itself, cannot be simplistically defined. Consequently, several definitions exist. One definition can be found from the National Library of Medicine, which describes the field as: "the study of the intersection of medicine and humanistic disciplines such as philosophy, religion, literature, and the fine and performing arts."[1] In another definition, medical humanities bases its ideological foundation on the values dictated by the *studia humanitatis*—the "study of man or humanity."[2] The historical origin of this academic viewpoint was brought about by the Italian Renaissance poet and humanist, Petrarch (1304–74).[3] His use of introspective writing and reflections that began when he was grieving losses brought about by the Black Plague provided an alternative means of scholasticism that melded the introspective self with a need to be involved and helpful towards the outside world.[4] This broad idea can be seen today in medical humanities,

---

1. "Collection Development Guidelines of the National Library of Medicine," National Library of Medicine.
2. Kutac et al., "Innovation Through Tradition," 374.
3. Whitfield, "Petrarch," 1.
4. Kutac et al., "Innovation Through Tradition," 374–75.

which emphasizes the humanist's reflective nature to provide a greater emphasis on morality for health care as a whole.[5]

The term "medical humanities" first appeared in academic literature within George Sarton's journal, *Isis*, in 1947.[6] Twenty years later, Pennsylvania State University's College of Medicine created their Department of Humanities in 1967, becoming the first of its kind found in any medical school.[7] In 1970, The Society for Health and Human Values (SHHV) established itself as an official member organization in the United States.[8] The establishment of the SHHV, coupled with the launch of the *Journal of Medical Humanities* in 1979 in the United States,[9] points to a more official recognition of medical humanities as a legitimate academic field, which is reflected in Edmund Pellegrino's work arguing for a larger focus on humanism in medical care and in his subsequent chairmanship of the Institute on Human Values in Medicine.[10]

In recent years, medical humanities has become increasingly relevant due to the medical field's shift from the traditional biomedical model towards a more human-centered model (i.e., bio-psycho-social).[11] Despite its relevance in medical education, the implementation of medical humanities has been variable across medical schools and is often de-emphasized compared to the traditional biomedical curricula taught in medical education.[12] In this context, the publication of Thomas Cole, Nathan Carlin, and Ronald Carson's *Medical Humanities: An Introduction* is a landmark in the pedagogy of medical education by being the first textbook that commmprehensively organizes the field.

Although medical humanities has been referenced since George Sarton's publication in 1947,[13] there are not many academic publications that attempt to broadly outline medical humanities in its entirety. There have been two key works in recent years that address this void in the

5. Kutac et al., "Innovation Through Tradition," 381.
6. "About," Health Humanities Consortium.
7. About," Health Humanities Consortium.
8. About," Health Humanities Consortium.
9. About," Health Humanities Consortium.
10. McElhinney and Pellegrino, "The Institute on Human Values in Medicine," 291–317.
11. Cole, Carlin, and Carson, *Medical Humanities*, 8.
12. Hvidt et al., "Weak Inclusion of the Medical Humanities"; Bentwich, "Medical Humanities and Active Learning"; Hackler, "University of Arkansas College of Medicine, Division of Medical Humanities."
13. "About," Health Humanities Consortium.

literature, *The Health Humanities Reader*[14] and *Medical Humanities*.[15] While both of these works are significant contributions to the corpus of the medical and health humanities, it is important to highlight their differences. A "reader" can be defined as an "anthology—a collection of selected literary pieces or passages or works of art or music,"[16] whereas a "textbook" can be defined as "a book used in the study of a subject: such as one containing a presentation of the principles of a subject."[17] While *The Health Humanities Reader* is important as the first collection of its kind that showcased works used in the Medical and Health Humanities, the first to add a framework of instruction and examples of works in the field was *Medical Humanities*.

This objective of this essay is to conduct a qualitative evidence synthesis of works that have cited *Medical Humanities* to demonstrate its impact. A qualitative evidence synthesis "is an umbrella term for the methodologies associated with the systematic review of qualitative research evidence."[18] The broad steps that must be followed for conducting a qualitative evidence synthesis include the following: "stating the objectives of research, defining eligibility criteria for studies to be included, identifying (all) potentially eiligible studies, applying eligibility criteria, assembling the most complete data set feasible including-data extraction and quality appraisal of incuded studies, analyzing this data set, using statistical synthesis and sensitivity analyses if appropriate and possible, and preparing a structured report of the research."[19] Additionally, it is important to mention that the process utilized for a qualitative evidence synthesis can be iterative or linear; the synthesis done here employed an iterative process.[20]

---

14. Jones et al., *Health Humanities Reader*.
15. Cole, Carlin, and Carson, *Medical Humanities*.
16. *Merriam-Webster's Online Dictionary*.
17. *Merriam-Webster's Online Dictionary*.
18. Flemming et al., "Qualitative Evidence Synthesis," 1.
19. Grimshaw, "A Knowledge Synthesis Chapter," 7–8.
20. Grimshaw, "A Knowledge Synthesis Chapter," 8.

METHODS

Search Strategy and Selection Criteria

The qualitative evidence sysnthesis focused on published scholarly works that cited *Medical Humanities*. One author (A.B.) searched for all works that cited the textbook via Google Scholar from the textbook's publication date in 2015 through December 15, 2022, when the literature search was conducted. The qualitative evidence synthesis included the following source types: books/textbooks, published theses/disertations, and scholarly journal articles. Scholarly works that were conference abstracts were excluded because the the authors felt that the brevity of the abstracts would provide inadequate qualitative data to be included in a qualitative evidence synthesis. Additionally, if the publication lacked an available English translation of the text, they were excluded because the authors did not possess the multi-linguistic expertise to conduct a proper qualitative analysis of the work in its primary lanaguage.

Screening and Data Abstraction

A.B. performed an initial screening and determined whether an English version of the scholarly work was available for any non-English publication via Harvard Countway Library. Both reviewers (I.C. and A.B.) read the abstracts and extracted the following information from published works: type of scholarly work (e.g., book or textbook, peer-reviewed journal article, thesis or dissertation), publication date, country of the author's academic affiliation, the section/chapter of *Medical Humanities* that was cited, and the context of the citation within the scholarly work (i.e., an excerpt of the text that included the citation). A.B. entered all data into Microsoft Excel, version 16.63.1 (Microsoft Corp), which was chosen due to its ability to both organize the qualitative data such that a content analysis could be performed and to conduct a descriptive analysis of the quantitative data. Continuous variables are reported as means (standard deviation), and categorical variables are reported as numbers (percentages).

Qualitative Analysis

We conducted a content analysis of excerpts of the scholarly works that cited *Medical Humanities*. A content analysis can be defined as a "family of systematic, rule-guided techniques used to analyze the informational contents of textual data."[21] In a content analysis, the "data are categorized using categories that are generated, at least in part, inductively (i.e., derived from the data) and in most cases applied to the data through close reading."[22] The general goal for content analyses is to "understand a phenomenon, rather than to make generalizations from study samples to populations based on statistical inference."[23] In essence, a content analysis works by breaking down the data into smaller segments by applying codes to the data which then allows for conclusions regarding the data to be found.[24]

The process of coding the data involved two reviewers (I.C. and A.B.) independently creating preliminary concepts based on how the scholarly work cited *Medical Humanities* within the text. Both authors reviewed each other's preliminary concepts and iteratively compared and clarified them to generate themes and subthemes until consensus was achieved.

RESULTS

Characteristics of Scholarly Works

From 148 unique records, 110 scholarly works met the inclusion criteria and were included in the qualitative evidence synthesis. A PRISMA flow diagram is presented in Figure 1.[25] Data abstracted from the publications are presented in Table 3. Characteristics of included publications are summarized in Table 1. Most publications that cited the textbook were academic journal articles, published between 2021–22; and included authors whose academic affiliations spanned North America, South

21. Mayring, "Qualitative Content Analysis," 1.

22. Forman et al., "Qualitative Content Analysis," 40; Morgan, "Qualitative Content Analysis," 112–12.

23. Forman et al., "Qualitative Content Analysis," 40; Morgan, "Qualitative Content Analysis," 60.

24. Forman et al., "Qualitative Content Analysis," 40; Morgan, "Qualitative Content Analysis," 60.

25. Tricco et al., "PRISMA extension."

America, Europe, Asia, the Middle East, and Oceana. Most authors were affiliated with academic institutions in North America and Europe. Citations increased from seven per year in 2015 to sixteen per year in 2022 (Figure 2).

Book Citation Characteristics

Most publications referenced *Medical Humanities* without citing a specific section of the book (n=57) (Figure 3).[26] The most cited sections of the book included the Introduction (n=29), followed by the Preface (n=7), Chapter 1: The Doctor-Patient Relationship (n=7) and Chapter 7: Narratives of Illness (n=7). Some publications cited several sections of the book, which is why the total number of key themes represented in the citations of the textbook (n=129) exceeds the total number of publications included in the qualitative evidence synthesis.

In our content analysis of citations, we identified six key themes that reflected how the book was cited in the text: (1) *understanding medical humanities* (52 [40.3 percent]); (2) *providing historical context for medical humanities* (27 [20.9 percent]); (3) *referencing works within the textbook* (7 [5.4 percent]); (4) *describing the value of medical humanities* (17 [13.2 percent]); (5) *supporting the author's argument* (13 [10.1 percent]); and (6) *establishing precedent in medical humanities* (13 [10.1 percent]) (Table 2).[27] Each publication included in the qualitative evidence synthesis could include more than one key theme, which is also why the total number of times key themes appear in citations (n=129) is greater than the total number of publications included in the analysis (n=110).

DISCUSSION

We performed this qualitative evidence synthesis to understand the influence *Medical Humanities* on the field by describing what works are citing the textbook and how the textbook was cited. Characteristics of the collected sources indicated that the textbook has been being utilized by academicians, writers, and authors across the globe, with the majority

26. n refers to the number times a specific section of textbook was cited.

27. n refers to the number of times a key theme emerged in the citation of the textbook. The denominator used to calculate the percentage is the total number of times the key themes appear in a citation.

being in North America and Europe. An increasing number of publications are citing this work each year. Most of the works citing the textbook did not reference a specific chapter, and the most cited parts of the book were the Introduction followed by the Preface, Chapter 1: The Doctor-Patient Relationship and Chapter 7: Narratives of Illness. Six key themes emerged from our qualitative analysis of the in-text citations; over 60% of citations contained the following two themes—*understanding medical humanities* and *providing historical context for medial humanities*.

The preponderance of North American and European scholars citing this textbook is unsurprising since the field of medical humanities emerged from the United States.[28] However, the global reach of this publication, especially to South America, the Middle East, and Asia, highlights the universal appeal of the subject matter covered in this textbook.[29] Several of these publications explore how to incorporate medical humanities into clinical training and education,[30] while others explore the essence of medicine itself and what it means to care for the sick.[31] Another publication, from India, reviewed the historical context of medical humanities in medical education to explore changing thematic ideas within the field.[32] Additionally, a Brazilian publication discussed the idea that learning about bioethics through illness narratives can create doctors who are better equipt to handle nuanced and controversial bioethical situations in their professional life.[33] It emphasized the idea that the medical humanities usage of literary analysis and reflective practices aim to inspire clinicians to be more empathetic and, therefore, more humanistic.[34]

Unsurprisingly, the introduction was the most cited section of the textbook (Figure 2). This section provides a succinct yet comprehensive

28. Cole, Carlin, and Carson, *Medical Humanities*, 1–18.

29. Mallee, "The Evolution of Health as an Ecological Concept"; Prabhu, "Medical Themes in a Literature Classroom"; Manchola, "Tres Apuestas Por Una Bioética Práctica."

30. Prabhu, "Medical Themes in a Literature Classroom"; Tekiner, "Why Teach Pharmacy Ethics Through Literary Fiction?" 203–6; Huffman and Inoue, "Establishing, Promoting and Growing the Health Humanities in Japan," 204–14; Haffman, "Vision for Health Humanities in Japan," 8–13.

31. Mallee, "The Evolution of Health as an Ecological Concept," 28–32; Ong and Anantham, "Medical Humanities," 233–37; Monajemi, "On the Nature of Medicine."

32. Prabhu, "Medical Themes in a Literature Classroom."

33. Manchola, "Tres Apuestas Por Una Bioética Práctica."

34. Manchola, "Tres Apuestas Por Una Bioética Práctica."

overview of medical humanities. Specifically, it defines the humanities; describes the origins of medical humanities; addresses debates with the term; provides comments on the conceptions and goals of medical humanities; and offers the authors' "own definition of the field and its implications for how the book is organized and presented."[35] The introduction creates well-defined paramaters for the reader to understand medical humanities, which is helpful given the plethora of available definitions in the literature.[36] For example, "is medical humanities a field or a discipline?"[37] and "what is the appropriate balance or tension between the practical/instrumental and the intellectual/critical forms of medical humanities?" The introduction lays out the authors' viewpoints around these complex issues,[38] which provides much needed guidance to scholars and medical practitioners alike.[39] Given the frequent citation of this section, it naturally follows that *understanding medical humanities* was the most common key theme that emerged among citations.

Following the introduction and the preface, chapters 1 and 7 were the next most cited sections of the book. For works that cited chapter 1,[40] the most cited key theme associated with these works was *providing historical context for medical humanities*. Chapter 1 explores how historical movements (e.g., the Renaissance), religion (e.g., Christianity), and other secular trends (e.g., corporate transformation of American medicine) have influenced our current assumptions about the doctor-patient relationship.[41] Interestingly, despite the evolving methods and philosophies of caring for the sick, the chapter highlights how managing the power imbalance between the doctor and patient remains a constant factor in the evolution of their relationship, leading to the creation of safeguards (e.g., Hippocratic oath, the American Medical Association Code of Ethics). It is no wonder why academics frequently cite this section since it provides a condensed yet thorough overview and timeline of this complex topic.

35. Cole, Carlin, and Carson, *Medical Humanities*, 1–18.

36. Olding et al., "Black, White, and Gray," 224; Schlamp, "Medical Humanities at Six Texas Medical Schools," 6; O'Doherty et al., "Humanities in Medicine," 1.

37. Evans and MacNaughton, "Should Medical Humanities Be a Multidisciplinary or an Interdisciplinary Study?" 1–4.

38. O'Doherty et al., "Humanities in Medicine," 1–2.

39. Olsen, "Curricular Opportunities and Constraints," xiii–xiv.

40. Wistrand, "Distressed Doctors," 250–56; Jones, "The Doctor-Patient Relationship in the Nineteenth Century French Novel"; MacQueen, "Vocal Pedagogy, Pathology, and Personality in Chervin's Journal La Voix Parlée et Chantée."

41. Cole, Carlin, and Carson, *Medical Humanities*, 36.

The frequent citations of chapter 7 (Narratives of Illness) underscores the effectiveness of narrative medicine as a pedagogical tool in medical education.[42] The chapter consists of summaries of notable illness narratives and describes how these stories provide additional dimensions to the human understanding of health and illness that the biomedical model simply cannot convey. Stories give readers a greater depth of emotional and perceptual understanding of human suffering due to poor health.[43] The textbook itself describes this phenomenon by stating, "Disease—what happens to the body—is understood through science. . . . Illness—what the person experiences—is understood through eliciting patient stories."[44] Therefore, these illness narratives aim to utilize creative ideas to act as a "bridge between science and experience."[45]

Reiterating the importance of *Medical Humanities* as the first textbook to exist in the field is crucial. Although this field has been in existence as far back as the late 1940s,[46] the first textbook emerged in 2015. A possible explanation for this delayed emergence includes the dominance of the biomedical model in medical pedagogy within western medicine since the late nineteenth century.[47] The publication of this textbook coincides with the growing acknowledgement that the mastery of biomedical knowledge alone is insufficient to train emotionally and intellectually competent healthcare providers.[48] Another possible reason for the delayed creation of a medical humanities textbook may stem from the sheer difficulty of properly integrating, organizing, and summarizing the multi-disciplinary field into a succinct yet comprehensive and digestible format.[49] Consequently, this textbook can therefore be viewed as the beginnings of a more standardized practice of organizing and teaching medical humanities, which may facilitate easier integration of medical humanities into medical school curricula in the future.[50]

This study has several limitations. First, only Google Scholar was utilized to identify published works that cited *Medical Humanities*. A

42. Milota et al., "Narrative Medicine as a Medical Education Tool," 802–10.
43. Cole, Carlin, and Carson, *Medical Humanities*, 136.
44. Cole, Carlin, and Carson, *Medical Humanities*, 9.
45. Cole, Carlin, and Carson, *Medical Humanities*, 9.
46. Bleakley, "When I Say . . . the Medical Humanities in Medical Education," 1.
47. Cole, Carlin, and Carson, *Medical Humanities*, 36.
48. Olsen, "Curicular Opportunities and Constraints," 2.
49. Ong et al., "The Medical Humanities," 235.
50. Isaac, "Role of Humanities in Modern Medical Education," 349.

more comprehensive search methodology that utilized multiple databases may have identified other works not included in this qualitative evidence synthesis. Second, the exclusion of all non-English works without an English translation and conference papers may have introduced some bias into the qualitative analysis. Additionally, the analysis of the data was constrained due to there only being two reviewers who coded the data and generated the themes. Typically, a third investigator is necessary to arbitrate any differences in opinion between the two coders. However, the two coders were able to successfully to come to consensus for any coding disagreements that arose.

CONCLUSION

The findings from our qualitative evidence synthesis of published scholarly works that cited *Medical Humanities* suggests that the textbook is being cited by an increasing number of scholars each year around the world. Moreover, as reflected by the most frequently cited sections of the book and most associated key themes, the primary purpose of citing the textbook is to clarify the definition and components of medical humanities as a scholarly field while providing historical context of the field and its respective disciplines.

Future examination of this textbook might include surveying medical educators to see how many medical institutions have incorporated this textbook into its curriculum and to understand how the textbook has impacted the students in their professional development via qualitative methods. As noted by the authors, "the book aims to stimulate and enhance both critical thinking and character development. We aim not only to bring the humanities *to* students but also to evoke the humanity *of* students."[51]

---

51. Cole, Carlin, and Carson, *Medical Humanities*, ix.

TABLE 1. CHARACTERISTICS OF PUBLICATIONS IN
QUALITATIVE EVIDENCE SYNTHESIS[a]

	N=110
Type of scholarly work	
Academic journal article	72 (65.5)
Textbook or book	26 (23.6)
Thesis/dissertation	12 (10.9)
Publication year	
2015–2016	17 (15.5)
2017–2018	25 (22.7)
2019–2020	32 (29.1)
2021–2022	36 (32.7)
Regions and countries of author affiliations	
North America	47 (42.7)
Canada	8 (7.3)
USA	39 (35.5)
South America	1 (0.9)
Brazil	1 (0.9)
Europe	31 (28.2)
Austria	1 (0.9)
Belgium	1 (0.9)
Finland	1 (0.9)
Germany	3 (2.72)
Ireland	2 (1.8)
Italy	1 (0.9)
Netherlands	2 (1.8)
Spain	1 (0.9)
Sweden	2 (1.8)
Switzerland	2 (1.8)
UK	15 (13.6)
Asia	12 (10.9)
China	2 (1.8)
India	3 (2.72)
Japan	5 (4.5)
Malaysia	1 (0.9)

Singapore	1 (0.9)
Middle East	4 (3.6)
Iran	1 (0.9)
Oman	1 (0.9)
Turkey	2 (1.8)
Oceania	1 (0.9)
Australia	1 (0.9)
Multiple countries	11 (10)
Other[b]	2 (1.8)
Not applicable[c]	1 (0.9)

[a]All data are n (%) otherwise noted. N=110 refers to the total number of publications included in the qualitative evidence synthesis and is the denominator used to calculate %.

[b]Both observations have 1 author without an academic affiliation but co-authors have academic affiliations in Sweden and the USA

[c]Solo author does not have an academic affiliation.

Table 2. Key Themes and Subthemes of Citations

Key Themes	Sub Themes	Examples
Understanding medical humanities	Defining medical humanities Citing the textbook as part of a general introduction of medical humanities Describing the content of medical humanities Differentiating between medical humanities and other disciplines Describing disciplines within medical humanities Describing the goals of medical humanities	"*Understanding health is covered more broadly in literature relating to medical humanities and health humanities (411,412), but it is also related to use of the arts within health to help the understanding of illness and disease.*" (Source #1) "*Cole, Carlin, and Carson define medical humanities as 'an inter- and multidisciplinary field that explores contexts, experiences, and critical and conceptual issues in medicine and health care, while supporting professional identity formation' among physicians and other healthcare professionals (12). Here exploring contexts means drawing on disciplines such as history and anthropology to investigate 'the temporal and cultural dimensions of medicine' (12).*" (Source #3) "*Cole, Carlin, and Carson note that 'humanities scholarship and education are dedicated to understanding human experience through the disciplined development of insight, perspective, critical understanding, discernment, and creativity.'*" (Source #6)

Providing historical context for medical humanities	Describing the origins, growth, and acceptance of medical humanities as an academic discipline	"Medical humanities were conceived in the context of what has become known as the contemporary crisis in medicine, a crisis which has challenged the epistemological status of medicine because "since the 1960s, the new fields of bioethics and medical humanities have grappled with problematic issues such as the protection of research subjects, the goals of health care, the definition of death, the rights of patients, the cessation of treatment, the meaning of illness, and the distribution of healthcare resources." (Source #65) "The US-based medical humanities movement that arguably started with Edmund Pellegrino in the 1970s has not made consistent, visible inroads in Japan." (Source #91) "Cole, Carlin, and Carson assert that "...the modern ideal of the doctor-patient relationship based on a personal connection, careful physical examination, and trust arose in the late nineteenth century." (Source #96)
	Providing historical context for development of doctor-patient relationship	
	Providing historical context for discrimination and abuse faced by minority groups within medicine	
	Providing historical context for long-standing relationship between literature and medicine	
	Providing historical context of hospice and palliative care	
	Providing historical context for integration of medical humanities into medical education	
	Providing historical and medico-legal context of epilepsy	
	Providing historical context of Edmund Pellegrino as a leader in the field of medical humanities	
	Providing historical context of pathography	
	Providing historical context for narrative medicine	
	Provides historical context for the term "acquaintance knowledge"	
	Provides historical context of concepts of health and disease	

Referencing works within the textbook	Referencing a specific section of the textbook	Beginners initiated a serious exploration of late-life sexuality and homosexuality." (Source #83)
	Referencing art featured in the textbook	"The cover of the textbook Medical Humanities: An Introduction displays an intriguing painting: Hypochondriac by Amy Bennett (Fig. 1)." (Source #42)
	Referencing primary text that is quoted in the textbook	
	Referencing philosophical terms defined in the textbook	
Describing the value of medical humanities	Utilizing medical humanities as a problem-solving tool	"Literature engages readers' moral imagination and allows them to "transport…into the lives of others in ways that enhance our empathetic understanding." (Source #95)
	Referencing the textbook to illustrate how medical humanities is being incorporated into medicine	
	Justifying the value of how medical humanities can foster professional and personal development among students and clinicians	"The value of MH teaching—not only for future clinicians but also for patients whose demographics and disease experience have so far been neglected by traditional biomedical models—is well documented." (Source #16)
	Describing the value of patient narratives to understand illness and disease	
	Highlighting the purpose of bioethics	
	Understanding the purpose and impact of poetry	

Supporting the author's argument	Supporting the author's views on doctor-patient relationships	"Physicians and other medical professionals find themselves in positions of power, particularly when it comes to patient-provider relationships, so a just provider would find themselves continuously working to respect patients and their background, protecting the vulnerable, and also working towards a future that promotes more equal access and the pursuit of justice." (Source #63)
	Asserting that the disease-based model of care does not consider social, emotional, spiritual, or cultural factors	
	Positing that open-mindedness and reflective thinking is important for healthcare providers	
	Contending there is no definitive integration of medical humanities into medical education	"While there is much literature supporting the value of the humanities in medical education, its standardized inclusion remains elusive." (Source #51)
	Maintaining the idea that healthcare is collaborative work environment	
	Critiquing how medical humanities views science fiction	"Consequently, social, emotional, spiritual, or other cultural factors are generally not major considerations accorded to etiology or treatment." (Source #40)
Establishing the precedent in medical humanities	Featuring Cole as a pioneer in medical humanities	"Moreover, Tom Cole, Nathan Carlin, and Ron Carson had published the first major textbook, Medical Humanities: An Introduction, to define, once again, the field and to describe its philosophical and pedagogical underpinnings for teachers and students." (Source #76)
	Citing the book as the groundbreaking text to teach medical humanities	
	Listing the textbook as an exemplar of medical humanities	
		"From the early 1960s, the writings of Ronald A. Carson and Thomas R. Cole established the term medical humanities as a comprehensive concept for a multidisciplinary field of research and study and expounded on its function and purpose." (Source #61)

A QUALITATIVE EVIDENCE SYNTHESIS OF MEDICAL HUMANITIES 203

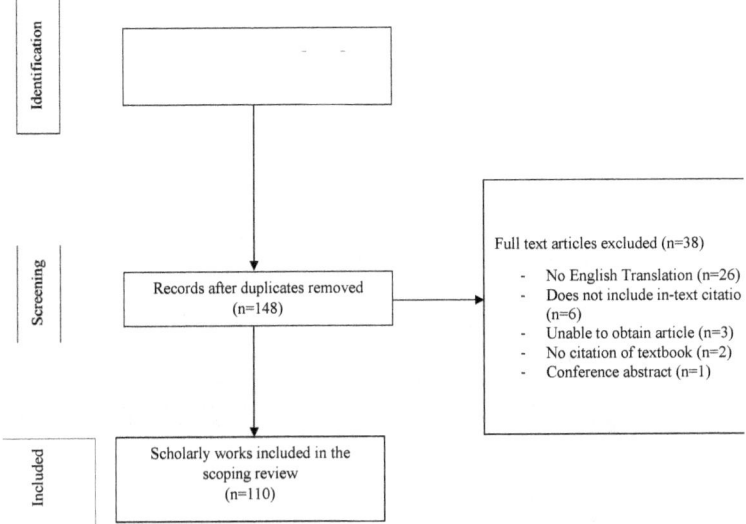

APPENDIX

FIGURE 2

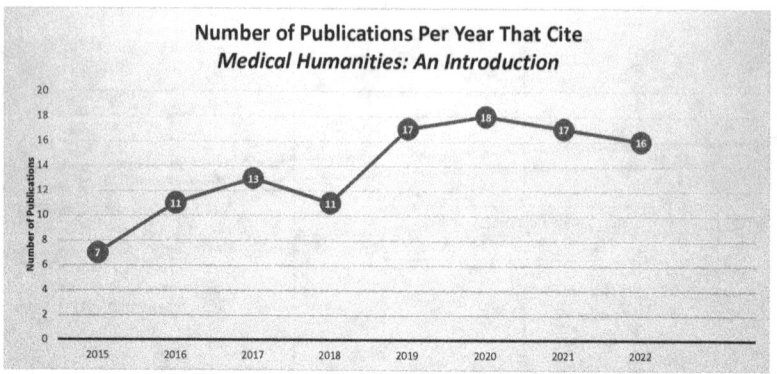

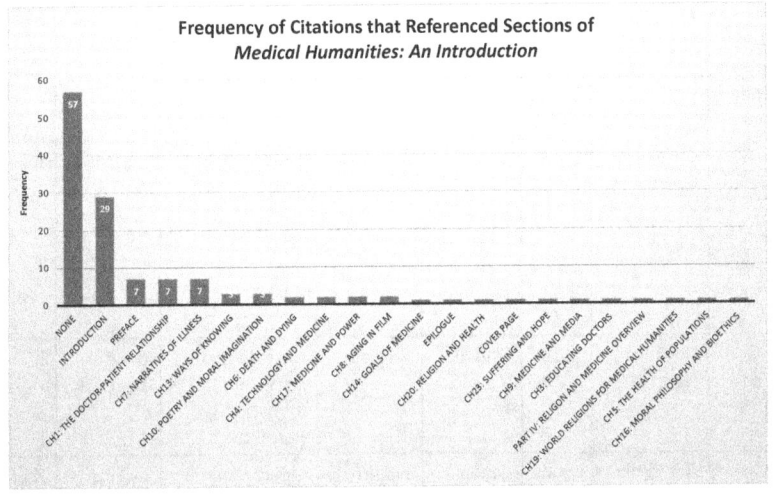

FIGURE 3

Table 3. Data Abstracted from Publications that Cited the Textbook

Source Title	First Author	Pub Date	Country	Language	Book Title or Journal Name	Source Type	Key Theme	Sub-Them
1) What is the Evidence on the Role of the Arts in Improving Health and Well-Being?	Daisy Fancourt	2019	Denmark	English	Health Evidence Network Synthesis Report 67	Book or Textbook	KT1	K1S:
2) Elisabeth Kubler-Ross and the "Five Stages" Model in a Sampling of Recent American Textbooks	Charles A. Corr	2018	United States	English	Omega	Journal Article	KT2	K2S:
3) Narratology Beyond the Human	David Herman	2018	United Kingdom	English	Inter-disciplinary E-Journal for Narrative Research	Book or Textbook	KT1	K1S: K1S:
4) Palliative Care	Abdulaziz Al-Mahrezi	2016	Oman	English	Oman Medical Journal	Journal Article	KT2	K2S:
5) Narratives of Survivorship	Asa Mohlin	2021	Sweden	English	Current Oncology	Journal Article	KT1	K1S: K1S:
6) Play and People Living with Dementia	Aagje Swinnen	2017	Netherlands	English	The Gerontologist	Journal Article	KT1	K1S:
7) The Evolution of Health as an Ecological Concept	Hein Mallee	2017	Japan	English	Current Opinion in Environmental Sustainability	Journal Article	KT2	K2S:
8) Pastoral Aesthetics	Nathan Carlin	2019	United States	English	Pastoral Aesthetics	Book or Textbook	KT2	K2S:
9) Introduction to the Special Issue	Elizabeth L. Angeli	2017	United States	English	Technical Communication Quartlerly	Journal Article	KT1	K1S:
10) Innovating through Tradition	Julie Kutac	2015	United States	English	Journal of Medical Humanities	Journal Article	KT2	K2S:
11) A Humanism for Nursing?	Graham McCaffrey	2019	Canada	English	Nursing Inquiry	Journal Article	KT1; KT2	K1S: K2S:
12) Using Co-Created Transdisciplinary Approach to Explore the Complexity of Air Pollution in Informal Settlements	Sarah E. West	2021	United Kingdom	English	Humanities and Social Sciences Communications	Journal Article	KT1	K1S:

Title	Author	Year	Country	Language	Journal/Source	Type	KT	KS
) Tales of Treatment and New Perspectives for Global Health Research on Antimicrobial Resistance	Marco J. Haenssgen	2020	United Kingdom; Thailand	English	BMJ Journals: Medical Humanities	Journal Article	KT4	K4S1
) Performance and the Medical Body	Alex Mermikides	2016	United Kingdom	English	Performance and the Medical Body	Book or Textbook	KT1	K1S1
) Introducing Urban Humanities	Dana Cuff	2020	United States	English	Urban Humanities	Book or Textbook	KT1; KT4	K1S2; K4S1
) Black, White and Gray	Madeleine Noelle Olding	2022	United Kingdom	English	Teaching and Learning in Medicine	Journal Article	KT4	K4S3
) Metascience Not Enough-A Plea for Psychological Humanities in the Wake of the Replication Crisis	Lisa Malich	2022	Germany	English	Review of General Psychology	Journal Article	KT1	K1S5
) Learning Medicine With, From, and Through the Humanities	Neville Chiavaroli	2019	Australia; Taiwan	English	Understanding Medical Education	Book or Textbook	KT1; KT4	K1S1; K4S3
) Introduction	Peter Fifield	2020	United Kingdom	English	Modernism and Physical Illness	Book or Textbook	KT4	K4S4
) A Review of Medical Humanities Curriculum in Medical Schools	Michael Lam	2015	Canada	English	Journal of Pain Management	Journal Article	KT1	K1S1
) Reflecting Art in Nursing Practice	Carlita Anglin	2020	United States	English	The Journal of Nursing Administration	Journal Article	KT1	K1S1; K1S3
) Healthcare Management and the Humanities	Nathan Gerard	2021	United States	English	International Journal of Environmental Research and Public Health	Journal Article	KT4	K4S2
) Novels as Data	Ad A. Kaptein	2022	Netherlands	English	Journal of Health Psychology	Journal Article	KT1	K1S2
) Pregnancy & Protest in Interwar British Women's Writing	Fran Bigman	2016	Japan	English	BMJ Journals: Medical Humanities	Journal Article	KT5	K5S6
) Medical Humanities	Brian Hurwitz	2015	United Kingdom	English	Anglo Saxonica	Journal Article	KT1; KT4	K1S1; K4S3

#	Title	Author	Year	Country	Language	Journal/Source	Type		
26) Reflective Writing about Near Peer Blogs	Rachel Conrad Bracken	2022	United States	English	Journal of Medical Humanities	Journal Article	KT6	K6S3
27) More to the Story	Nicole Piemonte	2017	United States	English	Review of Communication	Journal Article	KT1	K1S1
28) Introduction	Enda McCaffrey	2021	United Kingdom	English	L'Esprit Créateur	Journal Article	KT3	K3S3
29) Nonmaleficence and Hope	Nathan Carlin	2020	United States	English	Pastoral Psychology	Journal Article	KT1; KT2	K1S6 K2S3
30) Bearing Witness	Courtney S. Campbell	2019	United States	English	Bearing Witness	Book or Textbook	KT5	K5S1
31) Bioethics and Imagination	Camilo Hernán	2017	Brazil; Norway	English	BMJ: Medical Humanities	Journal Article	KT1	K1S4
32) Medical Humanities	Eng Koon Ong	2019	Singapore	English	Annals, Academy of Medicine, Singapore	Journal Article	KT4	K4S3
33) Reflections for Clinical Pastoral Education Students in Psychiatric Settings	Nathan Carlin	2017	United States	English	Journal of Religion and Health	Journal Article	KT1	K1S3
34) The Routledge Handbook of Translation and Health	Sebnem Susam-Sareva	2021	Canada	English	The Routledge Handbook of Translation and Health	Book or Textbook	KT1; KT2	K1S1 K2S1
35) The Meaning of Life	Nathan Carlin	2016	United States	English	Pastoral Psychology	Journal Article	KT2	K2S4
36) Introduction	Steven Wilson	2016	United States	English	Project Muse	Journal Article	KT1	K1S5
37) Palliative Design Meets Palliative Medicine	Rana Sagha Zadeh	2019	United States	English	Health Environments Research and Design Journal	Journal Article	KT2	K2S5
38) The Spirit Thickened	Nina Shevzov-Zebrun	2020	United States	English	Journal of Medical Humanities	Journal Article	KT1; KT2	K1S1 K2S1 K2S1 K2S1
39) Pathographies of Mental Illness	Nathan Carlin	2022	United States	English	Pathographies of Mental illness	Book or Textbook	KT3	K3S4
40) Are We Ready for Intercultural Cancer Care?	Patrick Crombez	2018	Belgium	English	Current Opinion in Oncology	Journal Article	KT5	K5S2
41) Three Approaches for a Practical Bioethics	Camilo Manchola	2017	Brazil	English, Spanish, Portuguese	Revista Bioética	Journal Article	KT4	K4S5

Title	Author	Year	Country	Language	Journal/Source	Type	KT	K
Amy Bennet's *pochondriac* as Narrative Painting that Teaches out Care	Gert Olthuis	2022	Netherlands	English	Journal of General Internal Medicine	Journal Article	KT3	K3S2
Evaluation Health and edical Humanies Education: Proposal for creditation	Sarah L. Berry	2022	United States	English	BMJ: Medical Humanities	Journal Article	KT6	K6S2
Narrating Museum to omote Empathy d Critical inking in Medi Science Stunts and Doctors rough Online tivities	Antonella Poce	2021	Italy, Switzerland	English	Italian Journal of Educational Technology	Journal Article	KT1	K1S2
Medical manities in nadian Medical ools	Allan Peterkin	2019	United States	English	Routledge Handbook of	Book or Textbook	KT1	K1S2
Compassion, cessity, and Pharma n of the Health manities	Graham McCaffrey	2016	Canada	English	Journal of Applied Hermeneutics	Journal Article	KT4	K4S3
Medical emes in a Litture Classroom	Gayathri Prabhu	2019	India	English	Indian Journal of Medical Ethics	Journal Article	KT2	K2S6
On the Arts d Humanis in Medical ucation	Danielle G. Rabinowitz	2021	United States	English	Philosophy, Ethics, and Humanities in Medicine	Journal Article	KT6	K6S2
No Country Old Men	Thomas R. Cole	2017	United States	English	Project Muse: Perspectives in Biology and Medicine	Journal Article	KT3	K3S1
What Can ademic Deopment Learn m the Health manities?	Daphne Loads	2018	United Kingdom	English	International Journal for Academic Development	Journal Article	KT5	K5S3
A (Un)Natural iance	Mary E. Kollmer Horton	2020	United States	English	A (Un)Natural Alliance	Thesis or Dissertation	KT5; KT6	K5S4; K6S3

52) Metaphors unto Themselves	Birgit Bunzel Linder	2015	United States	English	Project Muse: Literature and Medicine	Journal Article	KT4	K4S
53) Islamic Ethics in Engagement with Life, Health, and Medicine	Adi Setia	2022	Malaysia	English	Islam and Biomedicine	Book or Textbook	KT1	K1S
54) Entanglement of Racism and Medical Ethics	Zhenling Gan	2020	China	English	Forum for World Literature Studies	Journal Article	KT1; KT5	K1S; K5S
55) Transcultural Adoption Literature for Pediatricians and Parents	Marianne Novy	2018	United States	English	Project Muse: Adoption and Culture	Journal Article	KT1; KT6	K6S
56) Beyond Medical Paternalism	Anna Magdalena Elsner	2019	United States	English	Project Muse: Literature and Medicine	Journal Article	KT1; KT5	K1S; K5S
57) The Variety of Hope	Isabelle Wienand	2018	Switzerland	English	Spiritual Care	Journal Article	KT3	K3S
58) Ayurvedic Vision on Health and Environment	Raghul V. Rajan	2022	India	English	The Bloomsbury Handbook to the Medical-Environmental Humanities	Book or Textbook	KT5	K5S
59) The Geschlecht Complex	Oscar Jansson	2023	Sweden	English	The Geschlecht Complex	Book or Textbook	KT6	K6S
60) Distressed doctors	Jonatan E. G. Wistrand	2019	Sweden	English	BMJ Journals: Medical Humanities	Journal Article	KT2	K2S
61) Interactions between Medicine and the Arts	Wolfgang Schütz	2020	Austria	English	The Central European Journal of Medicine	Journal Article	KT6	K6S
62) Why Teach Pharmacy Ethics Through Literary Fiction?	Halil Tekiner	2017	Turkey	English	World Journal of Pharmaceutical Sciences	Journal Article	KT4	K4S
63) Medical Memoirs as a Teaching Tool within Narrative Medicine	Shelby McCubbin	2022	United States	English	Medical Memoirs as a Teaching Tool within Narrative Medicine	Thesis or Dissertation	KT5	K5S; K5S

Title	Author	Year	Country	Language	Source	Type	KT	KS
The Doctor-Patient Relationship and Encounter in the Nineteenth-Century French Novel	Sarah Jones	2019	United Kingdom	English	The Doctor-Patient Relationship and Encounter in the Nineteenth-Century French Novel	Thesis or Dissertation	KT2; KT5	K2S2; K5S1
Clinical Ethics in the Context of Medical Humanities	Mario Picozzi	2022	Italy	English	Introduction to Medical Humanities	Book or Textbook	KT1; KT2	K1S1; K2S1
Disability and Mental Health	Shivanee	2021	India	English	Media Watch	Journal Article	KT1	K1S1
Wearing a Cloak and Many Hats	Arlene L. Macdonald	2021	United States	English	Anthropology in Medical Education	Book or Textbook	KT1	K1S1
Writing and Healing in Saul Bellow's *Herzog*	Antti Ahonen	2022	Finland	English	Writing and Healing in Saul Bellow's *Herzog*	Thesis or Dissertation	KT1	K1S1; K1S5
Translation Without Medicalization	Sharon Rushing	2021	United States	English	Anthropology in Medical Education	Book or Textbook	KT2; KT4	K2S1; K4S2
The Arts and Humanities in Health Professional Education	Pam Harvey	2020	Australia; United Kingdom	English	Clinical Education for the Health Professions	Book or Textbook	KT4	K4S3
Epilepsy, Forgetting, and Convalescence in Ondaatje's *Warlight*	Jan Gresil S. Kahambing	2021	Philippines	English	Rupkatha Journal on Interdisciplinary Studies in Humanities	Journal Article	KT1; KT2	K1S3; K2S7
On the Nature of Medicine	Alireza Monajemi	2021	Iran	English	The Quarterly Journal of Philosophical Investigations-University of Tabriz	Journal Article	KT1	K1S3
Introduction	Steven Wilson	2020	United Kingdom	English	Modern and Contemporary France	Journal Article	KT2	K2S1
Book as Body	Darian Goldin Stahl	2021	Canada	English	Book as Body	Thesis or Dissertation	KT2	K2S3
Nursing and Humanities	Graham McCaffrey	2020	Canada	English	Nursing and Humanities	Book or Textbook	KT1; KT2; KT6	K1S6; K2S8; K2S1; K6S2
To Be or Not	Craig M. Klugman	2021	United States	English	Journal of Medical Humanities	Journal Article	KT6	K6S2

77) Healers, Innovators, Entrepreneurs: Healers	Sharon Strocchia	2020	United States	English	Annals of Science	Journal Article	KT2	K2S3
78) Humanities in Medicine	Diane O'Doherty	2019	Ireland	English	Creative Education	Journal Article	KT1	K1S1 K1S3
79) Narrative Medicine in Chekhov and Bulgakov	Melissa L. Miller	2021	United States	English	The Russian Medical Humanities	Book or Textbook	KT1; KT5	K1S6
80) Life and Times	Paul Craddock	2019	United Kingdom	English	British Journal of General Practice	Journal Article	KT5	K5S2
81) Self-Health	Emily Joan Waples	2016	United States	English	Self-Health	Thesis or Dissertation	KT2	K2S1
82) Piloting an Undergraduate Survey Course in Medical Humanities and Social Medicine	Eileen P. Anderson-Fye	2018	United States	English	Journal of Humanities in Rehabilitation	Journal Article	KT1	K1S3
83) Grandma	Thomas R. Cole	2016	United States	English	The Gerontologist	Journal Article	KT3	K3S1
84) Performing Cancer	Virginia Dakari	2016	Greece	English	Performing Cancer	Thesis or Dissertation	KT1	K1S1
85) The Philosophicum-Model Project of Philosophy of Medicine in Medical Education and Practice in Germany	Jonas Daub	2019	Germany	English	American Journal of Internal Medicine	Journal Article	KT1	K1S2 K1S3
86) John Wiltshire, Frances Burney and the Doctors	Virlana M. Shchuka	2020	Canada	English	Medical History (Cambridge)	Journal Article	KT2	K2S9
87) How the Humanities Shape Medical Culture	Lester Liao	2018	Canada	English	MedEd Publish	Journal Article	KT2	K2S1
88) Medical Humanities and the Eighteenth Century	Stephanie M. Hilger	2021	United States	English	Project Muse-Goethe Yearbook	Journal Article	KT1	K1S4
89) Exploring Creativity in Medical Students	James A. O'Hare	2019	Ireland	English	Creative Education	Journal Article	KT1	K1S2

1) Life, Science, and Power in History and Philosophy	Akihito Suzuki	2019	Japan	English	East Asian Science, Technology and Society	Journal Article	KT6	K6S2
2) Establishing, Promoting, and Growing the Health Humanities in Japan	Jeffrey Huffman	2020	United States	English	The Routledge Companion to Health Humanities	Book or Textbook	KT2	K2S8
3) Medical Humanities Education at Six Texas Medical Schools	Molly Schlamp	2020	United States	English	Medical Humanities Education at Six Texas Medical Schools	Thesis or Dissertation	KT6	K6S2
4) Aging Bodies and Minds in Shakespeare	Vicent Montalt	2020	Spain	English	Understanding the Discourse of Aging	Book or Textbook	KT3	K3S1
5) Teaching for Humanism	Nicole M. Piemonte	2019	United States	English	Teaching Health Humanities	Book or Textbook	KT4	K4S3
6) Healthcaring	Rebecca Amerisa Waters	2018	United States	English	Healthcaring	Thesis or Dissertation	KT4	K4S3
7) Vocal Pedagogy, Pathology, and Personality in Chervin's Journal La Voix Parlée et Chantée	Madeleine Matej MacQueen	2022	United States	English	Vocal Pedagogy, Pathology, and Personality in Chervin's Journal La Voix Parlée et Chantée	Thesis or Dissertation	KT2; KT6	K2S2; K6S3
8) Bodies and Transitions in the Health Humanities	Lisa M. DeTora	2019	United States	English	Bodies and Transitions in the Health Humanities	Book or Textbook	KT6	K6S3
9) AnArtomy	Ian Walsh	2018	United Kingdom	English	MedEd Publish	Journal Article	KT4	K4S3
10) The Technological Imperative and Medicine	Dennis Samson	2018	United States	English	Journal of Alabama Academy of Science	Journal Article	KT5	K5S1
11) Introduction	Stephanie M. Hilger	2017	United States	English	New Directions in Literature and Medicine Studies	Book or Textbook	KT1	K1S4
12) Representation of Medics in British and Bengali Literatures the 1850s-the 1950s	Pritha Kundu	2017	India	English	Representation of Medics in British and Bengali Literatures (the 1850s-the 1950s)	Thesis or Dissertation	KT1	K1S1; K1S2

102) Royal Ambitions	James Bradley	2015	Australia	English	Text Journal: Journal of Writing and Writing Courses	Journal Article	KT2	K2S1
103) Medicine, Value, and Knowledge in the Veterinary Clinic	Jane Desmond	2022	United States	English	Frontiers in Veterinary Science	Journal Article	KT1	K1S1 K1S2
104) Introduction	Rainer Brömer	2016	Turkey; Germany	English	Journal of Health and Culture	Journal Article	KT1	K1S4
105) Medical Humanities Education and Its Influence on Students' Outcomes in Taiwan	Bao Lan Hoang	2022	Taiwan; Australia	English	Frontiers in Medicine	Journal Article	KT1	K1S2
106) Biopolitics, Race, and Resistance in the Novels of Salman Rushdie	George William Twigg	2015	United Kingdom	English	Biopolitics, Race, and Resistance in the Novels of Salman Rushdie	Thesis or Dissertation	KT1	K1S2
107) Introduction	Monika Pietrzak-Franger	2017	Austria	English	Syphilis in Victorian Literature and Culture	Book or Textbook	KT1	K1S2
108) Je-sans-moi, Patients, Pain and Painlessness in Malraux's *Lazare*	Anna Magdalena Elsner	2016	United States	English	L'Esprit Créateur	Journal Article	KT1	K1S4
109) When I Say...the Medical Humanities in Medical Education	Alan Bleakley	2015	United Kingdom	English	ASME: Medical Education	Journal Article	KT1	K1S3
110) A Vision for Health Humanities in Japan	Jeffrey Huffman	2019	Japan	English	Bulletin of St. Luke's International University	Journal Article	KT1	K1S1

Key Themes and Sub-Themes

	Abbreviation	Key Themes / Sub-Themes
Key Theme 1	KT1	Understanding medical humanities
Sub-theme 1	K1S1	Defining medical humanities
Sub-theme 2	K1S2	Citing the textbook as part of a general introduction of medical humanities
Sub-theme 3	K1S3	Describing the content of medical humanities
Sub-theme 4	K1S4	Differentiating between medical humanities and other disciplines
Sub-theme 5	K1S5	Describing disciplines within medical humanities
Sub-theme 6	K1S6	Describing the goals of medical humanities
Key Theme 2	KT2	Providing historical context for medical humanities
Sub-theme 1	K2S1	Describing the origins, growth, and acceptance of medical humanities as an academic discipline
Sub-theme 2	K2S2	Providing historical context for development of doctor-patient relationship
Sub-theme 3	K2S3	Providing historical context for discrimination and abuse faced by minority groups within medicine
Sub-theme 4	K2S4	Providing historical context for long-standing relationship between literature and medicine
Sub-theme 5	K2S5	Providing historical context of hospice and palliative care
Sub-theme 6	K2S6	Providing historical context for integration of medical humanities into medical education
Sub-theme 7	K2S7	Providing historical and medico-legal context of epilepsy
Sub-theme 8	K2S8	Providing historical context of Edmund Pellegrino as leader in field of medical humanities
Sub-theme 9	K2S9	Providing historical context of pathography
Sub-theme 10	K2S10	Providing historical context for narrative medicine
Sub-theme 11	K2S11	Provides historical context for the term "acquaintance knowledge"
Sub-theme 12	K2S12	Provides historical context of concepts of health and disease
Key Theme 3	KT3	Referencing works within the textbook
Sub-theme 1	K3S1	Referencing a specific section of the textbook

Sub-theme 2	K3S2	Referencing art featured in the textbook
Sub-theme 3	K3S3	Referencing primary text that is quoted in the textbook
Sub-theme 4	K3S4	Referencing philosophical terms defined in the textbook
Key Theme 4	KT4	Describing the value of medical humanities
Sub-theme 1	K4S1	Utilizing medical humanities as a problem-solving tool
Sub-theme 2	K4S2	Referencing the textbook to illustrate how medical humanities is being incorporated into medicine
Sub-theme 3	K4S3	Justifying the value of how medical humanities can foster professional and personal development among students and clinicians
Sub-theme 4	K4S4	Describing the value of patient narratives to understand illness and disease
Sub-theme 5	K4S5	Highlighting the purpose of bioethics
Sub-theme 6	K4S6	Understanding the purpose and impact of poetry
Key Theme 5	KT5	Supporting the author's argument via citation
Sub-theme 1	K5S1	Supporting the author's views on doctor-patient relationships
Sub-theme 2	K5S2	Asserting that the disease-based model of care does not consider social, emotional, spiritual, or cultural factors
Sub-theme 3	K5S3	Positing that open-mindedness and reflective thinking is important for healthcare providers
Sub-theme 4	K5S4	Contending there is no definitive integration of medical humanities into medical education
Sub-theme 5	K5S5	Maintaining the idea that healthcare is collaborative work environment
Sub-theme 6	K5S6	Critiquing how medical humanities views science fiction
Key Theme 6	KT6	Establishing precedent in medical humanities
Sub-theme 1	K6S1	Featuring Cole as a pioneer in medical humanities
Sub-theme 2	K6S2	Citing the book as the groundbreaking text to teach medical humanities
Sub-theme 3	K6S3	Listing the textbook as an exemplar of medical humanities

Bibliography

"91st Academy Awards Special Rules for the Documentary Awards." Academy of Motion Pictures Arts & Sciences, 2018. Accessed February 5, 2023. https://www.oscars.org/sites/oscars/files/91aa_doc_features.pdf.

"2019 Alzheimer's Disease Facts and Figures." Alzheimer's Association. *Alzheimer's & Dementia* 15 (3) 321–87.

"About." Health Humanities Consortium. Accessed April 13, 2023. https://healthhumanitiesconsortium.com/about/.

Achenbaum, W. Andrew. "Afterword." In *Handbook of the Humanities and Aging*, edited by Thomas Cole, David Van Tassel, and Robert Kastenbaum, 419–32. New York: Springer, 1992.

———. "Conscious Aging, Spiritual Aging, and Soulful Aging: A Journey Toward the Vulnerability of Love." *Journal of Religion, Spirituality & Aging* 35, no. 3 (2023) 212–21.

———. *Crossing Frontiers: Gerontology Emerges as a Science*. New York: Cambridge University Press, 1995.

———. "The Humanities and Arts in the Gerontological Society of America." *The Gerontologist* 60, no. 4 (2020) 591–97.

———. *Safeguarding Social Security for Future Generations: Leaving a Legacy in an Aging Society*. New York: Routledge, 2023.

———. *Social Security: Visions and Revisions*. New York: Cambridge University Press, 1986.

Addis, Ilana B., Christine C. Ireland, Eric Vittinghoff, Feng Lin, Cynthia A. Stuenkel, and Stephen Hulley. "Sexual Activity and Function in Postmenopausal Women with Heart Disease." *Obstetrics and Gynecology* 106, no. 1 (2005) 121–27.

"Advancing Diversity, Equity, and Inclusion in Medical Education." AAMC. Accessed February 28, 2023. https://www.aamc.org/about-us/equity-diversity-inclusion/advancing-diversity-equity-and-inclusion-medical-education.

Ahonen, Antti. "Writing and Healing in Saul Bellow's "Herzog." PhD diss., University of Easter Finland, 2022.

Allen, Jon G. *Trusting in Psychotherapy*. Washington, D.C.: American Psychiatric Association, 2021.

Allen, Julie Ober, Erica Solway E, and Matthias Kirch M, et al. "Experiences of Everyday Ageism and the Health of Older US Adults." *JAMA Netw Open* 5, no. 6 (2022) e2217240.

Al-Mahrezi, Abdulaziz, and Zahid Al-Mandhari. "Palliative Care: Time for Action." *Oman Medical Journal* 31, no. 3 (2016) 161–63.

Alvarez, Al. *Risky Business: People, Pastimes, Poker and Books*. London: Bloomsbury, 2007.
American Association of Retired Persons (AARP). "The Aging Readiness & Competitiveness Report, United States," 2019. AARP International. Accessed November 30, 2023. https://www.aarpinternational.org/file%20library/arc/countries/full%20reports/arc-report--united-states.pdf.
Anderson-Fye, Eileen, Julia Knopes, and Hillary Villarreal. "Piloting an Undergraduate Survey Course in Medical Humanities and Social Medicine: Lessons, Tradeoffs, and Institutional Context." *Journal of Humanities in Rehabilitation* (2018) 1–14.
Andrews, Molly. "Critical and Reflective Gerontology." *Ageing & Society* 29 (2009) 649–58.
Angeli, Elizabeth L., and Richard Johnson-Sheehan. "Introduction to the Special Issue: Medical Humanities and/or the Rhetoric of Health and Medicine." *Technical Communication Quarterly* 27, no. 1 (2018) 1–6.
Anglin, Carlita, Carolyn Halpin-Healy, and Peri Rosenfeld. "Reflecting Art in Nursing Practice: Developing Visual Arts Programs to Transform and Strengthen Practice." *JONA: The Journal of Nursing Administration* 50, no. 5 (2020) 274–80.
Ankele, John, and Anne Macksoud. *Life Stories: Aging and the Human Spirit*. USA: Old Dog Documentaries, 2001. Film.
"Annual Juneteenth Ally Award Recipients." Center for the Healing of Racism. 2022. Accessed September, 28, 2023. https://www.centerhealingracism.org/annual-juneteenth-ally-award-recipients/.
Asad, Asad L., Michel Anteby, and Filiz Garip. "Who Donates Their Bodies to Science? The Combined Role of Gender and Migration Status among California Whole-Body Donors." *Social Science & Medicine* 106 (2014) 53–58.
Aufderheide, Patricia, Peter Jaszi, and Mridu Chandra. "Honest Truths: Documentary Filmmakers and Challenges in Their Work," 2009. Center for Social Media, American University. Accessed on November 30, 2023. https://web.archive.org/web/20210801235609/https://archive.cmsimpact.org/sites/default/files/Honest_Truths_--_Documentary_Filmmakers_on_Ethical_Challenges_in_Their_Work.pdf.
Baars, Jan. *Aging and the Art of Living*. Baltimore: The Johns Hopkins University Press, 2012.
———. "The Challenge of Critical Gerontology." *Journal of Aging Studies* 5, no. 3 (1991) 219–43.
Baars, Jan, Dale Dannefer, Chris Phillipson, and Alan Walker. *Aging, Globilization and Inequality: The New Critical Gerontology*. London: Routledge, 2006.
Back, Anthony, Elyse Park, Joseph Greer, Vicki Jackson, Juliet Jacobsen, Emily Gallagher, and Jennifer Temel. "Clinician Roles in Early Integrated Palliative Care for Patients with Advanced Cancer: A Qualitative Study." *Journal of Palliative Medicine* 17, no. 11 (2014) 1244–48.
Bakhtin, Mikhail. *Art and Answerability: Early Philosophical Essays*. Edited by Michael Holquist and Vadim Liapunov. Translated by Vadim Liapunov. Austin: University of Texas Press, 1990.
———. *Problems of Dostoevsky's Poetics*. Edited and translated by Caryl Emerson. Minneapolis: Minnesota University Press, 1984.
———. *Speech Genres and Other Late Essays*. Edited by Michael Holquist and Caryl Emerson. Translated by Vern McGree. Austin: University of Texas Press, 1986.

Baltes, Paul. "Facing our Limits: Human Dignity in the Very Old." *Daedalus* 135, no. 1 (2006) 32–39.
Baltes, Paul, and Jacqui Smith. "New Frontiers in the Future of Aging: From Successful Aging of the Young Old to the Dilemmas of the Fourth Age." *Gerontology* 49, no. 2 (2003) 123–35.
Bamberg, Michael. "Stories: Big or Small—Why Do We Care?" *Narrative Inquiry* 16, no. 1 (2006) 139–47.
Bamberg, Michael, and Alexandra Georgakopoulou. "Small Stories as a New Perspective in Narrative and Identity Analysis." *Text and Talk* 28, no. 3 (2008) 377–96.
Bass, Scott. "Gerontological Theory: The Search for the Holy Grail." *The Gerontologist* 46, no. 1 (2006) 139–44.
Bauer, Michael, Emily Haesler, and Deirdre Fetherstonhaugh. "Let's Talk About Sex: Older People's Views on the Recognition of Sexuality and Sexual Health in the Health-Care Setting." *Health Expectations* 19, no. 6 (2016) 1237–50.
Bauman, Zygmunt. *Mortality, Immortality, and Other Life Strategies*. Redwood City: Stanford University Press, 1992.
Behuniak, Susan M. "The Living Dead? The Construction of People with Alzheimer's Disease as Zombies." *Ageing and Society* 31, no. 1 (2011) 70–92.
Bentley, Allison, Tessa Morgan, Yakubu Salifu, and Catherine Walshe. "Exploring the Experiences of Living with Lewy Body Dementia: An Integrative Review." *Journal of Advanced Nursing* 77, no. 12 (2021) 4632–45.
Bentwich, Miriam. "Medical Humanities and Active Learning." In *Active Education for Future Doctors*, edited by N. Dickman and B. Schuster, 79–96. New York: Springer, 2020.
Berger, Arielle, Elizabeth Niedra, Stephanie Brooks, et al. "Teaching Professionalism in Postgraduate Medical Education: A Systematic Review." *Acad Med* 95, no. 6 (2020) 938–46.
Berman, David. *The Strange Demise of Jim Crow*. USA: California Newsreel, 1998. Film.
Berry, Sarah, Craig Klugman, Charise Adams, et al. "Health Humanities: A Baseline Survey of Baccalaureate and Graduate Programs in North America." *Journal of Medical Humanities* (2023). https://doi.org/10.1007/s10912-023-09790-5.
Berry, Sarah, Anna-leila Williams, Erin Gentry Lamb, and Craig M Klugman. "Evolution in Health and Medical Humanities Education: A Proposal for Accreditation." *Medical Humanities* 49, no. 1 (2023) 134–38.
Bigman, Fran. "Pregnancy as Protest in Interwar British Women's Writing: An Antecedent Alternative to Aldous Huxley's *Brave New World*." *Medical Humanities* 42, no. 4 (2016) 265–70.
Blackie, Michael, and Erin Gentry Lamb. "Courting Discomfort in an Undergraduate Health Humanities Classroom." In *The Health Humanities Reader*, edited by Therese Jones, Delese Wear, and Lester Friedman, 490–500. New Brunswick, NJ: Rutgers University Press, 2014.
Blair, Mervin, Cecile A. Marczinski, Nicole Davis-Faroque, and Andrew Kertesz. "A Longitudinal Study of Language Decline in Alzheimer's Disease and Frontotemporal Dementia." *Journal of the International Neuropsychological Society* 13, no. 2 (2007) 237–45.
Bleakley, Alan. "When I Say . . . the Medical Humanities in Medical Education." *Medical Education* 49, no. 10 (2015) 959–60.

Bookstein, Fred, and W. Andrew Achenbaum. "Aging as Explanation." In *Visions and Voices of Aging*, ed. Thomas R. Cole, W. Andrew Achenbaum, Patricia L. Jakobi, and Robert Kastenbaum, 20–45. *Voices and Visions of Aging: Toward a Critical Gerontology*. New York: Springer Publishing Company, 1993.

Boorse, Christopher. "Health as a Theoretical Concept." *Philosophy of Science* 44, no. 4 (1977) 542–73.

Booth, Wayne C. *The Company We Keep: An Ethics of Fiction*. Berkeley, CA: University of California Press, 1988.

Bordo, Susan. *Unbearable Weight: Feminism, Western Culture, and the Body*. Berkeley: University of California Press, 2003.

Bortz, Maggie. "Carrying the Fire: Individuation Toward the Mature Masculine and Telos of Cultural Myth in Cormac McCarthy's *No Country for Old Men* and *The Road*." *Jung Journal* 5, no. 4 (2011) 28–42.

Bracken, Rachel Conrad, Ajay Major, Aleena Paul, and Kirsten Ostherr. "Reflective Writing About Near-Peer Blogs: A Novel Method for Introducing the Medical Humanities in Premedical Education." In *The Medical/Health Humanities: Politics, Programs, and Pedagogies*, edited by Therese Jones and K. Pachucki, 23–57. New York: Springer, 2022.

Bradley, James, and Susan Bradley Smith. "Royal Ambitions: Creative Writing and the Secret Rules of Courtship in the Medical Humanities." *Text* 19, no. 1 (2015) 1–15.

Broncano, Manuel. *Religion in Cormac McCarthy's Fiction: Apocryphal Borderlands*. New York: Routledge, 2014.

Browne, Ken. *Why Doctors Write: Finding Humanity in Medicine*. USA: KBProductions, 2020. Film.

Buber, Martin. *I and Thou*. Translated by Ronald Gregor Smith. New York: Scribner Classics, 1958.

Bullivant, Stephen. *Mass Exodus: Catholic Disaffiliation in Britain and America since Vatican II*. Oxford: Oxford University Press, 2019.

Burke, Kenneth. *Permanence and Change: An Anatomy of Purpose*. 3rd ed. Los Angeles: University of California Press, 1984.

Burt, Stephanie. "Against Winning." *Georgia Review* Fall (2021). Accessed on November 30, 2023. https://thegeorgiareview.com/posts/against-winning/.

Bury, Mike. "Ageing, Gender and Sociological Theory." In *Connecting Gender and Ageing: A Sociological Approach*, edited by Sara Arber and Jay Ginn, 15–29. Buckingham: Open University Press, 1995.

Caddell, Lisa, and Linda Clare. "The Impact of Dementia on Self and Identity: A Systematic Review." *Clin Psychol Rev* 30, no. 1 (2010) 113–26.

Calasanti, Toni M., and Kathleen F. Slevin. *Gender, Social Inequalities, and Aging*. Walnut Creek: Rowman & Littlefield, 2001.

Calasanti, Toni, Kathleen F. Slevin, and Neal King. "Ageism and Feminism: From 'Et Cetera' to Center." *NWSA Journal* 18, no. 1 (2006) 13–30.

Callahan, Daniel. *Setting Limits: Medical Goals in an Aging Society*. With a response to my critics. Washington: Georgetown University Press, 1995.

Campbell, Courtney S. *Bearing Witness: Religious Meanings in Bioethics*. Eugene, OR: Wipf and Stock Publishers, 2019.

Campbell, Hugh, and M. Finney, eds. *Country Boys: Masculinity and the Country Life*. University Park: Pennsylvania State University, 2006.

Carlin, Nathan. "The Meaning of Life." *Pastoral Psychology* 65, no. 5 (2016) 611–30.

———. "Nonmaleficence and Hope: A Correlation." *Pastoral Psychology* 69, no. 4 (2020) 315–30.

———. *Pastoral Aesthetics: A Theological Perspective on Principlist Bioethics.* New York: Oxford University Press, 2019.

———. *Pathographies of Mental Illness. Elements in Bioethics and Neuroethics.* New York: Cambridge University Press, 2022.

———. "Reflections for Clinical Pastoral Education Students in Psychiatric Settings." *Journal of Religion and Health* 57, no. 2 (2018) 523–37.

Carlin, Nathan, and Thomas Cole. "The Aging Bodies of Mickey Rourke and Marisa Tomei in *The Wrestler.*" *Amerikastudien* 56, no. 1 (2011) 85–101.

Carson, Ronald. "Foreword." In *What Does It Mean to Grow Old? Reflections from the Humanities,* ed. Thomas R. Cole and Sally Gadow, xi–xiv. Durham: Duke University Press, 1986.

Castillo, Camilo Hernán Manchola, and Jan Helge Solbakk. "Bioethics and Imagination: Towards a Narrative Bioethics Committed to Social Action and Justice." *Medical Humanities* 43, no. 3 (2017) 166–71.

Centers for Disease Control and Prevention. "Life Expectancy." CDC/National Center for Health Statistics. February 7, 2023. Accessed on November 30, 2023. https://www.cdc.gov/nchs/fastats/life-expectancy.htm.

Centers for Disease Control and Prevention. "Sexually Transmitted Disease Surveillance." April 2021. Accessed on November 30, 2023. https://www.cdc.gov/std/statistics/2019/std-surveillance-2019.pdf.

Chambers, Tod S. "The Virtue of Incongruity in the Medical Humanities." *Journal of Medical Humanities* 30 (2009) 151–54.

Chattoo, Caty Borum. "Oscars So White: Gender, Racial, and Ethnic Diversity and Social Issues in U.S. Documentary Films (2008–2017)." *Mass Communication and Society* 21, no. 3 (2018) 368–94.

Chattoo, Caty Borum, Patricia Aufderheide, Kenneth Merrill, and Modupeola Oyebolu. "Diversity on U.S. Public and Commercial TV in Authorial and Executive-Produced Social-Issue Documentaries." *Journal of Broadcasting & Electronic Media* 62, no. 3 (2018) 495–513.

Chen, Po-Jui, Chien-Da Huang, and San-Jou Yeh. "Impact of a Narrative Medicine Programme on Healthcare Providers' Empathy Scores over Time." *BMC Medical Education* 17, no. 1 (2017) 1–8.

Chiavaroli, Neville, Chien-Da Huang, and Lynn Monrouxe. "Learning Medicine with, from, and through the Humanities." In *Understanding Medical Education: Evidence, Theory, and Practice,* edited by Tim Swanwick, Kirsty Forrest, and Bridget O'Brien, 223–37. 3rd ed. Oxford: Wiley Blackwell, 2019.

Churchill, John. "Odysseus's Bed; Agamemnon's Bath." *College Literature* 18, no. 1 (1991) 1–13.

Churchill, Larry. "Accepting and Embracing Our Human Mortality." *Perspectives in Biology and Medicine.* Forthcoming.

Clark, Katerina, and Michael Holquist. *Mikhail Bakhtin.* Cambridge, MA: Harvard University Press, 1984.

"CO_2 Emissions per Capita." Worldometer. Accessed on October 11, 2023. https://www.worldometers.info/co2-emissions/co2-emissions-per-capita/.

Cohler, Bertram J. "Aging, Morale, and Meaning." In *Visions and Voices of Aging,* ed. Thomas R. Cole, W. Andrew Achenbaum, Patricia L. Jakobi, and Robert

Kastenbaum, 107-33. *Voices and Visions of Aging: Toward a Critical Gerontology.* New York: Springer Publishing Company, 1993.

Cole, Thomas. "The Fall of Daedalus." *Generations* 25, no. 4 (2001) 66-68.

———. "The Flames of Oblivion." Unpublished. 1998.

———. "Grandma." *The Gerontologist* 56, no. 1 (2016) 155-57.

———. "The Humanities and Aging: An Overview." *Handbook of the Humanities and Aging*, ed. Thomas R. Cole, David D. Van Tassel, and Robert Kastenbaum, xi-xxiv. New York: Springer Publishing, 1992.

———. "Introduction." In *The Oxford Book of Aging*, edited by Thomas R. Cole and Mary Winkler. New York: Oxford University Press, 1994.

———. *The Journey of Life: A Cultural History of Aging in America.* New York: Cambridge University Press, 1992.

———. *No Color Is My Kind: The Life of Eldrewey Stearns and the Integration of Houston.* Austin, TX: University of Texas Press, 1997.

———. *Old Man Country: My Search for Meaning Among the Elders.* New York: Oxford University Press, 2020.

———. "The Tattered Web of Cultural Meaning." *What Does It Mean to Grow Old? Reflections from the Humanities*, edited by Thomas Cole and Sally Gadow, 3-7. Durham: Duke University Press, 1986.

Cole, Thomas, W. Andrew Achenbaum, Patricia L. Jakobi, and Robert Kastenbaum, eds. *Voices and Visions of Aging: Toward a Critical Gerontology.* New York: Springer Publishing Company, 1993.

Cole, Thomas, Nathan Carlin, and Ronald Carson. *Medical Humanities: An Introduction.* New York: Cambridge University Press, 2015.

Cole, Thomas R., and Sally Gadow, eds. *What Does It Mean to Grow Old? Reflections from the Humanities.* Durham: Duke University Press, 1986.

Cole, Thomas R., Robert Kastenbaum, and Ruth E. Ray. *Handbook of the Humanities and Aging.* 2nd ed. New York: Springer Publishing Company, 2000.

Cole, Thomas R., and Ruth E. Ray. "Introduction." In *Handbook of the Humanities and Aging*, edited by Thomas R. Cole, Robert Kastenbaum, and Ruth E. Ray, xi-xxii. 2nd ed. New York: Springer Publishing Company, 2000.

———. "Introduction: The Humanistic Study of Aging Past and Present, or Why Gerontology Still Needs Interpretive Inquiry." In *A Guide to Humanistic Studies in Aging: What Does It Mean to Grow Old*, ed. Thomas R. Cole, Ruth E. Ray, and Robert Kastenbaum, 1-29. Baltimore: The Johns Hopkins University Press, 2010.

Cole, Thomas R., Barbara Thompson, Linda Rounds. "In Whose Voice? Composing an Ethics Case as a Song of Life." *Journal of Long-Term Home Health Care* 14, no. 4 (1995) 23-31.

Cole, Thomas R., and Ben Saxton. "No Country for Old Men: Four Challenges for Men Facing the Fourth Age." *Perspectives in Biology and Medicine* 60, no. 4 (2017) 607-14.

Cole, Thomas R. and Mary Winkler, eds. *The Oxford Book of Aging.* New York: Oxford University Press, 1994.

Coleman, Peter. *Belief and Ageing: Spiritual Pathways in Later Life.* Bristol: Policy Press, 2011.

"Collection Development Guidelines of the National Library of Medicine." National Library of Medicine (US); 2019-. Medical Humanities. Updated July 30, 2004. https://www.ncbi.nlm.nih.gov/books/NBK518708/.

"Completed Life Euthanasia Proposal Needs for Safeguards against Misuse." *NL Times.* May 20, 2022. Accessed on December 15, 2023. https://nltimes.nl/2022/05/20/completed-life-euthanasia-proposal-needs-safeguards misuse-council-state.

Conley, Terri D., and Verena Klein. "Women Get Worse Sex: A Confound in the Explanation of Gender Differences in Sexuality." *Perspectives on Psychological Science* 17, no. 4 (2022) 960–78.

Cooper, Lydia. *No More Heroes: Narrative Perspective and Morality in Cormac McCarthy's Novels.* Baton Rouge: Louisiana State University Press, 2011.

Corbin, Juliet, and Anselm Strauss. *Basics of Qualitative Research: Techniques and Procedures for Developing Grounded Theory.* 4th ed. Thousand Oaks: Sage, 2015.

Corr, Charles A. "Elisabeth Kübler-Ross and the 'Five Stages' Model in a Sampling of Recent American Textbooks." *OMEGA* 82, no. 2 (2020) 294–322.

Cowdry, Edmund. *The Problems of Aging.* Baltimore: Williams and Wilkins, 1939.

Craddock, Paul, Arti Maini, Jo Horsburgh, and Sonia Kumar. "Lifetimes of the Clinical Consultation: The Current Situation of Healthcare Consultations." *British Journal of General Practice* 69, no. 687 (2019) 506–7.

Crombez, Patrick, Sandra Michiels, and Dominique Bron. "Are We Ready for Intercultural Cancer Care?" *Current Opinion in Oncology* 30, no. 4 (2018) 205–11.

Cruess, Richard, Sylvia Cruess, J. Donald Boudreau, et al. "Reframing Medical Education to Support Professional Identity Formation." *Acad Med* 89, no. 11 (2014) 1446–51.

Cruikshank, Margaret. *Learning to Be Old: Gender, Culture, and Aging.* 3rd ed. New York: Rowman & Littlefield. 2013.

Cuff, Dana, Anastasia Loukaitou-Sideris, Todd Presner, Maite Zubiaurre, and Jonathan Jae-an Crisman. *Urban Humanities: New Practices for Reimagining the City.* Boston: MIT Press, 2020.

Curiel, Himeka "Meyer Remembers for Shaping Curriculum in History Department." *The Wesleyan Connection*, June 5, 2018. Accessed on October 19, 2023. https://newsletter.blogs.wesleyan.edu/2018/06/05/meyer-remembered-for-shaping curriculum-in-history-department/.

Dakari, Virginia. "Performing Cancer: Toward an Aesthetic of the Unpresentable." PhD diss., Aristotle University of Thessaloniki, 2016.

D'Angelo, Chris. "Climate Change is Supercharging Most Infectious Diseases, New Study Funds." *Huffington Post*, August 8, 2022. https://www.huffpost.com/entry/climate-change-infectious-disease paper_n_62dfeac9e4b03dbb991d9a9e.

"Data Reference Card Details." University of Texas Medical Branch, 2022. Accessed September 29, 2023. https://www.utmb.edu/facts.

Daub, Jonas, Hans Christoph Aster, Hannah Gauger, Till Gallasch, Michael Schmidt, Johann Heinrich Koenigshausen, and Thomas Bohrer. "The Philosophicum-Model Project of Philosophy of Medicine in Medical Education and Practice in Germany Perspective Article." *American Journal of Internal Medicine* 7, no. 3 (2019) 72–76.

Davie, Grace. *Religion in Britain since 1945: Believing without Belonging.* Oxford: Blackwell, 1996.

———. "Vicarious Religion: A Methodological Challenge." *Everyday Religion: Observing Modern Religious Lives* (2007) 21–36.

de Medeiros, Kate. "Beyond the Memoir: Telling Life Stories Using Multiple Literary Forms." *Journal of Aging, Humanities, and the Arts* 1, no. 2 (2007) 159–67.

———. "The Complementary Self: Multiple Perspectives on the Aging Person." *Journal of Aging Studies* 19, no. 1 (2005) 1–13.
———. *Narrative Gerontology in Research and Practice*. New York: Springer, 2013.
Denninger, Tina, and Lea Schütze, eds. *Alter(n) und Geschlecht: Neuverhandlungen eines sozialen Zusammenhangs*. Münster: Westfälisches Dampfboot, 2017.
Desmond, Jane. "Medicine, Value, and Knowledge in the Veterinary Clinic: Questions for and from Medical Anthropology and the Medical Humanities." *Frontiers in Veterinary Science* 9 (2022). https://www.frontiersin.org/articles/10.3389/fvets.2022.780482/full.
DeTora, Lisa, and Stephanie Hilger. "Introduction: Bodies and Transitions in the Health Humanities." In *Bodies in Transition in the Health Humanities*, edited by Lisa DeTora and Stephanie Hilger, 1–8. New York: Routledge, 2019.
Donnelly, Colleen. "Claiming Chaos Narrative, Emerging from Silence." *Disability and Society* (2021) 1–15.
Döring, Nicola, and M. Rohangis Mohseni. "The Gender Orgasm Gap: A Critical Research Review on Gender Differences in Orgasm Frequency during Heterosex." *Z Sex Forsch* 35, no. 2 (2022) 73–87.
Drummond, Claudia, Gabriel Coutinho, Marina Monteiro, et al. "Narrative Impairment, White Matter Damage and CSF Biomarkers in the Alzheimer's Disease Spectrum." *Aging* 11, no. 20 (2019) 9188–9208.
Dürrenmatt, Friedrich. *Der Besuch der alten Dame*. Zürich: Arche, 1956.
Eddens, Ann. "Gender Stereotypes: Definitions & Examples." Study.com. July 23, 2018. Accessed on December 1, 2023. https://study.com/academy/lesson/the-impact-of-socialization-on-gender.html.
Eliot, George. *Middlemarch*. Houlton, ME: The New American Library, 1964.
Ellor, James, and Susan McFadden. "Perceptions of the Roles of Religion and Spirituality in the Work and Lives of Professionals in Gerontology: Views of the Present and Expectations about the Future." *Journal of Religion, Spirituality & Aging* 23, no. 1–2 (2011) 50–61.
Elsner, Anna Magdalena. "Beyond Medical Paternalism: Undoing the Doctor-Patient Relationship in Simone De Beauvoir's *A Very Easy Death*." *Literature and Medicine* 37, no. 2 (2019) 420–41.
———. "'Je-Sans-Moi' Patients, Pain, and Painlessness in Malraux's *Lazare*." *L'Esprit Créateur* 56, no. 2 (2016) 25–37.
Emanuel, Ezekiel. "Why I Hope to Die at 75." *The Atlantic* 314, no. 3 (2014) 74–81.
Emerson, Ralph Waldo. *Essays: Second Series*, edited by Brooks Atkinson. *The Selected Writings of Ralph Waldo Emerson*. New York: The Modern Library, 1950.
Engelhardt, H. Tristam, Jr. "The Birth of the Medical Humanities and the Rebirth of the Philosophy of Medicine: The Vision of Edmund D. Pellegrino." *Journal of Medicine and Philosophy* 15, no. 3 (1990) 237–41.
EPA. "Global Greenhouse Gas Emissions Data." United States Environmental Protection Agency. Accessed on October 11, 2023.
Global Greenhouse Gas Emissions Data | US EPA.
Epictetus. *The Art of Living*. Interpreted by Sharon LeBell. New York: HarperCollins, 1994.
Epstein, Rob, and Jeffrey Friedman. *End Game*. USA: Netflix, 2018. Film.

Esteban-Guitart, Moisès. "Towards a Multimethodological Approach to Identification of Funds of Identity, Small Stories and Master Narratives." *Narrative Inquiry* 22 (1) 173–80.

Evans, H. M., and J. Macnaughton. "Should Medical Humanities Be a Multidisciplinary or an Interdisciplinary Study?" *Medical Humanities* 30, no. 1 (2004) 1–4.

Falcus, Sarah, and Katsura Sako. *Contemporary Narratives of Dementia: Ethics, Ageing, Politics.* Abingdon: Routledge, 2019.

Fancourt, Daisy, and Saoirse Finn. *What Is the Evidence on the Role of the Arts in Improving Health and Well-Being? A Scoping Review.* World Health Organization. November 5, 2019. Accessed on December 1, 2023. https://www.who.int/europe/publications/i/item/9789289054553.

Faulkner, William. *Absalom! Absalom!* New York: Random House, 1936.

Fellowship, Lutheran Peace. "Transcript of Walter Wink's Nonviolence for the Violent." Accessed on December 1, 2023. https://www.lutheranpeace.org/articles/transcript-of-walter-winks-nonviolence-for-the violent.

Fernandez, Alicia. "Further Incorporating Diversity, Equity, and Inclusion into Medical Education Research." *Acad Med* 94, no. 11S (2019) S5-S6.

Fideler, David. *Breakfast with Seneca: A Stoic Guide to the Art of Living.* New York: W.W. Norton, 2022.

Fifield, Peter. *Modernism and Physical Illness: Sick Books.* New York: Oxford University Press, 2020.

"Films—Life Stories." Accessed February 20, 2023. http://www.thomasrcole.com/film.

Flaherty, Frances H. *Nanook of the North.* USA: Pathé Exchange, 1922. Film.

Flemming, Kate et al., "Qualitative Evidence Synthesis for Complex Interventions and Guideline Development: Clarification of the Purpose, Designs and Relevant Methods." BJM Global Health 4, no. 1 (2019) https://doi.org/10.1136/bmjgh-2018-000882.

Flexner, Abraham. *Medical Education: A Comparative Study* New York, NY: MacMillan, 1925.

———. *Medical Education in the United States and Canada: A Report to the Carnegie Foundation for the Advancement of Teaching Bulletin No. 4.* Boston: Updyke, 1910.

Forman, Jane, and Laura Damschroder. "Qualitative Content Analysis." In *Empirical Methods for Bioethics: A Primer*, edited by Liva Jacoby and Laura Siminoff, 39–62. Leeds: Emerald, 2007.

Foucault, Michel. *The Birth of the Clinic: An Archaeology of Medical Perception.* New York: Vintage Books, 1975.

Frank, Arthur. *The Wounded Storyteller: Body, Illness, and Ethics.* Chicago: University of Chicago Press, 1995.

Fraser, Kathleen, Jed Meltzer, and Frank Rudzicz. "Linguistic Features Identify Alzheimer's Disease in Narrative Speech." *Journal of Alzheimer's Disease* 49, no. 2 (2016) 407–22.

Freeman, Mark. "Life on Holiday? In Defense of Big Stories." *Narrative Inquiry* 16, no. 1 (2006) 131–38.

Friedman, Lester. "The Precarious Position of the Medical Humanities in the Medical School Curriculum." *Academic Medicine* 77, no. 4 (2002) 320–22.

Fuchs, Elinor. "Estragement: Towards an 'Age Theory' Theatre Criticism." *Performance Research* 19, no. 3 (2014) 69–77.

———. "Rehearsing Age." *Modern Drama* 59, no. 2 (2016) 143–54.

Gagnon, John H., and William Simon. *Sexual Conduct: The Social Sources of Human Sexuality*. 2nd ed. Abingdon: Routledge, 2017.

Gan, Zhenling, and Robin Chen-Hsing Tsai. "Entanglement of Racism and Medical Ethics: Cee's Illness and Healing in Toni Morrison's *Home*." *Forum for World Literature Studies* 12, no. 2 (2020). https://go.gale.com/ps/i.do?id=GALE%7CA635178563&sid=googleScholar&v=2.1&it=r&linkaccess=abs&issn=19498519&p=LitRC&sw=w&userGroupName=anon%7E552ec6a1&aty=open-web-entry.

Garcia, Justin, Chris Reiber, Sean Massey, and Ann Merriwether. "Sexual Hookup Culture: A Review." *Review of General Psychology* 16, no. 2 (2012) 161–76.

Gardiner, Stephen. *The Perfect Moral Storm: The Ethical Tragedy of Climate Change*. New York: Oxford University Press, 2011.

Geertz, Clifford. "Blurred Genres: The Refiguration of Social Thought." *The American Scholar* 49, no. 2 (1980) 165–79.

Gentili, Angela and Michael Godschalk. "Chapter 57: Sexuality." *Geriatric Review Syllabus*. 10th Ed. New York: American Geriatric Society, 2019.

Georgakopoulou, Alexandra. "Small Stories Research: Methods—Analysis—Outreach." *The Handbook of Narrative Analysis*, edited by Anna De Fina and Alexandra Georgakopoulou, 255–71. London: Wiley-Blackwell, 2015.

George, Daniel R. "Overcoming the Social Death of Dementia through Language." *The Lancet* 376, no. 9741 (2010) 586–87.

Gerard, Nathan. "Healthcare Management and the Humanities: An Invitation to Dialogue." *International Journal of Environmental Research and Public Health* 18, no. 13 (2021) 6771.

Gerike, Ann. E. "On Gray Hair and Oppressed Brains." *Journal of Women and Aging* 2, no. 2 (1990) 35–46.

Gilleard, Chris. "Finitude, Choice and the Right to Die: Age and the Completed Life." *Ageing and Society* 42, no. 6 (2022) 1241–51.

Gilleard, Chris, and Paul Higgs. "Aging without Agency: Theorizing the Fourth Age." *Aging and Mental Health* 14, no. 2 (2010) 121–28.

———. *Contexts of Aging: Class, Cohort and Community*. Cambridge: Polity, 2005.

———. "The Fourth Age and the Concept of a 'Social Imaginary': A Theoretical Excursus." *Journal of Aging Studies* 27, no. 4 (2013) 368–76.

———. *Cultures of Ageing: Self, Citizen and the Body*. Harlow: Prentice Hall, 2000.

———. "The Third Age: Field, Habitus or Identity?" In *Consumption and Generational Change*, edited by Ian Jones, Paul Higgs, and David Ekerdt, 23–36. London: Routledge, 2017.

Goffman, Erving. *The Presentation of Self in Everyday Life*. Edinburgh, UK: University of Edinburgh Press, 1956.

Goldberg, Natalie. *Writing Down the Bones: Freeing the Writer Within*. Boston: Shambhala, 1986.

Goldman, Marlene, Kate de Medeiros, and Thomas Cole, eds. *Critical Humanities and Ageing: Forging Interdisciplinary Dialogues*. 4th ed. New York and London: Taylor & Francis, 2022.

Greenberg, Charles J. "Review *Still Life: The Humanity of Anatomy* 2001." *Educational Media Reviews Online*. November 9, 2018. Accessed February 4, 2023. https://emro.libraries.psu.edu/record/index.php?id=1087.

Grierson, John. "The Documentary Producer." *Cinema Quarterly* 2, no. 1 (1933) 7–9.

Grimshaw, Jeremy. "A Knowledge Synthesis Chapter." Canadian Institutes of Health Research. 2010. Accessed on December 19, 2023. https://cihr-irsc.gc.ca/e/documents/knowledge_synthesis_chapter_e.pdf.

Grogan, Sarah. "Age, Ethnicity, Social Class, and Sexuality." In *Body Image*, 149–19. 3rd ed. London: Routledge, 2017.

Grogan, Sarah, and Nicola Wainwright. "Growing Up in the Culture of Slenderness: Girls' Experiences of Body Dissatisfaction." *Women's Studies International Forum* 19, no. 6 (1996) 665–73.

Gubrium, Jaber. "Voice and Context in a New Gerontology." In *Visions and Voices of Aging*, ed. Thomas R. Cole, W. Andrew Achenbaum, Patricia L. Jakobi, and Robert Kastenbaum, 46–63. *Voices and Visions of Aging: Toward a Critical Gerontology*. New York: Springer Publishing Company, 1993.

Gullette, Margaret Morganroth. *Aged by Culture*. Chicago: University of Chicago Press, 2004.

Gutierrez, Kevin J., and Sayantani DasGupta. "The Space That Difference Makes: On Marginality, Social Justice and the Future of the Health Humanities." *Journal of Medical Humanities* 37, no. 4 (2016) 435–48.

Häberlen, Joachim. *Beauty is in the Street: Protest and Counterculture in Post-War Europe*. London: Penguin UK, 2023.

Habermas, Jürgen. *An Awareness of What is Missing: Faith and Reason in a Post-secular Age*. Cambridge: Polity, 2010.

Hackler, Chris. "University of Arkansas College of Medicine, Division of Medical Humanities." *Academic Medicine* 78, no. 10 (2003) 1059.

Haenssgen, Marco, Nutcha Charoenboon, Patthanan Thavethanutthanawin, and Kanokporn Wibunjak. "Tales of Treatment and New Perspectives for Global Health Research on Antimicrobial Resistance." *Medical Humanities* 47, no. 4 (2021) e10-e10.

Haffman, Jeffrey. "A Vision for Health Humanities in Japan: A Proposed Definition and Potential Avenues for Application in Nursing Education and Beyond." 聖路加国際大学紀要 5 (2019) 8–13.

Hamilton, Heidi. "Language and Dementia: Sociolinguistic Aspects." *Annual Review of Applied Linguistics* 28 (2008) 91–110.

Haraway, Donna. "Situated Knowledges: The Science Question in Feminism and the Privilege of Partial Perspective." *Feminist Studies* 14, no. 3 (1988) 575–99.

Hartmann, Uwe, Susanne Philippsohn, Kristina Heiser, and Claudia Rüffer-Hesse. "Low Sexual Desire in Midlife and Older Women: Personality Factors, Psychosocial Development, Present Sexuality." *Menopause* 11, no. 6, part 2 of 2 supplement (2004) 726–40.

Hartung, Heike, Oddgeir Synnes, Sarah Falcus, Rüdiger Kunow, Matthew Sweney, Olga Lehmann, and Maricel Oró-Piqueras, eds. *Ageing Masculinities, Alzheimer's and Dementia Narratives*. London: Bloomsbury Academic, 2022.

Harvey, Pam, Neville Chiavaroli, and Giskin Day. "Arts and Humanities in Health Professional Education." *Clinical Education for the Health Professions: Theory and Practice*, edited by Debra Nestel, Gabriel Reedy, Lisa McKenna, and Suzanne Gough, 1–18. New York: Springer, 2020.

Hearn, Jeff. "The Place and Potential of Crisis/Crises in Critical Studies on Men and Masculinities." *Global Discourse* 12, no. 3–4 (2022) 563–85.

Henry, Julie, John Crawford, and Louise Phillips, "Verbal Fluency Performance in Dementia of the Alzheimer's Type: A Meta-Analysis." *Neuropsychologia* 42, no. 9 (2004) 1212–22.
Herman, David. *Narratology Beyond the Human: Storytelling and Animal Life.* New York: Oxford University Press, 2018.
Higgs, Paul, and Chris Gilleard. "Frailty, Abjection and the 'Othering' of the Fourth Age." *Health Sociology Review* 23, no. 1 (2014) 10–19.
———. *Personhood, Identity and Care in Advanced Old Age.* Bristol: Policy Press, 2016.
———. *Rethinking Old Age: Theorising the Fourth Age.* London: Bloomsbury, 2017.
Hilger, Stephanie M. "Introduction: Bridging the Divide between Literature and Medicine." In *New Directions in Literature and Medicine Studies*, edited by Stephanie Hilger, 1–12. New York: Springer, 2017.
———. "Medical Humanities and the Eighteenth Century." *Goethe Yearbook* 28, no. 1 (2021) 301–6.
Hillier, Russell M. *Morality in Cormac McCarthy's Fiction: Souls at Hazard.* Ashland, OH: Palgrave, 2017.
Hillman, James, and Glen Elder, eds. *Senex and Puer*. 3rd ed. Washington, D.C.: Spring Publications, 2005.
Hoang, Bao Lan, Lynn Valerie Monrouxe, Kuo-Su Chen, Shu-Ching Chang, Neville Chiavaroli, Yosika Septi Mauludina, and Chien-Da Huang. "Medical Humanities Education and Its Influence on Students' Outcomes in Taiwan: A Systematic Review." *Frontiers in Medicine* 9 (2022) 857488.
Homer. *The Odyssey of Homer.* Translated by Richmond Lattimore. New York: Harper & Row, 1965.
Hornaday, Ann. "Emma Thompson Wants Us To Like Our Bodies. She Knows It's Hard." *The Washington Post.* June 17, 2022. https://www.washingtonpost.com/movies/2022/06/17/emma-thompson-interview-leo-grande/.
Horowitz, Robert, Robert Gramling, and Timothy Quill. "Palliative Care Education in U.S. Medical Schools." *Med Educ* 48, no. 1 (2014) 59–66.
Horton, Mary F. Kollmer. "A (Un)Natural Alliance: Medical Education and the Humanities the Rise and Fall of the Institute on Human Values in Medicine 1971–1981." PhD diss., Emory University, 2021.
Huffman, Jeffrey, and Mami Inoue. "Establishing, Promoting, and Growing the Health Humanities in Japan: A Review and a Vision for the Future." *The Routledge Companion to Health Humanities*, edited by Paul Crawford, Brian Brown, and Andrea Charise, 204–14. London: Routledge, 2020.
Hughes Julian. "A Situated Embodied View of the Person with Dementia: Where Does the Spiritual Come In?" In *Spirituality and Personhood in Dementia*, edited by Albert Jewell, 198–206. London: Jessica Kingsley Publishers, 2011.
Hume, David. *A Treatise of Human Nature.* 2nd ed. Vol. II, Part III. Oxford: Oxford University Press, 1978.
Hurwitz, Brian. "Medical Humanities: Origins, Orientations and Contributions." *Revista Anglo Saxonica* 10 (2015) 11–31.
Hvidt, Elisabeth, Anne Ulsø, Cecilie Thorngreen, et al. "Weak Inclusion of the Medical Mumanities in Medical Education: A Qualitative Study among Danish Medical Students. *BMC Med Educ* 22, no. 1 (2022) 660. doi: 10.1186/s12909-022-03723-x.
Hyde, Sophie. *Good Luck to You, Leo Grande.* Align Genesius Pictures, 2022. Film.

Hydén, Lars-Christer. *Entangled Narratives: Collaborative Storytelling and the Re-Imagining of Dementia.* New York: Oxford University Press, 2017.
Isaac, Mohan. "Role of Humanities in Modern Medical Education." *Current Opinion in Psychiatry* 36, no. 5 (2023) 347–51.
Jansson, Oscar, and David LaRocca. *The Geschlecht Complex: Addressing Untranslatable Aspects of Gender, Genre, and Ontology.* New York: Bloomsbury, 2022.
Jecker, Nancy. "Justice and Mother Love." In *Visions and Voices of Aging*, ed. Thomas R. Cole, W. Andrew Achenbaum, Patricia L. Jakobi, and Robert Kastenbaum, 275–88. *Voices and Visions of Aging: Toward a Critical Gerontology.* New York: Springer, 1993.
Jenkins, Richard. "Disenchantment, Enchantment and Re-Enchantment: Max Weber at the Millennium." *Max Weber Studies* 1, no. 1 (2000) 11–32.
Johnson, Malcolm. "Spirituality, Biographical Review and Biographical Pain at the End of Life in Old Age." In *Spiritual Dimensions of Ageing*, edited by Malcolm Johnson and Joanna Walker, 198–214. Cambridge: Cambridge University Press, 2016.
Jonas, Hans. *The Imperative of Responsibility.* Chicago: University of Chicago Press, 1985.
Jones, Ian, and Paul Higgs. "The Natural, the Normal and the Normative: Contested Terrains in Ageing and Old Age." *Social Science & Medicine* 71, no. 8 (2010) 1513–19.
Jones, Malcolm. *Dostoevsky after Bakhtin.* Cambridge: Cambridge University Press, 1990.
Jones, Norma, and Bob Batchelor. *Aging Heroes: Growing Old in Popular Culture.* Washington, DC: Rowman & Littlefield, 2015.
Jones, Sarah. "The Doctor-Patient Relationship and Encounter in the Nineteenth-Century French Novel." PhD diss., University of Oxford, 2019.
Jones, Therese. "Another Kind of DNR: Titicut Follies." In *The Picture of Health: Medical Ethics and the Movies*, edited by Henri Colt, Silvia Quadrelli and Lester Friedman, 90–95. New York: Oxford University Press, 2011.
———. "Moving Pictures: Visual Culture/Visual Activism in the Health Humanities Classroom." In *Teaching Health Humanities*, edited by Olivia Banner, Nathan Carlin, and Thomas Cole, 283–307. New York: Oxford University Press, 2019.
Jones, Therese, Delese Wear, and Lester Friedman, eds. *Health Humanities Reader.* New Briswick, NJ: Rutgers University Press, 2014.
Kahambing, Jan Gresil S. "Epilepsy, Forgetting, and Convalescence in Ondaatje's Warlight." *Rupkatha Journal on Interdisciplinary Studies in Humanities* 13, no. 2 (2021) 1–11.
Kaptein, Ad. "Novels as Data: Health Humanities and Health Psychology." *Journal of Health Psychology* 27, no. 7 (2022) 1615–25.
Kastenbaum, Robert. "Encrusted Elders." In *Visions and Voices of Aging*, ed. Thomas R. Cole, W. Andrew Achenbaum, Patricia L. Jakobi, and Robert Kastenbaum, 160–83. *Voices and Visions of Aging: Toward a Critical Gerontology.* New York: Springer, 1993.
Katz, Stephen. "Critical Gerontology for a New Era." *The Gerontologist* 59, no. 2 (2019) 396–97
———. *Disciplining Old Age.* Charlottesville: University Press of Virginia, 1996.

Katz, Stephen, W. Andrew Achenbaum, Thomas R. Cole, and Brian de Vries. "Inside Aging Masculinities and Gerontological Careers." A Roundtable Discussion. *Journal of Aging Studies* 63 (2022) 101032.

Katz, Stephen, and Toni Calasanti. "Critical Perspectives on Successful Aging: Does It 'Appeal More Than It Illuminates'?" *The Gerontologist*, vol. 55, no. 1 (2015) 26–33.

Katz, Stephen, and Peter Whitehouse. "Legacies, Generations, and Ageing Futures." In *Planning Later Life*, ed. Mark Sweder et al., 240–54. New York: Routledge, 2017.

Kearney, Matthew D., Shawn C. Chiang, and Philip M. Massey. "The Twitter Origins and Evolution of the Covid-19 "Plandemic" Conspiracy Theory." *Misinformation Review* 1 (Oct 9, 2020). Accessed on December 8, 2023. https://misinforeview.hks.harvard.edu/article/the-twitter-origins-and-evolution-of-the-covid-19-plandemic-conspiracy-theory/.

Kim, Janna, C., Lynn Sorsoli, Katherine Collins, Bonnie A. Zylbergold, Deborah Schooler, and Deborah L. Tolman. "From Sex to Sexuality: Exposing the Heterosexual Script on Primetime Network Television." *The Journal of Sex Research* 44, no. 2 (2007) 145–57.

King, Nancy, Gail Henderson, and Larry R. Churchill. *Bioethics Reenvisioned: A Path Toward Health Justice*. Chapel Hill, NC: University of North Carolina Press, 2022.

Kinsey, Alfred C., William B. Pomeroy, Clyde E. Martin, & Paul H. Gebhard. *Sexual Behavior in the Human Female*. Bloomington, IN: Indiana University Press, 1998.

Klein, Verana, and Terri D. Conley. "The Role of Gendered Entitlement in Understanding Inequality in the Bedroom." *Social Psychological and Personality Science* 13, no. 6 (2021) 1047–57.

Klugman, Craig. M. "How Health Humanities Will Save the Life of the Humanities." *J Med Humanit* 38, no. 4 (2017) 419–30.

Klugman, Craig, Rachel Bracken, Rosemary Weatherston, Catherine Konefal, and Sarah Berry. "Developing New Academic Programs in the Medical/Health Humanities: A Toolkit to Support Continued Growth." *J Med Humanit* 42, no. 4 (2021) 523–34.

Klugman, Craig, and Therese Jones. "To Be or Not: A Brief History of the Health Humanities Consortium." *J Med Humanit* 42, no. 4 (2021) 515–22.

Klugman, Craig, and Erin Gentry Lamb. "Introduction." In *Research Methods in Health Humanities*, edited by Craig M. Klugman and Erin Gentry Lamb, 1–11. New York: Oxford University Press, 2019.

Krauss, Dan. *Extremis*. USA: Netflix, 2016. Film.

Kripal, Jeffrey. *The Superhumanities: Historical Precedents, Moral Objections, New Realities*. Chicago: University of Chicago Press, 2022.

Krishnan, Armin. *What Are Academic Disciplines?* National Centre for Research Methods, University of Southampton, Southampton, UK. January 2009. Accessed on December 6, 2023. http://eprints.ncrm.ac.uk/783/1/what_are_academic_disciplines.pdf.

Krznaric, Roman. *The Good Ancestor*. New York: The Experiment, 2020.

Kubler-Ross, Elizabeth. *Death: The Final Stage of Growth*. New York Scribner, 1986.

Kuckartz, Udo. *Qualitative Inhaltsanalyse: Methoden, Praxis, Computerunterstützung*. 4th ed. Weinheim, Basel: Beltz Juventa, 2018.

Kuhn, Thomas S. *The Structure of Scientific Revolutions*. 3rd ed. Chicago: University of Chicago Press, 1996.

Kumagai, Arno K., and Delese Wear. "'Making Strange': A Role for the Humanities in Medical Education." *Academic Medicine* 89, no. 7 (2014) 1–5.

Kundu, Pritha, and Debashis Bandyopadhyay. "Representation of Medics in British and Bengali Literatures (the 1850s-the 1950s): A Comparative Study." PhD diss., Vidyasagar University, 2018.
Kutac, Julie, Rimma Osipov, and Andrew Childress, "Innovation Through Tradition: Rediscovering the 'Humanist' in the Medical Humanities." *The Journal of Medical Humanities* 37, no. 4 (2016) 371–87.
Labov, Williams, and Joshua Waletzky. "Narrative Analysis: Oral Versions of Personal Experience." In *Sociolinguistics: The Essential Readings*, edited by Christina Bratt Paulston and G. Richard Tucker. Oxford: Blackwell Publishing, 1967.
Laceulle, Hanne, and Jan Baars. "Self-Realization and Cultural Narratives about Later Life." *J Aging Stud* 31 (2014) 34–44.
Lam, Michael, Breanne Lechner, Ronald Chow, Leonard Chiu, Nicholas Chiu, Henry Lam, Marko Popovic, et al. "A Review of Medical Humanities Curriculum in Medical Schools." *Journal of Pain Management* 8, no. 4 (2015) 289–97.
Laman, Douglas. "'Nanook of the North' at 100: How Documentaries Can Warp Reality." *Collider*. June 11, 2022. Accessed February 4, 2023. https://collider.com/nanook-of-the-north-100-anniversary-documentary-robert-flaherty/.
Lamb, Erin Gentry. "Not Your Grandmother's Ageism: Ageism Across the Life Course." In *Cultural Perspectives on Aging: A Different Approach to Old Age and Aging*, edited by Andrea von Hülsen-Esch, 65–80. Berlin: De Gruyter, 2021.
Lamb, Erin G., Sarah L. Berry, and Therese Jones. "Baccalaureate Programs in Health Humanities in the United States and Canada, 2022." December 6, 2023. https://healthhumanitiesconsortium.com/publications/hhc-toolkit/.
Langer-Most, Orli, and Nieli Langer. "Aging and Sexuality: How Much Do Gynecologists Know and Care?" *Journal of Women & Aging* 22, no. 4 (2010) 283–89.
Lasch, Christopher. *The Culture of Narcissism: American Life in an Age of Diminishing Expectations*. New York: W. W. Norton & Company, 2018.
Laslett, Peter. *A Fresh Map of Life: The Emergence of the Third Age*. New Haven: Harvard University Press, 1991.
———. "The Third Age, the Fourth Age and the Future." *Ageing and Society* 14, no. 3 (1994) 436–47.
Lattanzio, Ryan. "On This Day in 1895, the Lumière Brothers Debuted Their First Film, and Changed the World." *IndieWire*. March 22, 2020. Accessed December 12, 2023. https://www.indiewire.com/2020/03/lumiere-brothers-workers-leaving-factory-anniversary-1202219698/.
Laumann, Edward, John Gagnon, Robert Michael, and Stuart Michaels. "The Social Organization of Sexuality Sexual Practices in the United States." Chicago: University of Chicago Press, 1994.
Lee, David, James Nazroo, Daryl B. O'Connor, Margaret Blake, and Neil Pendleton. "Sexual Health and Well-Being Among Older Men and Women in England: Findings from the English Longitudinal Study of Ageing." *Archives of Sexual Behavior* 45, no. 1 (2016) 133–44.
Levac, Danielle, Heather Colquhoun, and Kelly O'Brien. "Scoping Studies: Advancing the Methodology. *Implementation Science* 5, no. 1 (2010) 1–9.
Levertov, Denise. *This Great Unknowing: Last Poems*. New York: New Directions Books, 1999.

Liang, Jiayin, and Baozhen Luo. "Toward a Discourse Shift in Social Gerontology: From Successful Aging to Harmonious Aging." *Journal of Aging Studies* 26, no. 3 (2012) 327–34.

Liao, Lester, and Dax Gerard Rumsey. "How the Humanities Shape Medical Culture: Knowing Wegener and Other Nazi Eponyms." *MedEdPublish* 7 (2018) 175.

Lindau et al., "A Study of Sexuality and Health Among Older Adults in the United States." *New England Journal of Medicine* 357 (2007) 762–74.

Linder, Birgit Bunzel. "Metaphors Unto Themselves: Mental Illness Poetics in Contemporary Chinese Poetry." *Literature and Medicine* 33, no. 2 (2015) 368–92.

Loads, Daphne. "What Can Academic Development Learn from the Health Humanities?" *International Journal for Academic Development* 23, no. 3 (2018) 256–59.

Luttrull, Daniel. "Prometheus Hits *The Road*: Revising the Myth." *The Cormac McCarthy Journal* 8, no. 1 (2010) 20–33.

MacDonald, Arlene, and Jerome Crowder. "Wearing a Cloak and Many Hats: Expectations of Anthropologists in an Academic Health Science Center in Texas." In *Anthropology in Medical Education*, 239–67. New York: Springer, 2021.

MacKinlay, Elizabeth. "Ageing and Spirituality across Faiths and Cultures." In Malcolm Johnson and Joanna Walker, eds. *Spiritual Dimensions of Ageing*, 32–50. Cambridge: Cambridge University Press, 2016.

———. "Baby Boomers Ageing Well? Challenges in the Search for Meaning in Later Life." *Journal of Religion, Spirituality & Aging* 26, no. 2–3 (2014) 109–21.

Macoir, Joël. "The Cognitive and Language Profile of Dementia with Lewy Bodies." *American Journal of Alzheimer's Disease and Other Dementias* 37 (2022). doi: 15333175221106901.

MacQueen, Madelaine Matej. "Vocal Pedagogy, Pathology, and Personality in Chervin's Journal La Voix Parlée Et Chantée." PhD diss., Case Western Reserve University, 2022.

Maierhofer, Roberta. "Aging as Continuity and Change: Age as Personal and Social Transformation." *Identities on the Move*, edited by Flocel Sabaté, 387–402. Frankfurt am Main: Peter Lang, 2014.

———. "Feminism and Aging in Literature." *Encyclopedia of Gerontology and Population Aging*, edited by Danan Gu and Matthew Dupre, 1–8. New York: Springer, 2019.

———. "The Graying of American Feminism." In *Values in American Society*, edited by Tibor Frank, 113–21. Budapest: Eötvös Loránd University, 1995.

———. *Salty Old Women: Frauen, Alter und Identität in der amerikanischen Literatur*. Essen: Di Blaue Eule, 2015.

Malich, Lisa, and Christoph Rehmann-Sutter. "Metascience Is Not Enough—A Plea for Psychological Humanities in the Wake of the Replication Crisis." *Review of General Psychology* 26, no. 2 (2022) 261–73.

Mallee, Hein. "The Evolution of Health as an Ecological Concept." *Current Opinion in Environmental Sustainability* 25 (2017) 28–32.

Manchola, Camilo. "Tres Apuestas Por Una Bioética Práctica." *Revista Bioética* 25 (2017) 264–74.

Mankewicz, Joseph L. *People Will Talk*. USA: 20th Century Studios, 1951. Film.

Markov, Čedomir, and Youngmin Yoon. "Diversity and Age Stereotypes in Portrayals of Older Adults in Popular American Primetime Television Series." *Ageing and Society* 41, no. 12 (2021) 2747–67.

Martin, Douglas. "Walter Wink, Theologian and Author, Dies at 76." *The New York Times*, May 19, 2012. Accessed on December 12, 2023. https://www.nytimes.com/2012/05/20/us/walter-wink-theologian-who-challenged-orthodoxy-dies-at-76.html.

Maschler, Yael, and Deborah Schiffrin. "Discourse Markers Language, Meaning, and Context." *The Handbook of Discourse Analysis*, edited by Deborah Tannen, Heidi Hamilton, and Deborah Schiffrin,189–221. Hoboken, NJ: Wiley-Blackwell, 2015.

Maslow, Abraham. *Religions, Values and Peak Experiences*. Columbus, OH: Ohio State University Press, 1964.

Matthews, Pia. "Religion and the Secularization of Spirituality: A Catholic Perspective on Spirituality in the Care of the Elderly." *Journal of Religion, Spirituality & Aging* 22, no. 4 (2010) 283–90.

Mattson, Kevin. "The Historian as a Social Critic: Christopher Lasch and the Uses of History." *The History Teacher* 36, no. 3 (2003) 375–96.

Mayring, Philipp. "Qualitative Content Analysis." *Forum on Qualitative Social Research* 1, no. 2 (2000). doi: https://doi.org/10.17169/fqs-1.2.1089.

McAdams, Dan. *The Stories We Live By: Personal Myths and the Making of the Self*. New York City: The Guilford Press, 1993.

McAdams, Dan, and Jen Guo. "Narrating the Generative Life." *Psychol Sci* 26, no. 4 (2015) 475–83.

McCaffrey, Enda, and Steven Wilson. "Introduction: Death and/as Relationality." *L'Esprit Créateur* 61, no. 1 (2021) 1–12.

McCaffrey, Graham. "Compassion, Necessity, and the Pharmakon of the Health Humanities." *Journal of Applied Hermeneutics* (2016). doi: https://doi.org/10.11575/jah.v0i0.53292.

———. "A Humanism for Nursing?" *Nursing Inquiry* 26, no. 2 (2019) e12281. doi: 10.1111/nin.12281.

———. *Nursing and Humanities*. London: Routledge, 2020.

McCarthy, Cormac. *No Country for Old Men*. New York: Vintage International, 2005.

———. *The Road*. New York: Vintage International, 2006.

McCubbin, Shelby. "Medical Memoirs as a Teaching Tool within Narrative Medicine." PhD diss., University of Kentucky, 2022.

McCullough, Laurence B. "Arrested Aging." In *Visions and Voices of Aging*, ed. Thomas R. Cole, W. Andrew Achenbaum, Patricia L. Jakobi, and Robert Kastenbaum, 184–204. *Voices and Visions of Aging: Toward a Critical Gerontology*. New York: Springer Publishing Company, 1993.

McElhinney, Thomas, Edmund Pellegrino, "The Institute on Human Values in Medicine: Its Role and Influence in the Conception and Evolution of Bioethics." *Theor Med Bioeth* 22 (2001) 291–317.

Mellyn, Elizabeth W. "Healers, Innovators, Entrepreneurs: Women in Early Modern Healthcare." Review of Sharon Strocchia's *Forgotten Healers: Women and the Pursuit of Health in Late Renaissance Italy*. *Annals of Science* 78, no. 2 (2021) 252–59.

Menand, Louis. "Nanook and Me." *The New Yorker*. August 1, 2004. Accessed on Decemember 12, 2023. https://www.newyorker.com/magazine/2004/08/09/nanook-and-me.

Mermikides, Alex, and Gianna Bouchard. *Performance and the Medical Body*. London: Bloomsbury Publishing, 2016.

Merriam Webster's Online Dictionary. https://www.merriam-webster.com/.
Meyers, Nancy. *Something's Gotta Give*. Waverly Films, 2003. Film.
Miller, Melissa L. "Narrative Medicine in Chekhov and Bulgakov." In *The Russian Medical Humanities: Past, Present, and Future*, edited by Melissa Miller and Konstantin Starikov, 99–188. Washington, DC: Rowman and Littlefield, 2021.
Milota, M. M., G. J. M. W. van Thiel, and J. J. M. van Delden. "Narrative Medicine as a Medical Education Tool: A Systematic Review." *Medical Teacher* 41, no. 7 (2019) 802–10.
Mohlin, Åsa, and Katarina Bernhardsson. "Narratives of Survivorship: A Study of Breast Cancer Pathographies and Their Place in Cancer Rehabilitation." *Current Oncology* 28, no. 4 (2021) 2840–51.
Montaigne, Michel. *The Complete Essays of Montaigne*. Translated by Donald M. Frame. Stanford, CA: Stanford University Press, 1957.
Moody, Harry. "Overview: What is Critical Gerontology and Why Is It Important?" In *Visions and Voices of Aging*, ed. Thomas R. Cole, W. Andrew Achenbaum, Patricia L. Jakobi, and Robert Kastenbaum, xv-xli. *Voices and Visions of Aging: Toward a Critical Gerontology*. New York: Springer Publishing Company, 1993.
———. "Toward a Critical Gerontology." In *Emergent Theories of Aging*, ed. Vern Bengtson and James E. Birren, 19–40. *Emergent Theories of Aging*. New York: Springer Publishing Company, 1988.
Monajemi, Alireza. "On the Nature of Medicine: Necessities, Approaches, and Challenges." *Philosophical Investigations* 15, no. 37 (2021) 153–77.
Montalt, Vicent. "Aging Bodies and Minds in Shakespeare." In *Understanding the Discourse of Aging: A Multifaceted Perspective*, edited by Vicent Salvador and Agnese Sampietro, 199–216. Newcastle upon Tyne, UK: Cambridge Scholars, 2020.
Morgan, D. L. "Qualitative Content Analysis: A Guide to Paths Not Taken." *Qualitative Health Research*, 3, no. 1 (1993) 112–21.
Nichols, Bill. *Introduction to Documentary*. 3rd ed. Bloomington, IN: Indiana University Press, 2017.
Noddings, Nel. "The Language of Care Ethics." *Knowledge Quest* 40, no. 5 (2012) 52–56.
Nouwen, Henri, and Walter J. Gaffney. *Aging: The Fulfillment of Life*. New York: Image, 1974.
Novy, Marianne. "Transcultural Adoption Literature for Pediatricians and Parents." *Adoption & Culture* 6, no. 1 (2018) 135–61.
Nussbaum, Martha. *The Fragility of Goodness: Luck and Ethics in Greek Tragedy and Philosophy*. New York: Cambridge University Press, 1986.
O'Doherty, Diane, James A O'Hare, Sarah Hyde, and Deirdre McGrath. "Humanities in Medicine: A Qualitative Study of Graduate and Student Experiences of Completing a Student Selected Component." *Creative Education* 10, no. 2 (2019) 273–87.
O'Hare, James A, Diane O'Doherty, Sarah Hyde, and Deirdre McGrath. "Exploring Creativity in Medical Students: Themes and Media in a Compulsory Humanities Student Selected Component." *Creative Education* 10, no. 2 (2019) 407–22.
Olding, Madeleine Noelle, Freya Rhodes, John Humm, Phoebe Ross, and Catherine McGarry. "Black, White, and Gray: Student Perspectives on Medical Humanities and Medical Education." *Teaching and Learning in Medicine* 34, no. 2 (2022) 223–33.

Olsen, Lauren. "Curricular Opportunities and Constraints: The Incorporation of the Humanities and Social Sciences into Contemporary U.S. Medical Education. PhD diss., University of California, San Diego, 2019.
Olthuis, Gert. "Amy Bennett's Hypochondriac as a Narrative Painting That Teaches About Care." *Journal of General Internal Medicine* 37, no. 7 (2022) 1791-92.
Ong, Eng Koon, and Devanand Anantham. "The Medical Humanities: Reconnecting with the Soul of Medicine." *The Annals, Academy of Medicine, Singapore* 48, no. 7 (2019) 233-37.
O'Neill, Desmond. "Geriatric Medical Humanities: Fresh Insights into Ageing and Geriatric Medicine." *European Geriatric Medicine*, 10, no. 3 (2019) 337-38.
Oransky, Ivan. "Obituary: Joanne Trautmann Banks." *The Lancet* 370, no. 9584 (2007) 132.
Oxfam International. "Carbon Emissions of Richest 1 Percent More than Double the Emissions of the Poorest Half of Humanities." September 21, 2020. Accessed on December 12, 2023.
"Carbon Emissions of Richest 1 Percent More than Double the Emissions of the Poorest Half of Humanity." Oxfam International. September 21, 2020. Accessed on December 15, 2023. oxfam.org.
Oxford English Dictionary. https://www.oed.com/?tl=true.
Parfit, Derek. "Personal Identity." *The Philosophical Review* 80, no. 1 (1971) 3-27.
Pargament, Kenneth, and Julie Exline. *Working with Spiritual Struggles in Psychotherapy: From Research to Practice.* New York: Guilford Press, 2021.
Park, Hyung Wook. *Old Age, New Science: Gerontologists and Their Biosocial Visions.* Pittsburgh: University of Pittsburgh Press, 2016.
Patton, Paul. "McCarthy's Fire." In *Styles of Extinction: Cormac McCarthy's The Road*, edited by Julian Murphet and Mark Stevens, 131-43. New York: Continuum, 2012.
Pearlman, Sarah. "Late Mid-Life Astonishment: Disruptions to Identity and Self-Esteem." *Women and Therapy* 14, no. 1-2 (1993) 1-12.
Pearson, Jennifer. "High School Context, Heterosexual Scripts, and Young Women's Sexual Development." *Journal of Youth and Adolescence* 47, no. 7 (2018) 1469-85.
Pellegrino, Edmund D. *Humanism and the Physician.* Knoxville: University of Tennessee Press. 1997.
Peterkin, Allan, Natalie Beausoleil, Monica Kidd, Bahar Orang, Hesam Noroozi, and Pamela Brett-Maclean. "Medical Humanities in Canadian Medical Schools: Progress, Challenges and Opportunities." In *Routledge Handbook of the Medical Humanities*, edited by Alan Bleakley, 364-79. London: Routledge, 2019.
Phinney, Alison. "Fluctuating Awareness and the Breakdown of the Illness Narrative in Dementia." *Dementia* 1, no. 3 (2002) 329-44.
Pickard, Susan. *Age Studies: A Sociological Examination of How We Age and Are Aged Through the Life Course.* Los Angeles: Sage, 2016.
Picozzi, Mario, and Federico Nicoli. "Clinical Ethics in the Context of Medical Humanities." In *Introduction to Medical Humanities*, 17-29. New York: Springer, 2022.
Piemonte, Nicole. "More to the Story: How the Medical Humanities Can Learn from and Enrich Health Communication Studies." *Review of Communication* 17, no. 3 (2017) 137-48.

Piemonte, Nicole, and Arno Kumagai. "Teaching for Humanism." *Teaching Health Humanities*, edited by Olivia Banner, Nathan Carlin, and Thomas Cole, 38–60. New York: Oxford University Press, 2019.

Pietrzak-Franger, Monika. "Introduction: Ways of Seeing." In *Syphilis in Victorian Literature and Culture*, 1–25: New York: Springer, 2017.

Pistono, Aurélie, M. Jucla, C. Bézy, et al. "Discourse Macrolinguistic Impairment as a Marker of Linguistic and Extralinguistic Functions Decline in Early Alzheimer's Disease." *Int J Lang Commun Disord* 54, no. 3 (2019) 390–400.

Poce, Antonella, Massimo Mancone, Maria Rosaria Re, Mara Valente, Carlo De Medio, Francesca Amenduni, and Viviana Maestrini. "Narrating the Museum to Promote Empathy and Critical Thinking in Medical Science Students and Doctors through Online Activities: A Pilot Research Experience." *Italian Journal of Educational Technology* 29, no. 3 (2021) 20–36.

Polkinghorne, Donald. *Narrative Knowing and the Human Sciences*. SUNY Series in Philosophy of the Social Sciences. Albany: State University of New York Press, 1988.

Poppy, Nick. "Frederick Wiseman: The Grandfather of Cin." *Salon*. January 30, 2002. Accessed February 5, 2023. https://www.salon.com/2002/01/30/wiseman_2/.

Potts, Matthew L. *Cormac McCarthy and the Signs of Sacrament: Literature, Theology, and the Moral of Stories*. New York: Bloomsbury, 2015.

Prabhu, Gayathri. "Medical Themes in a Literature Classroom: An Alternate Perspective on Medical Humanities Pedagogy in India." *Indian Journal of Medical Ethics* 4, no. 1 (2018) 35–38.

Rabinowitz, Danielle G. "On the Arts and Humanities in Medical Education." *Philosophy, Ethics, and Humanities in Medicine* 16, no. 1 (2021) 1–5.

Rajan, Raghul. "Ayurvedic Vision on Health and Enviroment." In *The Bloomsbury Handbook to the Medical-Environmental Humanities*, edited by Scott Slovic, Swarnalatha Rangarahan, and Vidya Sarveswaran, 263–76. London: Bloomsbury, 2022.

Ratzenböck, Barbara. *Media Relations: How and Why Older Women Care for Information and Communication Technologies*. Graz: UniPub, 2020.

Ratzenböck, Barbara, Florian Pirker, Nicole Haring, and Roberta Maierhofer. "Aging Masculinities in Austria: Social Realities and Cultural Representations." *Journal of Aging Studies*, no. 63 (2022). doi: org/10.1016/j.jaging.2022.101035.

Ray, Keisha. "Who Gets to Tell Our Stories? Health Narratives and Privilege." *Bioethics Today*. June 27, 2018. Accessed October 3, 2023. https://bioethicstoday.org/blog/who-gets-to-tell-our-stories-health-narratives-and-privilege/.

Ray, Ruth E. "Foreword: Coming of Age in Critical Gerontology." *Journal of Aging Studies* 2, no. 22 (2008) 97–100.

Reid, David. *Doing Relationship-Centered Dementia Care: Learning from Each Other for Better Dementia Support*. London: Jessica Kingsley Publishers, 2021.

Ricoeur, Paul. *Living Up to Death*. Translated by David Pellauer. Chicago: The University of Chicago Press, 2007.

Riefenstahl, Leni. *Triumph of the Will*. Germany: UFA GmbH, 1935. Film.

Rimer, Sara. "Turning to Autobiography for Emotional Growth in Old Age." *The New York Times*. February, 9 2000. Accessed on December 12, 2023. https://www.nytimes.com/2000/02/09/us/turning-to-autobiography-foremotional-growth-in-old-age.html.

Romm, Joseph. *Climate Change: What Everyone Needs to Know*. 3rd ed. New York: Oxford University Press, 2022.

Rovelli, Carlo. *There Are Places in the World Where Rules Are Less Important than Kindness*. New York: Riverhead Books, 2018.

Roy, Meghna, and Minati Panda. "Is Generativity Erikson's Answer to Human Ageing in the Neoliberal World?" *Journal of Aging Studies* 62 (2022). doi: 101057.

Rubinstein, Robert, Laura Girling, Kate de Medeiros, Michael Brazda, and Susan Hannum. "Extending the Framework of Generativity Theory Through Research: A Qualitative Study." *The Gerontologist* 55, no. 4 (2015) 548–59.

Rubinstein, Robert, and Kate de Medeiros. "Ecology and the Aging Self." In *Annual Review of Gerontology and Geriatrics*, edited by Hans-Werner Wahl, Rick J. Schiedt and Paul G. Windely, 59–82. New York: Springer, 2003.

Rushing, Sharon, and Juliet Mcmullin. "Translation without Medicalization: Ethnographic Notes on the Planning and Development of a Health Humanities Program in California." In *Anthropology in Medical Education*, 217–38: New York: Springer, 2021.

Sabat, Steven, and Michelle Collins. "Intact Social, Cognitive Ability, and Selfhood: A Case Study of Alzheimer's Disease." *American Journal of Alzheimer's Disease* 14, no. 1 (1999) 11–19.

Sabat, Steven, Ann Johnson, Caroline Swarbrick, and John Keady. "The 'Demented Other' or Simply 'A Person'? Extending the Philosophical Discourse of Naue and Kroll through the Situated Self." *Nursing Philosophy* 12, no. 4 (2011) 282–92.

Sacks, Oliver. *Gratitude*. New York: Alfred A. Knopf, 2016.

Sansom, Dennis Lee. "The Technological Imperative and Medicine." *The Journal of the Alabama Academy of Science* 89, no. 2 (2018) 127–27.

Sarton, George. "Seventy-First Critical Bibliography of the History and Philosophy of Science and of the History of Civilization to January (to October 1947)." *Isis* 39, no. 1 and 2 (1948) 70–139.

Saxton, Benjamin. "Grotesque Subjects: Dostoevsky and Modern Southern Fiction, 1930–1960." PhD diss., Rice University, 2012.

———. "Tolkien and Bakhtin on Authorship, Literary Freedom, and Alterity." *Tolkien Studies* 10 (2013) 167–83.

Saxton, Benjamin, and Thomas R. Cole. "*No Country for Old Men*: A Search for Masculinity in Later Life." *International Journal of Ageing and Later Life* 7, no. 2 (2012) 97–116.

Schalko, David. *Bad Regina*. Cologne: Kiepenheuer & Witsch, 2022.

Scheffler, Samuel. *Death and the Afterlife*. Edited by Niko Kolodny. New York: Oxford University Press, 2016.

Schenck, David, and Larry R. Churchill. "Six Maxims for a Marginally Inhabitable Planet." *Perspectives in Biology and Medicine* 64, no. 4 (2021) 494–510.

Schlamp, Molly. "Medical Humanities Education at Six Texas Medical Schools." Plan II Honors Thesis, University of Texas at Austin, 2020.

Schütz, Wolfgang. "Interactions between Medicine and the Arts." *Wiener klinische Wochenschrift* 132, no. 1 (2020) 1–65.

Segal, Lynne. *Out of Time: The Pleasures and the Perils of Ageing*. London: Verso, 2013.

Setia, Adi. "Islamic Ethics in Engagement with Life, Health, and Medicine." In *Islam and Biomedicine*, edited by Afifi al-Akiti and Aasim Padela, 79–109. New York: Springer, 2022.

Sharpe, Christina. *In the Wake: On Blackness and Being*. Durham, NC: Duke University Press, 2016.

Shchuka, Virlana. "John Wiltshire, *Frances Burney and the Doctors: Patient Narratives Then and Now*." Review Essay. *Medical History* 64, no. 4 (2020) 545–46.

Shevzov-Zebrun, Nina, Elizabeth Barchi, and Katie Grogan. "'The Spirit Thickened': Making the Case for Dance in the Medical Humanities." *Journal of Medical Humanities* 41, no. 4 (2020) 543–60.
Shields, Christopher. "Aristotle." *The Stanford Encyclopedia of Philosophy*, edited by Edward N. Zalta. Revised August 25, 2020. Accessed on December 8, 2023. https://plato.stanford.edu/archives/spr2022/entries/aristotle/.
Shivanee, and Manoj Kumar Yadav. "Disability and Mental Health: Reflections on the Contemporary Hindi Cinema." *Media Watch* 12, no. 1 (2021) 7–19.
Sims, Deborah. "Genre, Fame, and Gender: The Middle-Aged Ex-Wife Heroine of Nancy Meyer's *Something's Gotta Give*." In *Star Power: The Impact of Branded Celebrity*, edited by Aaron Barrow, 191–205. Santa Barbara, CA: ABC-Clio, 2014.
Slater, Glen, ed. *James Hillman Uniform Edition*. 3rd ed. Thompson, CT: Spring Publications, 2021.
Small, Jeff, Kathy Geldart, Gloria Gutman, and Mary Ann Clarke Scott. "The Discourse of Self in Dementia." *Ageing & Society* 18, no. 3 (1998) 291–316.
Snow, Charles Percy. *The Two Cultures: And a Second Look: An Expanded Version of The Two Cultures and the Scientific Revolution*. New York: Cambridge University Press, 1961.
Spike, Jeffrey, Thomas Cole, and Richard Buday, eds. *The Brewsters*. 2nd ed. Houston: UTHealth, 2012.
Stahl, Darian Goldin. "Book as Body: The Meaning-Making of Artists' Books in the Health Humanities." PhD diss., Concordia University, 2021.
Statistik Austria. "Demographisches Jahrbuch." Wein 2022. Accessed on December 18, 2023. Demographisches-JB-2020.pdf (statistik.at).
Stevens, Wallace. *The Collected Poems of Wallace Stevens*. New York: Alfred A. Knopf, 1954.
Susam-Saraeva, Şebnem, and Eva Spišiaková. *The Routledge Handbook of Translation and Health*. London: Routledge, 2021.
Suzuki, Akihito, and Akinobu Takabayashi. "Life, Science, and Power in History and Philosophy." *East Asian Science, Technology and Society* 13, no. 1 (2019) 9–16.
Swinnen, Aagje, and Kate de Medeiros. "'Play' and People Living with Dementia: A Humanities-Based Inquiry of Timeslips and the Alzheimer's Poetry Project." *The Gerontologist* 58, no. 2 (2018) 261–69.
Taylor, Charles. *Modern Social Imaginaries*. Durham NC: Duke University Press, 2004.
Taylor, Janelle. "On Recognition, Caring, and Dementia." *Medical Anthropology Quarterly* 22, no. 4 (2008) 313–35.
Tekiner, Halil. "Why Teach Pharmacy Ethics through Literary Fiction?" *World Journal of Pharmaceutical Sciences* 5, no. 6 (2017) 203–6.
Thomas, Bronwen. "Whose Story Is It Anyway? Following Everyday Accounts of Living with Dementia on Social Media." *Style* 51, no. 3 (2017) 357–73.
Thomas, Holly, Rachel Hess, and Rebecca C. Thurston. "Correlates of Sexual Activity and Satisfaction in Midlife and Older Women." *Ann. Fam. Med.* 13 (2015) 336–42.
Thomas, Nicholas. "Becoming Undisciplined: Anthropology and Cultural Studies." In *Anthropological Theory Today*, edited by Henrietta L. Moore, 262–79. Cambridge UK: Polity Press, 1999.
Thurman, Howard. *The Growing Edge*. New York: Harper, 1956.
Timmermans, Elisabeth, and J. Van den Bulck. "Casual Sexual Scripts on the Screen: A Quantitative Content Analysis." *Archives of Sexual Behavior* 47, no. 5 (2018) 1481–96.

Tornstam, Lars. "Gerotranscendence: The Contemplative Dimension of Aging." *Journal of Aging Studies* 11, no. 2 (1997) 143–54.
Tricco, Andrea C., Erin Lillie, Wasifa Zarin, Kelly K. O'Brien, Heather Colquhoun, Danielle Levac, David Moher et al. "PRISMA Extension for Scoping Reviews (PRISMA-ScR): Checklist and Explanation." *Annals of Internal Medicine* 169, no. 7 (2018) 467–73.
Trotignon, Beatrice. "The Persisting Relic of Prayer in *The Road* by Cormac McCarthy." *Revue Française d'Études Américaines* 141, no. 4 (2014) 197–209.
Ttwēak. *Still Life The Humanity of Anatomy*. USA: Fanlight Productions, 2001. Film.
———. *Stroke: Conversations and Explanations*. USA: Terra Nova Films, 2007. Film.
Turner, Bryan. "Discipline." *Theory, Culture & Society* 23, no. 2–3 (2006) 183–97.
———. *Religion and Modern Society: Citizenship, Secularisation and the State*. Cambridge, Cambridge University Press, 2011.
Twain, Mark. *The Wit and Wisdom of Mark Twain*. Garden City, NY: Dover Publications, 1998.
Twigg, George William. "Biopolitics, Race and Resistance in the Novels of Salman Rushdie." PhD diss., University of Exeter, 2016.
Twigg, Julia, and Wendy Martin. "The Challenge of Cultural Gerontology." *The Gerontologist* 55, no. 3 (2015) 353–59.
van Dyk, Silke. *Soziologie des Alters*. Bielefeld: Transcript, 2015.
———. "Zur Interdependenz und Analyse von Alter(n) und Geschlecht. Theoretische Erkundungen und zeitdiagnostische Überlegungen." *Alter(n) und Geschlecht. Neuverhandlungen eines sozialen Zusammenhangs. Forum Frauen-und Geschlechterforschung*. Münster: Westfälisches Dampfboot, 2017.
van Wijngaarden, Els, Anne Goossensen, and Carlo Leget. "The Social–Political Challenges behind the Wish to Die in Older People who Consider Their Lives to be Completed and No Longer Worth Living." *Journal of European Social Policy* 28, no. 4 (2018) 419–29.
Vincent, John. *Old Age*. London: Routledge, 2003.
von Gunten, Charles, Patricia Mullan, Richard Nelesen, et al. "Development and Evaluation of a Palliative Medicine Curriculum for Third-Year Medical Students." *J Palliat Med* 15, no. 11 (2012) 1198–217.
Waite, Linda, Edward O. Laumann, Aniruddha Das, and L. Philip Schumm. "Sexuality: Measures of Partnerships, Practices, Attitudes, and Problems in the National Social Life, Health, and Aging Study." *Journal of Gerontology* 64B, S1 (2009) i56–i66.
Walsh, Ian, Joseph Quinn, Andrea Spencer, and Helen Noble. "Anartomy: Arts, Anatomy and Medicine-Human Beings Being Human." *MedEdPublish* 7 (2018) 1–19.
Waples, Emily Joan. "Self-Health: The Politics of Care in American Literature, 1793–1873." PhD diss., University of Michigan, 2016.
Ward, L. Monique, Danielle Rosenscruggs, and Erick R. Aguinaldo. "A Scripted Sexuality: Media, Gendered Sexual Scripts, and Their Impact on Our Lives." *Current Directions in Psychological Science* 31, no. 4 (2022) 369–74.
Waters, Rebecca Amerisa. "Healthcaring: Learning to Resist the Logic of Letting Go through Arts-Based Curriculum in a Student-Run Free Clinic." PhD diss., Univeristy of Texas Medical Branch (UTMB Health), 2018.

Weicht, Bernhard, and Bernhard Forchtner. "Negotiating Euthanasia: Civil Society Contesting 'The Completed Life.'" *Current Sociology* 71, no. 3 (2021) 432–49.
Weitz, Rose. "Changing the Scripts: Midlife Women's Sexuality in Contemporary U.S. Film." *Sexuality & Culture* 14, no. 1 (2010) 17–32.
West, Sarah, Cressida Bowyer, William Apondo, Patrick Büker, Steve Cinderby, Cindy Gray, Matthew Hahn, et al. "Using a Co-Created Transdisciplinary Approach to Explore the Complexity of Air Pollution in Informal Settlements." *Humanities and Social Sciences Communications* 8, no. 1 (2021) 1–13.
Whitfield, J. Humphreys. "Petrarch." *Encyclopedia Britannica*. Accessed on October 6, 2023. https://www.britannica.com/biography/Petrarch.
Whitman, Walt. *Leaves of Grass*. Edited by Emory Holloway. Garden City, NY: Doubleday, 1926.
Wienand, Isabelle, Milenko Rakic, Sandra Eckstein, Monica Escher, Nadia Pacurari, Susanne Zwahlen, and Bernice Elger. "The Variety of Hope: Findings in Palliative Care Patients' Medical Records." *Spiritual Care* 7, no. 2 (2018) 181–85.
Wilson, Edward O. "Biophilia and the Conservation Ethics." In *The Biophilia Hypothesis*, edited by Stephen R. Kellert and Edward O. Wilson, 31–69. Washington, D.C.: Island Press, 1993.
Wilson, Steven. "Introduction: Connecting Medicine and Religion in Modern French Literature." *Modern & Contemporary France* 28, no. 4 (2020) 357–64.
———. "Introduction: Embodiment, Identity, and the Patient's Story." *L'Esprit Créateur* 56, no. 2 (2016) 1–11.
Wistrand, Jonatan. "Distressed Doctors: A Narrative and Historical Study of Work-Related Mental Discomfort among Practising Physicians." *Medical Humanities* 46, no. 3 (2020) 250–56.
Woodward, Kathleen. *Figuring Age: Women, Bodies, Generations*. Bloomington, Indianapolis: Indiana UP, 1999.
———. "Magical Moments in a Beloved Community." *The Gerontologist* 42, no. 3 (2002) 429–30.
Wright Morton, Lois, Sanford Eigenbrode, and Timothy Martin. "Architectures of Adaptive Integration in Large Colaborative Projects." *Ecolody and Society* 20, no. 4 (2015). https://www.jstor.org/stable/26270306.
Yarbrough, Scott D. "Tricksters and Lightbringers in McCarthy's Post-Appalachian Novels." *The Cormac McCarthy Journal* 10, no. 1 (2012) 46–55.
Young, Jessica A., Christopher Lind, J. B. Orange, and Marie Y. Savundranayagam. "Expanding Current Understandings of Epistemic Injustice and Dementia: Learning from Stigma Theory." *Journal of Aging Studies* 48 (2019) 76–84.
Zadeh, Rana Sagha, and Paul Eshelman. "Palliative Design Meets Palliative Medicine: A Strategic Approach to the Design, Construction, and Operation of Healthcare Facilities to Improve Quality of Life and Reduce Suffering for Patients, Families, and Caregivers." *HERD: Health Environments Research & Design Journal* 12, no. 3 (2019) 179–86.
Zeilig, Hannah. "Dementia as a Cultural Metaphor." *The Gerontologist* 54, no. 2 (2014) 258–67.

Index

Abel, Oliver, 171
Achenbaum, Andrew, 4, 10
Advance Directives (film), 92
afterlife, 168–71
ageism, 22–23, 38–39, 136, 144–46
ageless aging, 160
agency, 154–56
aging
    ageism, 22–23, 38–39, 136, 144–46
    ageless aging, 160
    aging masculinities, 31, 45–47, 50, 126
    body image, 138–42
    completed life, 158–60
    Fuch on experience of aging, 43–44
    gendered male aging, 39–51
    handbooks focusing on the humanities and aging, 24–27
    humanistic gerontology, 3–4, 26, 37–38
    life's meanings, 168–72
    meaning in, 21–23, 35–42, 172–75, 180–81
    secularization, 160–64
    sexuality, 136–42
    See also self and identity in dementia narratives
Aging (Nouwen), 20
alterity, 88–89
Alzheimer's disease, 36–37, 59–60
anocriticism, 47
Anthropocene, 175–81, 175n18
assisted suicide, 159

Atlantic magazine, 159
Austria, 45–51
autonomy, 154, 158–60, 164, 167

Baars, Jan, 30, 57, 58
baby boomers, 156–57, 163–64
Bad Regina (Schalko), 45, 49–51
Bakhtin, Mikhail, 74–75, 81–82, 88–89
Baltes, Paul, 157, 158–59
Bamberg, Michael, 57–58
Bauman, Zygmunt, 162
big stories, 57–58, 63, 69
bioethics, 153–54
biographical pain, 166
biomedical model, 195
biophilia, 178
body image, 138–42
Booth, Wayne, 109
Bourdieu, Pierre, 156
Brecht, Bertolt, 43–45
The Brewsters (Cole), 6
broken stories, 63
B-roll, 95–96, 110
Broncano, Manuel, 121
Browne, Ken, 91
Buber, Martin, 101
Burke, Kenneth, 8

Callahan, Daniel, 153–54, 167
Callahan, Sidney, 154, 167
carbon footprint, 181
care, imperative to, 165–66
Carlin, Nathan, 6, 33, 83, 188
Carson, Ronald, 2, 6, 21–22, 83, 188

cathedral thinking, 179–80
Center for Healing, Hope and the Human Spirit at Beth Israel, 33
Chambers, Tod, 8
chaos narrative, 62, 69, 72
China, 176, 181
Christianity, 160–61, 164–66, 178
"A Clearing" (Levertov), 183
climate change, 175–78
Cole, Bert (stepfather), 76–78
Cole, Thomas R.
    aging masculinities, 45–47
    biographical sketch, 1–3
    Callahan interview, 153–54
    critical gerontology, 28–31
    dialogic masculinity, 79–82
    documentary films, 91–111
    and father/stepfather, 75–78
    filmography, 93
    formative years, 17–21
    handbooks focusing on the humanities and aging, 24–27
    humanistic gerontology, 3–4, 26, 37–38
    intergenerational justice, 178
    listening and telling, 73–75
    loving care, 184–85
    McCarthy's *No Country for Old Men*, 123
    meaning in aging, 21–23, 35–42, 172–75, 180–81
    medical humanities, 4–6, 21, 83–84, 188–216
    narrative construction of Wink, 62–72
    as *puer-senex*, 15–34
    spiritual journey, 31–33
    and Stearns, 10, 42–44, 78–79, 88, 101–4
    undisciplined, becoming, 6–10
completed life, 158–61
Cooper, Lydia, 121, 125
critical gerontology, 27, 28–31
cultural narratives, 57–59, 63, 71
The Culture of Narcissism (Lasch), 19

Cultures of Ageing (Gilleard and Higgs), 156
"Cultures of Aging" approach, 155–57
A Cure for Dying (film), 92

Davie, Grace, 163
death, 99–100, 160–62, 173–75
Death and the Afterlife (Scheffler), 168–69
deathstyles, 160
"decline narrative" of aging, 47, 50
deep-time humility, 179
de Medeiros, Kate, 17–18, 31, 95–98
dementia, 165–66. See also Alzheimer's disease; self and identity in dementia narratives
dementia with Lewy bodies (DLB), 55, 60, 64, 65–66
dialogic masculinity, 79–82
dialogism, 74–75
discipline(s), 6–10, 183–85
discrimination, 144–46
documentary films, 91–111
    Cole filmography, 93
    defined, 93–94
    diversity in film, 107–9
    filmic reality, 94–99
    identity, 102–4
    relationships, 99–102
    social justice, 104–7
Donnelly, Colleen, 62
Döring, Nicola, 138
double standards for men, 146

elders, 178–80
Eliot, George, 185
Ellor, James, 162
Emanuel, Ezekiel J., 159
End Game (film), 91
environment, 175–78
Epictetus, 177
Erikson, Erik, 116, 163
Esteban-Guitart, Moisès, 58–59
ethics, 177–78
Extremis (film), 91

INDEX   243

Falcus, Sarah, 71–72
first-person pronouns, 61
Flaherty, Robert, 94–95
Flexner, Abraham, 5
Forchtner, Bernhard, 159–60
Fourth Age, 153–67
Frank, Arthur, 62
Frankfurt, Harry, 168–69
A Fresh Map of Life (Laslett), 155–56
Fuchs, Elinor, 43–45, 48

Gadow, Sally, 21–23
Geertz, Clifford, 8
gendered male aging, 39–51
gender socialization, 150
Generations (periodical), 23
generativity/generative work, 115–34
genre mixing, 8
Georgakopoulou, Alexandra, 57–58
Gerontological Society of America (GSA), 4, 28–30
GHGs (greenhouse gases), 175–76, 179
Gilleard, Chris, 153–59
global warming, 175–78, 180
Goldberg, Natalie, 98
The Good Ancestor (Krznaric), 179–80
good death, 160, 161–62
Good Luck to You, Leo Grande (film)
   aging and body image, 139
   analysis of, 144–49
   gender socialization, 150
   plot summary, 143–44
Goodrich, Thelma Jean, 2, 33, 184
Grace and Frankie (television series), 149
Greek mythologies, 44–45
greenhouse gases (GHGs), 175–76, 179
Grierson, John, 93–94
Gubrium, Jaber, 29
Gullette, Margaret Morganroth, 47, 50
Guo, Jen, 58

Habermas, Jurgen, 162

Handbook of the Humanities and Aging (Cole, Kastenbaum, Ray), 24–26
handbooks focusing on the humanities and aging, 24–27
Haraway, Donna, 37–39
Harding, Sandra, 39
Haring, Nicole, 45–49
Harvey, Bob, 101, 105–6
The Health Humanities Reader, 189
Hearn, Jeff, 45–46
Homer, 44, 174
Hughes, Julian, 166
humanistic gerontology, 3–4, 26, 37–38
"Human Values and Aging" conference, 19
Hume, David, 169
Hydén, Lars-Christer, 63

identity, 40, 58–59, 102–4. *See also* self and identity in dementia narratives
imagined author, 109
implied author, 109
incarnational theology, 170
An Inconvenient Truth (film), 106
infectious diseases, 176
Institute for the Medical Humanities, 2–3, 6, 21, 92, 97, 110
intergenerational justice, 178–80
Intergovernmental Panel on Climate Change (IPCC), 176
intersectionality, 20
interviews, 88–89
"In Whose Voice?" (Cole), 36
IPCC (Intergovernmental Panel on Climate Change), 176
I-Thou relationship, 101–2, 109

Johnson, Malcolm, 166
Jones, Therese, 105–6
Journal of Medical Humanities, 188
The Journey of Life (Cole), 3–4, 23, 39–41, 178

Karff, Rabbi Samuel, 32–33

Kastenbaum, Robert, 24, 26–27, 28–29
Katz, Stephen, 30
Kinsey, Alfred, 137
Krznaric, Roman, 179–80
Kubler-Ross, Elizabeth, 184–85
Kuckartz, Udo, 46–47

Labov, Williams, 56
Laceulle, Hanne, 57, 58
Lake, Robert, 103
Langer, Nieli, 138
Langer-Most, Orli, 138
Lasch, Christopher "Kit," 2, 18–19
Laslett, Peter, 155–56, 157
Laumann, Edward, 138
Leaves of Grass (Whitman), 170
legalized euthanasia, 160
Levertov, Denise, 183
LGBT community, 149–50
life course, 29, 72, 155–57, 162–64
life expectancy, 136
life's meanings, 168–72
Life Stories (film), 92, 95–99, 102, 108, 109–11
Lindau, S. T., 136–37, 140
linear personal narratives, 56–57
Living After Stroke: Conversations with Couples, 102–3
Living Up to Death (Ricoeur), 171
longevity, 158–59
longtermism, 179–80

MacKinlay, Elizabeth, 163
Mannheim, Karl, 156
MascAge project, 45–46
masculinity, 39–51, 79–82
Maslow, Abraham, 170
May, William F., 22
McAdams, Dan, 58
McBride, William, 18
McCarthy, Cormac, 31, 41–42, 80–82, 85, 115–34
McCullough, Laurence B., 29
McFadden, Susan, 162
McGovern Center for Humanities and Ethics, 3, 33, 73

meaning in aging, 35–42, 172–75, 180–81
"The Meaning of Life and the Meaning of Old Age" (Moody), 22
"The Meanings of Life and the Meaning of Old Age" (Moody), 35
Medical Education in the United States and Canada (Flexner), 5–6
medical humanities, 4–6, 9, 21, 83–84, 187–216
Medical Humanities (Cole, Carlin, and Carson), 6, 188–216
medical immortality, 161
medical schools, 5, 188
metaphors, 39–41, 57, 60, 63, 66, 127–28, 158
Meyer, Donald, 18
Michel, Burton David (father), 1–2, 75–76, 89–90
Middlemarch (Eliot), 185
Mohseni, M. Rohangis, 138
monologism, 74–75
monologues in *No Country for Old Men*, 118–24
Moody, Harry R., 4, 22–23, 29–30, 35

Nanook of the North (film), 94–95, 107
narrative. *See* self and identity in dementia narratives
narrative gerontology, 27, 30, 55–72
Netherlands, 159
new aging, 157
No Color Is My Kind (Cole), 10, 42–44, 101–2
No Country for Old Men (McCarthy), 31, 41–42, 80–82, 85, 115–16, 117–26, 134
"No Country for Old Men" (Cole and Saxton), 32–33
"Nonviolence for the Violent" (Wink), 70
non-violent resistance, 70–71
Nouwen, Henri, 20

INDEX   245

The Odyssey (Homer), 44, 174
older women's sexuality, 135–50
Old Man Country (Cole), 10, 33, 44, 45, 55, 64–71, 85–89, 153–54, 180–81
orgasms, 136–38, 143–44
Oxford Book of Aging (Cole), 31

Panda, Minati, 134
Parfit, Derek, 102
Paris Agreement of 2015, 175–76
pastoral role of religion, 166
Pellegrino, Edmund, 188
People Will Talk (film), 103
persistent generativity, 117, 126, 134
Petrarch, 187
Phinney, Alison, 62, 71
Plandemic (film), 105–6
plasticity of cognitive function, 157
Polkinghorne, Donald, 57
polyphony, 75
Ponet, Rabbi James, 32
power, 45–49
professional identity, 103
Psalmist, 174
puer-senex, 15–34

qualitative evidence synthesis, 187–216

Ratzenböck, Barbara, 45–49
Ray, Ruth, 25–26, 30
real-life author, 109–10
"Rehearsing Age" (Fuchs), 43–45
religion, 160–66
representation, 144, 147, 149
Ricoeur, Paul, 171
right-to-die, 159
rituals, 166
The Road (McCarthy), 115–16, 126–34
Roth, Phillip, 73–74
Roy, Meghna Datta, 134
Rubinstein, Robert, 116–17, 125–26

Sabat, Steven, 61, 69
Sako, Katsura, 71–72
Salk, Jonas, 179

Sarton, George, 5, 188
Saxton, Benjamin, 123, 126
Scheffler, Samuel, 168–69, 174–75
Search for Meaning Among the Elders in Old Man Country (Cole), 41
secularization, 160–64
self and identity in dementia narratives, 55–72
    "big" and "small" stories, 57–58
    cultural narratives, 57–58
    dementia and narrative, 59–61
    linear personal narratives, 56–57
    narrative and identity, 58–59
    narrative construction of Wink, 62–72
    narrative in dementia, 62–64
    self in dementia, 61–62
Seneca, 177–78
Sermon on the Mount, 70–71
sexism, 144–46
sexual behaviors of women, 147–48
sexual dysfunctions, 139–41
Shalko, David, 45, 49–51
"Share Your Life Story" writing workshops, 96–99
SHHV (Society for Health and Human Values), 188
small stories, 56, 57–58, 64, 69–71, 72
social actors, 94–95
social imaginary of a Fourth Age, 155, 157–58, 165–67
social justice, 104–7
Society for Health and Human Values (SHHV), 188
Something's Gotta Give (film)
    analysis of, 144–49
    plot summary, 142–43
spiritual care, 164
spiritual development, 164, 167
spirituality, 32, 162–63, 167, 169–71
Stearns, Eldrewey, 10, 42–44, 78–79, 88, 101–4
stereotypes of older women, 145–46
Stevens, Wallace, 173–74

Still Life: The Humanity of Anatomy (film), 92, 99–101, 103, 105–6, 110–11
Stoicism, 177–78
The Strange Demise of Jim Crow (film), 10, 92, 95, 101–2, 104, 106–8, 109–11
Stroke: Conversations and Questions (film), 92–93, 96, 105, 108, 109–11
student-cadaver relationship, 99–101, 103, 105–6
Sunday Morning (Stevens), 173–74

television, 144–50
Third Age, 154–58, 160–64
Thomas, Bronwen, 63–64
Thompson, Barbara, 23
Tornsam, Lars, 163
transcendent goals, 180
Transparent (television series), 149
Triumph of the Will (film), 105–6
Trotignon, Beatrice, 128–29, 131–33
Turner, Bryan, 6–7, 163

Uit Vrije Wil (Of Free Will), 159
unbearable suffering, 164
undisciplined, becoming, 6–10. See also *puer-senex*
University of Pennsylvania, 5

University of Texas Medical Branch (UTMB), 2, 5, 21, 108
University of the Third Age (U3A), 156
UTMB (University of Texas Medical Branch), 2, 5, 21, 108

Van Tassel, David, 19, 24–25
van Wijngaarden, Els, 160
Vincent, John, 161–62
"The Virtues and Vices of the Elderly" (May), 22
"voice-of-god" commentary in film, 95
Voices and Visions of Aging (Cole), 28–29
voluntary euthanasia, 154, 159, 167

Waletzky, Joshua, 56
Weber, Max, 160–61
Weicht, Bernhard, 159–60
Wesleyan University, 18–19
Westphal, Merold, 17–18
What Does It Mean to Grow Old? (Cole and Gadow), 22–23
Whitman, Walt, 170
Wilson, E. O., 178
Wink, Walter, 55–56, 64–71
Wiseman, Frederick, 106–7